Lost in Heaven

THE STORY OF 1ST LT. JAMES R. POLKINGHORNE JR., USAAF, EARLY BLACK AVIATION HISTORY AND THE TUSKEGEE AIRMEN

Dr. Leo F. Murphy

Published by Pensacola Bay Flying Machines Ltd Co
leomurphy18@gmail.com

ISBN: 978-0-9743487-2-8
Library of Congress Control Number: 2018951644
First Edition: October 2018

Printed in the United States of America by BluewaterPress LLC
Book Design and Layout by Tanya Hughes of Hughes Design Group

Lost in Heaven

By Robert Frost

The clouds, the source of rain, one stormy night

Offered an opening to the source of dew;

Which I accepted with impatient sight,

Looking for my old skymarks in the blue.

But stars were scarce in that part of the sky,

And no two were of the same constellation---

No one was bright enough to identify;

So 'twas with not ungrateful consternation,

Seeing myself well lost once more, I sighed,

"Where, where in Heaven am I? But don't tell me!

O opening clouds, by opening on me wide.

Let's let my heavenly lostness overwhelm me."

Dedication

For my wife Denise and our four children, Kelli and her husband Shaun,
Benjamin and his fiancée Nicole, Joel and Colin, whose loving
support and heartfelt encouragement allow me to pursue my
passionate study of aviation history

Dedicated to the memory of 1st Lt. James R. Polkinghorne Jr., USAAF,
and all of the Tuskegee Airmen who made tremendous personal
sacrifices in defense of our country during World War II

Table of Contents

Missing in Action May 1944,
near Terracina, Italy

1st Lt. James R. Polkinghorne Jr.
301st Fighter Squadron
332nd Fighter Group
Pensacola, Florida.

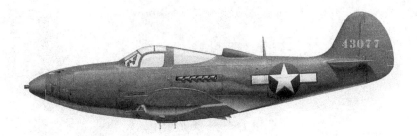

Prologue

Dawn broke gently into cloudy skies on the early morning of May 5, 1944 as twelve war-weary Bell P-39 *Airacobra's* from the U.S. Army Air Forces' 301st Fighter Squadron lifted off from the captured Luftwaffe airfield at Montecorvino, Italy. Lead by Capt. Lee Rayford, an experienced air combat veteran, the formation launched precisely at 05:04 a.m. and was divided into three flights, appropriately named Red, White, and Blue.

Their mission was to strafe ground targets in support of Lt. Gen. Mark Clark's Fifth Army's advance along the shoreline roads toward Rome. During the bitter winter months, the Italian Campaign had deteriorated into a terrible stalemate with Allied forces unable to penetrate well-fortified German defensive lines. With the arrival of spring, the Allies were ready to resume their full-scale ground offensive against what they hoped were now weakened German forces.

As the strike package winged its way across southern Italy, the designated target area slowly came into view but was veiled by a dark cloud bank. Sighting an opening in the overcast, Capt. Rayford ordered Red and Blue flights to descend below the clouds with him for an attack while White flight was directed to remain overhead to protect against marauding German fighters.

But the break in the clouds was short-lived, and mist quickly enveloped the descending fighters, now in a spread formation for their strafing mission. Visibility deteriorated to near zero, and wingmen lost sight of one another. With no indication they would break out under the overcast, Capt. Rayford ordered the attack formation to get on their flight instruments and climb, tracers from automatic weapons and flak bursts from a now-alerted enemy bracketing their ascent.

As the P-39's regrouped above the clouds and began their journey back to base, it soon became painfully clear that one aircraft was missing. The time was now 05:40 a.m. They had been airborne 36 minutes. ■

Aviation cadet James R. Polkinghorne Jr.

Foreword

It was such a surprise when Dr. Murphy first contacted me about writing a book about my brother. It only took a short while into the conversation to realize the magnitude of his research into the background of my brother. It was obvious that much time and effort was devoted to it.

I was only ten years old when we received a telegram informing my parents that James was missing in action. Although many years have passed, I vividly remember the pain and sorrow of my parents, especially my mother. Many years passed before she was able to accept it.

On behalf of my family, I thank Dr. Murphy for his dedication, hard work, and time required to produce a book like this.

This book will help to preserve the memory of my brother, 1st Lt. James Reed Polkinghorne Jr., and for that, I shall be eternally grateful to Dr. Leo Murphy.

Maggie Polkinghorne Wilson

INTRODUCTION AND ACKNOWLEDGEMENTS

Dr. Leo F. Murphy, Daytona Beach, Florida

Photograph of an unidentified black aviator held in the archives of the University of West Florida Historic Trust.

A mong the constellation of aviation heroes that grace the heavens above Pensacola, none shine brighter than Pensacola-born Tuskegee Airman 1st Lt. James R. Polkinghorne, U.S. Army Air Forces. Yet he is virtually unknown, even in his hometown, and he is rarely mentioned in books or articles about the Tuskegee Airmen.

The idea for this book was created in 2010 when I was being interviewed by Robert Hill on his radio show WRNE 980-AM while on a promotional tour for the Pensacola International Airport's 75th-anniversary celebration. I had just published my book on the history of the airport, and my second on the history of aviation in Pensacola, when during the interview Robert asked if I had ever come across any early black Pensacola aviators. I replied that I had not, other than one unidentified photograph of a black aviator taken by Pensacola photographer H. Lee Bell and held in the archives of the University of West Florida Historic Trust.

Fast forward two years later to 2012 and the release of George Lucas' motion picture *Red Tails* about the Tuskegee Airmen of World War II. This triggered a recollection that during an exhausting review of old *Pensacola News-Journal* back issues for clues to Pensacola's aviation past, I had read about a black U.S. Army Air Forces aviator who had been killed during World War II.

Scanning through faint pages of microfilm, I had barely noticed the headline which only stated, "Lost Negro Flier Declared Dead." Published on November 3, 1945 and buried deep within the paper, I could have easily missed the story or ignored it entirely as his death was one of many routinely reported in Pensacola's newspapers during those terrible years of war.

Although my research focused on Naval aviation and the development of commercial aviation in Pensacola, providence guided my hand, and I printed a copy of the article for my files and thought no more of it until *Red Tails* appeared in theaters. I then wondered if the unknown black aviator was related to Pensacola and whether he was a Tuskegee Airman.

I relocated the article and was thrilled to discover that it was about Pensacola-born 1st Lt. James R. Polkinghorne Jr., who was indeed a Tuskegee Airman, earning his silver wings as a U.S. Army Air Forces aviator on February 16, 1943. In comparison, the first African-American Naval aviator, Ensign Jesse L. Brown, was not awarded his golden wings until October 21, 1948; the first U.S. Marine Corps African-American aviator, 2nd Lt. Frank E. Petersen, not until October 22, 1952; and the first U.S. Coast Guard African-American aviator, Ensign Bobby C. Wilks, not until March 25, 1957.

This small newspaper article now drew my research interests to the history of the Tuskegee Airmen and 1st Lt. Polkinghorne's place in their history. But I have found this to be an exceptionally challenging book to research, primarily because there is so much erroneous and conflicting information published about the Tuskegee Airmen and their predecessors. Primary source materials are difficult to find, and many factual errors are perpetuated from one reference to another, including one author who confused in a photograph the wife of Tuskegee Institute president Dr. Frederick D. Patterson with Eleanor Roosevelt, the wife of U.S. President Franklin D. Roosevelt. As a result, untold hours of personal research has been required to attempt to unravel the ties between truth and invention. Nonetheless, any errors, mistakes or omissions in this book are the sole responsibility of the author.

The second challenge was properly positioning Polkinghorne

VIEWPOINT

We forgot one of our own in Black history

S ince the month of February is now notable as Black History Month, I often wonder why some of the old-timer veterans and citizens of this city, like me, haven't mentioned the heroic actions of Lt. James R. Polkinghorne Jr. before.

He was one of the original Tuskegee Airmen and the first black Airman and officer from Pensacola.

I remember vividly how enlisted personnel (whites) would turn their backs, pretending not to see him, so they would not have to salute when passing him on the streets of Pensacola in uniform,

HORACE DUKES

when shopping or visiting his parents or other members of the family.

During those earlier days all enlisted personnel would have to salute an officer in the military anywhere in uniform.

Nothing to be taken away from Daniel "Chappie" James, Rosamond Johnson, Capt. Scott Jones, son of Mrs. Corrine Jones — I knew them all.

It was Lt. James R. Polkinghorne

Jr. who shot down a German fighter pilot on the tail of another famous black pilot, Col. Benjamin O. Davis Jr., now retired at the rank of lieutenant general of the Army Air Force, saving his life.

Unfortunately, Lt. Polkinghorne was one of the Tuskegee Airmen shot down over Italy while serving his and our country, making the supreme sacrifice during World War II. He was never mentioned, noted or remembered by the press in Pensacola, his native and birth city.

Not even a street, building, plaque or anything has been dedicated to him or his name — but re-

membered by only me and his family (Calvin Harris and wife — Mr. Harris, now deceased, was a flying instructor at Tuskegee. Mrs. Harris resides in Lincoln Park).

If you happen to see the movie or video of "The Tuskegee Airmen" you will see Lt. Polkinghorne at the end of the film in the still picture (snapshot) as the credit rolls by, kneeling in the first row, dead center.

How soon some of us forget!

Horace L. Dukes is a resident of Pensacola.

As so ably expressed in this 1997 article published in the *Pensacola News-Journal*, formal recognition of 1st Lt. James R. Polkinghorne's achievements are long overdue.

with respect to the much broader historical narrative of those early black aviators who only wanted to fly and their followers who strived to serve their country as military combat pilots. From the first successful flight of the Wright Brothers in 1903 to the first entry of the Tuskegee Airmen into aerial combat in 1943, it was as if each pioneering black aviator laid a single cobblestone on a narrow, bumpy path that allowed a young James R. Polkinghorne Jr. to walk up to a U.S. Army recruiting station during World War II and enlist as an aviation cadet.

Personally, I knew very little about black aviation history when I began this book, and I have provided a detailed background story for readers who are likewise unfamiliar with the topic. Where possible, I have let the various participants, experts, and individuals tell their stories in their own-recorded words. I have found them to be more eloquent than I could ever hope to be.

The final challenge was establishing a somewhat reasonable chronology of events that the reader could follow. There were many twists, turns, reverses and parallel paths that influenced the history of the Tuskegee Airmen and it is all too easy to lose one's place in the chase down various rabbit holes.

As it turned out, the saving grace for all of these challenges was the discovery of several remarkable papers that documented the establishment of the Tuskegee Airmen program and 1st Lt. Polkinghorne's training and combat service. The most important of these was a chronological memoir prepared by Tuskegee Institute faculty member George L. Washington, who served as the school's Director of Aviation Training from 1939 to 1945 and who can be considered the single most influential person in the development and operation of Tuskegee's civilian and military flight training programs.

The next most important documents were the official histories and combat records of the 332nd Fighter Group and

301st Fighter Squadron, to which 1st Lt. Polkinghorne was assigned. Mostly written by junior officers, these narratives are chockablock with incisive wit, unimaginable sadness, the momentous and the mundane. These logbooks provide uncensored insight into the daily life of fighter pilots preparing for and conducting overseas combat operations during World War II.

In the interest of scale, this book focuses primarily on 1st Lt. Polkinghorne and the units in which he served. Not mentioned are the various service groups and support squadrons that reinforced the Tuskegee Airmen, as well as the 477th Bombardment Group, the first all-black bomber squadron activated in 1944, and liaison pilots, the first black aviators assigned to U.S. Army ground forces as aerial field artillery observers.

Also not discussed is Pensacola's most famous Tuskegee Airman, Gen. Daniel "Chappie" James Jr., whose own illustrious U.S. Air Force career has been well-documented in several biographies. James earned his U.S. Army Air Forces wings on July 28, 1943, more than five months after Polkinghorne was awarded his wings on February 16, 1943.

Of interest, two additional Tuskegee Airmen were also identified who cited Pensacola as their hometown. Grover Crumbsy, who graduated with Tuskegee Class 44-K, was raised in Pensacola but was born in Pine Hill, Alabama; and Benjamin J. Brown Jr. who started flight training in Tuskegee Class 42-D but failed to finish.

During my research, I was very privileged to have met some extraordinary people who provided me with invaluable assistance. In particular, I would like to thank George Cully for his work with the Air Force Historical Research Agency; Dr. Merle Dawson of the Southeastern Regional Black Archives Research Center; Christine Biggers with the Tuskegee Airmen National Historic Site; Jacquelyn Wilson of the University of West Florida

Historic Trust; Dean DeBolt of the University of West Florida Archives and West Florida History Center; and Lani Suchcicki of the *Pensacola News-Journal*.

I was very honored to have come in contact with Angie Colasanti, who provided me invaluable insight on her mother, Emeldia Zaragoza of Pensacola, who served with the Tuskegee Airmen. I was also very fortunate to meet artist Susan Rothschild, who provided me an original painting of Polkinghorne's final mission. I am also grateful beyond words to Tanya Hughes, my book designer, whose patience and enthusiasm for my projects knows no bounds.

A special thank you to Dana Chandler, Archivist, Tuskegee University, who kindly opened his files to me on a trip to Tuskegee, and his assistant, Jared McWilliams, who diligently researched the university's photographic holdings. I am deeply indebted to Brett Stolle, Curator, National Museum of the United States Air Force Research Division, who provided me copies of all the Tuskegee Airmen photographs held by the museum.

My sincerest thank you to Dr. Daniel L. Haulman, Chief, Organizational History Branch at the Air Force Historical Research Agency, an expert on the Tuskegee Airmen who graciously volunteered to review my manuscript before publication. I am deeply indebted to him for his insight, wisdom and gentle guidance.

But the most special person I met during my research was Maggie Beatrice (Polkinghorne) Wilson, the youngest sister of James R. Polkinghorne. Just 10 years old when her only brother was killed in combat, she provided me an incredible window into the past on what life was like growing up in Pensacola in the Polkinghorne family, and the heartbreaking impact of James' death on her mother and father. ∎

Chapter One
Before the
Tuskegee Airmen

James Reed Polkinghorne Jr. was born on June 16, 1921 in Pensacola, Florida, the only son and second eldest child of six children born to Dr. James Reed Polkinghorne Sr. and Maggie Ridley Polkinghorne.[1]

During his childhood, Pensacola was host to the largest Naval Air Station in the United States and perhaps the largest air facility in the world. Since 1914 all of the U.S. Navy's lighter-than-air and heavier-than-air aviation had been stationed in Pensacola and a host of aviation greats had visited the area, including Charles Lindbergh and Amelia Earhart. With nearby Eglin Field hosting U.S. Army aviators, commercial aviation well-established at a new civilian airport, and a swarm of barnstormers and flying circuses cycling through the city, Pensacolians enjoyed an exclusive front-row seat to aeronautical marvels that most people in the world could not even imagine. For a young man growing up in Pensacola, it would be nearly impossible not to become enthralled with the possibilities of a career in aviation.

But while a passion for flight might be ignited by the many airplanes flying overhead, for a young African-American in the South, the opportunity to obtain flight training was nearly impossible. This exclusion went well beyond state and local Jim Crow laws that mandated racial segregation. Often enforced by vigilante violence, institutionalized racism barred all African-Americans from civilian and military flight training in the United States. Although this was the Golden Age of Aviation, there was not a single African-American role model for a young James Reed Polkinghorne Jr. among the hundreds of U.S. Army, U.S. Marine Corps, U.S. Navy, U.S. Coast Guard and commercial aviators who walked the streets of Pensacola.

Even biographical histories of famous American pilots and contemporary lists of Who's Who in American Aeronautics failed to list the achievements of early African-American pilots.[2,3] To inspire young African-Americans toward careers in aviation, they needed their own black Charles Lindbergh and black Amelia Earhart with their adoring public and enormous press coverage,

> If, for the present, race prejudice closes to Negroes the avenues of air mail and the army and commercial service, we must open other channels. We have pilots who are willing

to compensate their limited experience with more daring, extra intelligence and if need be, greater sacrifice.[4]

And sacrifices were made. Journalist Enoch Waters of the *Chicago Weekly Defender*, one of the biggest African-American daily papers in the United States, noted,

> Chicagoans discovered how deeply racial discrimination had permeated all aspects of aviation. Blacks were denied instruction, they experienced difficulty in renting aircraft and even those owning planes were often denied parking space and service at private airfields.[5]

Yet some passionate African-Americans refused to be denied the opportunity to enjoy the splendors of flight. Each in their own unconquerable manner found a way to get airborne.

A study of these pioneering, trailblazing early African-American aviators reveals a small, tight-knit group of pilots whose fates were often intertwined as they sought to circumvent discriminatory regulations and practices. They taught themselves how to fly, shared their airplanes with each other, built their own segregated airports, held joint air shows, and together formed professional African-American aerospace organizations to advance their cause.[6]

One significant trait common among these early African-American aviators, women and men alike, was that many were skilled automobile mechanics and accomplished small business owners, using their talents and personal funds as a stepping stone into the world of aviation. Additionally, many were born in the Deep South but moved to northern cities to escape violent racism. As a result, three great centers of early African-American aviation emerged: Chicago, Illinois; Los Angeles, California; and Pittsburgh, Pennsylvania.

Yet despite some modest degree of success, it appeared that even the world economy conspired against early African-American aviators. Charles Lindbergh's 1927 flight across the Atlantic ignited unprecedented interest in the development of private and commercial aviation. But only a few years later, the crushing economic hardships of the Great Depression precipitated by the stock market crash of 1929, crushed the hopes of many young African-

Americans who hoped to fly. Even if they found someone who was willing to provide flight instruction, flight lessons were, and still are, extremely expensive. In August 1936, the Department of Commerce reported that there were fewer than 70 certificated black pilots in the United States among an estimated total population of some 12 million African-Americans.[7]

First African-American Pilot: Charles Wesley Peters

Determining who was the first African-American to pilot an airplane is a nearly impossible task as the earliest flight attempts were rarely documented. In 1889 Thomas Crump, a graduate of Fisk University living in Chicago, became the first African-American ever recorded to have built an airplane, although it never flew.[8]

Following the triumphant flight of the Wright brothers in 1903 and the widely-publicized flight of their arch-rival Glenn Curtiss in 1908, fledgling black and white aviators across the country built and successfully flew dozens of their own flying machine inventions, perhaps drawing local attention but rarely national headlines. The first African-American to pilot a heavier-than-air aircraft may very well have been Charles Wesley Peters of Pittsburgh, Pennsylvania who made several glider flights in 1906 and several powered flights in 1911.[9]

Establishing precisely who was the first African-American to earn a pilot certificate, while still a complicated task, is made easier by the fact that the Aero Club of America, the United States representative of the Paris-based international aeronautics governing body Fédération Aéronautique Internationale (FAI), began issuing pilot certificates as early as 1911.

First African-American Military Fighter Pilot: Eugene James Bullard

There is no question that the first African-American military fighter pilot in the history of the United States was Eugene James Bullard (October 9, 1895 to October 12, 1961) who was born in Columbus, Georgia and received his coveted military aviator wings (#6,950) on May 5, 1917.[10] But they were not the military brevet of a United States pilot but rather those of his adopted country France, because at that time African-Americans were barred from serving as pilots in the U.S. military.

The grandson of a slave, as a young boy Bullard fled the United States as a stowaway on a ship bound to Europe, seeking to replace the violent racism of the Deep South with the equality and respect for human rights embraced by the French.

When World War I erupted, he enlisted in the French Foreign Legion and spent two horrifying years as a rifleman fighting the Germans in the slaughter that was trench warfare. Wounded multiple times and decorated with several awards for heroism,

including the Médaille Militaire and Croix de Guerre, while on convalescent leave he was offered the opportunity to transfer into the French Air Service Aeronautique Militaire.[11]

Initially assigned as a student aviation machine gunner, he reported to the French aviation training school on October 6, 1916 but he was able to get his designator changed to student pilot, and he flew Bleriot and Cauldron G-3's airplanes between 1916 and 1917.[12]

While Bullard spoke fluent French, other American student aviators trained by the French did not. One American student pilot recalled,

> None of us had had any ground school instruction and few of us had any idea about the theory of flight. Our instructors did not speak English and we did not speak French.
>
> After each flight, the instructor would pull out a pasteboard card with a line drawn down the center. One side was written in English and the other in French. The instructor would explain all the mistakes you had made while in flight. He gave you hell in French while pointing to the English translation. Perhaps it was just as well we did not understand his words.[13]

American-born Eugene Jacques Bullard flew in combat as a fighter pilot with two French squadrons during World War I. On his right breast, he is wearing French military pilot wings; on his left breast he is wearing the Croix de Guerre, awarded for his heroism during the battle of Verdun.

Bullard recalled his flight test for his pilot's certificate in his personal journal,

> When the day came for my first solo flight, I don't know what in the world came over me. After listening to about fifteen minutes of explanations and being told that if you do this, you are dead, and if you should do that, you are dead, and, "Bullard, whatever you do, don't forget one thing. I have tried to teach you and your comrades here in this school all that I know about aviation, and I have been flying since 1911. So, now, Bullard, you have your own life in your hands. You know I can't do anything for you when you are up there alone. So, don't forget that one thing: When you are going to land, after you fly around, just over the field twice, you must piquer et couper."
>
> Piquer et couper means to push and cut on the handle. But which did you do first? I went up for my flight confused. I did not know whether I should piquer and then couper, or couper and then piquer. I had been told so many do's and don't-do's that when it was time for me to come down, I could not make up my mind which to do first. After the third time around the field, I had to do something, anything. What I did was to couper and then piquer.
>
> When I landed all right, you can just imagine I was wild with joy, and not just because I had passed the test for my pilot's certificate. Later, we pilots had a lot of laughs over my worry because it doesn't make any difference at all whether you piquer and couper or couper and piquer.
>
> I received my pilot's certificate on May 5, 1917. I was also granted six days leave in Paris.[14]

It was on a subsequent visit to Paris before Bullard was assigned to his first squadron that he purchased a small rhesus monkey, which he named Jimmy, as a personal mascot,

> I bought Jimmy while I was in Paris from a nice girl who had taken me for a monkey financially. I didn't mind that; only I wanted to take someone else for a monkey. So I bought Jimmy from the girl. When we arrived "en escadrille," I don't remember which of the two of us had the more success, Jimmy or me. But I must say sincerely that we both were made to feel at home.[15]

Jimmy flew with Bullard on nearly every one of his combat missions, safely tucked into his master's fur-lined flight jacket. In August 1917 he was assigned to the French squadron L'escadrille SPAD 93. His first combat mission was in the early morning on September 8, 1917 over the Verdun sector where he had fought as an infantryman,

> I was determined to do all that was in my power to make good, as I knew that the eyes of the world were watching me as the first Negro military pilot in the world. I felt the same way the Frenchman Pegoud must have felt when he was the first to do a loop-the-loop in an airplane, or the way Lindbergh felt when he was the first to fly from New York to Paris, France. I had to do or die, and I didn't die.[16]

Bullard also served with L'escadrille SPAD 85 and completed more than 20 combat missions. Bullard always believed that while piloting a Newport 27 in November 1917, he shot down at least two German aircraft, a Fokker Dr.I triplane from Richthofen's Flying Circus and a German Pfalze D.III. [17,18] But a lack of witnesses and corroborating evidence due to the aircraft falling behind enemy lines prevented awarding of official kill status to him.[19,20]

With the entry of the United States into World War I in April 1917, the U.S. Army announced that all American pilots currently flying for France could transfer into the U.S. Army Air Service. But because Bullard was an African-American, he was denied this opportunity to become a commissioned pilot in the U.S. Army, the only member of the Lafayette Flying Corps and Lafayette Escadrille to be so rejected. Bullard recalled,

> I was more and more puzzled until suddenly it came to me that all my fellow countrymen who were transferred were white. Later I learned that in World War I, Negroes were not accepted as fliers by the U.S. Army. This hurt me very much. Then as now my love for my own country was strong. I got some comfort out of knowing that I was able to go on fighting on the same front and in the same cause as other citizens of the U.S. and so in a round-about way I was managing to do my duty and serve it.[21]

Bullard's military flying service ended on November 11, 1917 and after a successful career as a nightclub owner in Paris, he eventually returned to the United States to virtual anonymity.

First African-American Male Civilian Pilot Certificate: Emory Conrad Malick

Recently discovered documentation has revealed that Emory Conrad Malick (December 29, 1881 to January 23, 1959) was the first African-American to receive a pilot certificate in the United States.[22] Born in Seven Points, Pennsylvania, he attended the Curtiss Aviation School on North Island, San Diego and on March 20, 1912 earned his pilot certificate (#105) from the Aero Club of America, a representative of the Fédération Aéronautique Internationale (FAI) in the United States. In 1927, he also became the first African-American to earn a commercial transport pilot certificate (#1,716).

Documents only recently discovered authenticate that Emory C. Malick was the first African-American to earn a pilot's certificate in the United States.

Aviation historians are unclear on how Malick was able to obtain his pilot certificates from the Aero Club of America since other prospective African-American aviators during that era were forced to travel overseas to get their certificates. However, in census and military draft records he self-identified as white, which may explain his unprecedented achievements.[23]

After obtaining his pilot certificate, Malick purchased a Curtiss pusher biplane, barnstormed, and helped form the Flying Dutchman Air Service with Ernie H. Buehl, Sr., a German-born aviator.[24] One of their pilots was Charles A. Anderson, who later played a significant role as the chief flight instructor for the Tuskegee Airmen.[25] Malick stopped flying in 1928 after a crash involving a passenger fatality, and he never flew again although he lived to the age of 77.[26]

First African-American Female Civilian Pilot Certificate: Bessie Coleman

Until the discovery of Malick's documentation, aviatrix Bessie Coleman (January 26, 1892 to April 30, 1926) was considered to be the first African-American to obtain a civilian pilot certificate. One of 13 children, she was born in Atlanta, Texas, and moved to Chicago in 1915 to live with two of her brothers.[27] Trained as a beautician and manicurist, she became enthralled about aviation, but as an African-American woman, she was not able to find anyone willing to teach her to fly. So she decided to go overseas

for her training.

With financing provided by two African-American philanthropists, in November 1920 she sailed for France where she learned to fly in a French Nieuport Type 82 biplane in the École d'Aviation des Fréres Caudron at Le Crotoy, France.[28,29] After completing several months of training, she was awarded her pilot certificate (#18.310) on June 15, 1921 from the Fédération Aéronautique Internationale headquartered in Paris.

Before leaving France, Coleman ordered a 130-horsepower Nieuport de Chasse airplane that was to be shipped to the United States, as she was intending to earn a living by putting on exhibitions flights to paying audiences[30] She returned to the United States in September 1921 where she was greeted with much fanfare by the press.

For whatever reason, the Nieuport she ordered never arrived from France, and due to her race, no one was willing to employ her as a commercial pilot or sell her an airplane so that she could begin her exhibition flights. Realizing that her only hope for an aviation career was as a barnstorming pilot in the many flying circuses crisscrossing the United States, she sought advanced aerobatic training but again was unable to find anyone willing to train her because of her race and gender.

So, in early 1922 Coleman returned to Europe to receive advanced flight instruction in aerobatics and to develop her personal air show routine. On a whirlwind tour, she trained in France, Germany, and Holland before returning to Chicago in August 1922

Known as "Queen Bess," Bessie Coleman stands atop the wheel of the Curtiss JN-4 "Jenny" that she flew as a barnstormer.

to a celebrity's welcome.[31]

Provided an airplane by a local white entrepreneur, Coleman then embarked on a series of very successful air shows, traveling across the country, including the Deep South, to perform and lecture, conduct parachute jumps and provide paying-passenger rides.[32]

Coleman's career rollercoastered for the next several years, including an airplane crash in 1925 that left her severely injured.[33] However, she could now afford her own airplane and found a willing seller in Texas where she purchased a Curtiss JN-4 *Jenny* from the Curtiss Southwestern Airplane and Motor Company.[34]

She spent the winter of 1926 recuperating with friends in Orlando, Florida and was hired by the Negro Welfare League of Jacksonville, Florida to perform an air show on May 1st, which included her making a parachute jump. Unable to rent an airplane in the local area due to her race, she directed the Curtiss Southwestern Airplane and Motor Company to send her personal airplane to Jacksonville from Texas. Flown by William D. Wills, an employee of Curtiss Southwestern, the airplane arrived on April 28, 1926.[35]

Two days later, on April 30, 1926, she took a practice flight with Wills at the controls, letting him fly while she sat in the back so that she could familiarize herself with the area before her performance. She was not wearing a seatbelt when the airplane suddenly spun out of control and inverted, ejecting Coleman, who fell to her death. Wills was unable to regain control of the spinning airplane and was killed in the subsequent crash and a postcrash fire caused by a careless spectator who lit a cigarette that ignited gasoline fumes from the wreck.[36]

First African-American U.S. Department of Commerce Pilot Certificate: J. Herman Banning

James Herman Banning (November 5, 1900 – February 5, 1933) is recognized as the first African-American to obtain a pilot certificate from the newly established U.S. Department of Commerce.

Born in Canton, Oklahoma, his family moved to Ames, Iowa where he became a skilled mechanic and owned his own successful automotive repair shop.[37] After briefly studying electrical engineering at Iowa State College, in 1924 he became "air-minded" and traveled 30 miles each way during the winter of 1924 to receive flight instruction from World War I aviation veteran Raymond C. Fisher at his flying school located in Des Moines, Iowa.[38]

Just before Banning was due to solo, Fisher died in an airplane crash. While the airplane was completely destroyed, the engine was only slightly damaged. So Banning purchased the motor and secured an old fuselage and a set of wings, which may have been from a two-seat 1926 White Aircraft Company *Hummingbird*.[39] He then acquired an aircraft manual from the Curtis Aeroplane Company and with the assistance of several white mechanically-inclined friends, rebuilt the airplane, which he christened *Miss Ames*.

Unfortunately, after one look at this Phoenix, no experienced pilot was willing to test fly it for him, so Banning decided to try it out himself even though he had never flown alone,

> The one big moment in a pilot's life is the day he is allowed to solo. He remembers this event until his dying day, and in rare cases this has been known to be one and the same day. This is the day on which, for the first time, the novice soars up and into the blue sky all alone—sole commander of his craft. The day of days. The moment toward which all of his weary hours of training have been pointed. This is the time when the student pilot conclusively proves to the world at large that he has both nerve and ability. To himself he proves that he is nothing but a scared, witless fool who hasn't had half enough flying lessons.[40]

He then completed his required solo hours and in 1930 earned

J. Herman Banning, the first African-American to earn a pilot certificate from the U.S. Department of Commerce.

his limited commercial pilot certificate (#1,324) from the U.S. Department of Commerce, a first as all of his predecessors had received their pilot certificates from the Aero Club of America or the Fédération Aéronautique Internationale.[41]

Banning became a successful barnstormer, and in 1929 he left Iowa to live in Los Angeles and served as the chief pilot for the Bessie Coleman Aero Club, an organization formed in memory of the famous aviatrix by William J. Powell, another celebrated early African-American aviator.[42] Banning gained national fame in 1932 when he and fellow pilot Thomas C. Allen became the first African-American pilots to fly coast-to-coast from California to New York, to be discussed in the next chapter.

On February 5, 1933, less than five weeks after his return from his transcontinental flight, Banning, one of the most experienced African-American pilots in the world, was killed in an airplane crash during an air show in San Diego. Banning was scheduled to perform at the air show but at the moment did not have an airplane. Due to his race, he was refused a rental airplane because the local flying school did not believe him to be a capable pilot and he was forced to sit in the back seat of a two-seat Travelair with a less experienced pilot at the controls. Eyewitnesses reported that the airplane stalled and entered a spin, a maneuver the more experienced Banning would have recovered from with ease. The newspaper reported,

> Victim of a prejudice as old as the nation itself, Banning went to his death today without a fighting chance to save his life.[43]

John Charles Robinson

The second black military pilot in American history to engage in aerial combat was John "Johnnie" Charles Robinson (November 26, 1905 to March 26, 1954) who was born in Carrabelle, Florida but raised in Gulfport, Mississippi.[44] On December 21, 1910 as a five-year-old boy he became captivated with flight after witnessing early aviation pioneer John Moisant make the first airplane landing in Gulfport's history.[45]

After graduating from high school, he attended the Tuskegee Normal and Industrial Institute (typically shortened to Tuskegee Institute and later renamed Tuskegee University) and graduated in 1923 with a college degree in automotive sciences. Tuskegee did not offer any aviation programs at that time, but Robinson recognized that a solid background in automobile mechanics would prove to be a valuable credential and a viable means of breaking racial barriers in the aviation industry. As will be discussed later, as a certificated pilot and aerial combat veteran Robinson returned to his alma mater several times in an attempt to ignite a flame of interest in flight training or to serve as a faculty member, but budgetary constraints and a call to war disrupted his plans.

After graduating from Tuskegee, Robinson left deeply

segregated Mississippi for better opportunities available in the more racially tolerant north, eventually finding a position as an automobile mechanic in Detroit, where he opened up his own automobile repair garage.[46] In 1926 he drove to a nearby airport in hopes of taking flight lessons, but he was rebuffed due to his race. Robinson learned, however, that a JN-4D Curtiss *Jenny* at the field had engine troubles. He offered to make repairs in exchange for a free flight, to which the white pilot agreed, sources differing on whether this was the first airplane flight of Robinson's life.[47] Although the pilot refused to provide Robinson flight instruction, he did suggest that Robinson consider moving to Chicago and enrolling in an aeronautical course of instruction there.

In 1927, Robinson did just that and eventually opened his own automobile repair garage, which proved to be quite successful. By mail, he applied to and was accepted at the prestigious all-white Curtis-Wright Aeronautical University (in 1933 renamed Aeronautical University of Chicago) which offered aviation ground school and aviation maintenance laboratory courses that complemented actual flight instruction provided about 20 miles away at the Curtiss-Reynolds Airport in Glenview, Illinois.[48] While women were encouraged to enroll, the school did not admit African-American students and Robinson was denied admission when he appeared in person, and school officials realized that he was black.[49]

Refusing to be denied, he persisted until the school's director eventually hired him as a weekend janitor when aviation ground school courses were offered. Robinson surreptitiously observed classes, copied lecture notes from blackboards in empty classrooms, studied classroom textbooks, assisted the engine instructors, and generally impressed instructors and students with his aeronautical and mechanical knowledge.

Robinson also managed to locate a white flight instructor by the name of Warren Melvicke at Acres Field (also referred to as Akers Airport), located about 15 miles away in Melrose Park, who was willing to provide him flight instruction.[50] On February 1, 1930 Robinson made his first solo flight and that same year earned his private pilot certificate (#26,042), followed later by his transport pilot certificate.[51]

While accounts vary as to the exact reason, Robinson was eventually allowed to enroll full-time in the school.[52] In May 1931, after two years of intensive study, Robinson became the first African-American graduate of the Curtiss-Wright Aeronautical University.[53]

After graduation, Robinson's proposal to serve as a faculty member to create and teach the first all-black class in the school's history during the academic year 1931-32 was accepted, as long as he could recruit a minimum of 25 African-American students.[54] Robinson was successful and the class, which included six women, began an intensive year-long night course that included aviation ground school and hands-on aviation maintenance training. Only eight students successfully graduated, including two women, Willa Brown and Janet Bragg.

Known as the "Brown Condor of Ethiopia," John C. Robinson is pictured during his service as a colonel in the Ethiopian Imperial Air Force.

Tireless in his promotion of black aviation in Chicago, Robinson continued to shatter racial barriers. In 1933 he built the first Department of Commerce's accredited African-American airfield, and in 1935 he established what some consider to be the first all-black military aviation unit in U.S. history, the Illinois state-chartered "Military Order of Guard, Aviation Squadron," comparable to that of a state militia.[55] He also helped organized three aeronautical clubs for African-Americans, in 1927 the Aero Study Club, in 1929 the Brown Eagle Aero Club; and in 1931 the Challenger Aero Club, later renamed the Challenger Air Pilots' Association.[56]

In a rather unusual turn of events, Robinson's reputation also attracted the attention of Ethiopian Emperor Haile Selassie, whose country was on the verge of war with Benito Mussolini's fascist Italy. Selassie wanted black aviators in his country's air force, and in April 1935 he offered Robinson an officer's commission and a position in the Imperial Ethiopian Air Force.[57]

Upon his arrival in May 1935 Robinson initially served as a flight instructor. But in August 1935, he was advanced to full colonel and given command of the entire air force, which consisted of a handful of obsolete airplanes, some equipped with machine guns for self-defense but none truly capable of air-to-air combat against modern Italian fighters.[58] Robinson himself had no air-to-air combat training.

On October 3, 1935, Mussolini invaded Ethiopia without warning and launched a bomber attack against the defenseless Ethiopian town of Adowa, devoid of military targets but the site of a humiliating Ethiopian victory over the Italians in 1896 that protected Ethiopian sovereignty and prevented Italian colonization.[59] Robinson was staying in Adowa, flying dispatches between Selassie and his frontline commanders, when Italian six-engine Caproni Ca 90 bombers, at that time the largest airplane in the world, bombed and strafed the town twice.[60] The Italian Air Force quickly established air supremacy across Ethiopia and Robinson's airplanes were relegated to furtive reconnaissance, medical evacuation, supply, and transportation missions.

Robinson's first exposure to aerial combat occurred the day after the Adowa attack on October 4, 1935 as he dashed from Adowa to deliver messages to Selassie at Addis Ababa, the nation's capital. Flying a French Potez 25 biplane, a 1920s design, twin-seat, single-engine biplane, he was attacked by two Italian fighters. He managed to fire a few shots at his adversaries and narrowly escaped only by employing a series of low-level maneuvers. As he recalled,

> The day after {the bombing of Adowa} I started back to Addis Ababa with some important papers and was attacked by two Italian airplanes {and now} I really had the closest call I have ever had in my life...I didn't mind being attacked , but I wish my airplane had been of a later type, I think I would have given them a wonderful lesson.[61]

He was pursued by various Italian fighters throughout his trip to Addis Ababa, managing to evade them only by flying low between the rocky crags of the mountainous terrain. Upon landing, one small section of his Potez's wing was found to have ten bullet holes in it.[62] While this account differs from a press interview Robinson gave on October 5, 1935 when he stated that he saw no Italian airplanes on his return to Addis Ababa, there is little doubt that every time Robinson flew in Ethiopia, he was under constant threat of attack by Italian fighters.[63]

During the next several months Robinson flew himself to exhaustion, flying 700 hours between June 1935 and April 1936.[64] In December 1935, he sighted and attacked a lone Caproni bomber, raking it with machine gun fire until driven off by Italian fighters flying to its rescue.[65,66] It was Robinson's last air-to-air combat mission in a futile war. Robinson departed Ethiopia on April 30, 1936 just before the final Italian advance that captured Addis Ababa and occupied Ethiopia.

Robinson returned to the United States to a hero's welcome

Cornelius R. Coffey was the first African-American to hold both a pilot certificate and a mechanic certificate.

from black America and on September 28, 1936 he opened his own aviation school in Chicago, named the John C. Robinson National Air College and School of Automotive Engineering.[67] Courses offered encompassed all aspects of an aviation ground school, including airplane engine mechanics, automotive mechanics, and flight instruction.[68]

For the next several years he passionately promoted aviation to African-Americans and in 1940 at the request of the U.S. Army Air Corps Robinson served as an aviation instructor at Keesler Field and Chanute Field.[69] In 1944 he returned to Ethiopia at the request of Emperor Selassie after the country's liberation towards the end of World War II. At the young age of 48, he died there as a result of injuries from an airplane accident on March 27, 1954 and he is buried in Addis Ababa.

Cornelius Robinson Coffey

Cornelius Robinson Coffey (September 6, 1903 to March 2, 1994) was born in Newport, Arkansas and after graduating from high school moved to Chicago, Illinois for instruction as an automobile mechanic. Upon successful completion of training, he moved to Detroit where he owned and operated an automobile and motorcycle repair shop.

In 1925 in Detroit he met John C. Robinson, a fellow automobile mechanic who shared his passion for flight.[70] Robinson convinced Coffey to return to Chicago where together they worked in Robinson's garage to rebuild a three-seat open cockpit biplane Waco 9. They used kit parts purchased from the Heath Airplane Company and also converted a used motorcycle engine for aviation use.[71]

When the aircraft was complete, they moved it to Acres Airport where the two expert mechanics exchanged free work on the white owners' and customers' airplanes and automobiles for free working space.[72] After an inspection by a night school instructor at the nearby Curtiss-Wright Aeronautical University, the aircraft was deemed airworthy and flew perfectly on its first flight.[73] It appears that this is the airplane that Robinson and Coffey learned to fly in.[74]

Here is where the story diverges. In one version, Robinson enrolled in the Curtiss-Wright Aeronautical University alone. Then after graduation when Robinson taught his first all-black aeronautical course at the Curtiss-Wright Aeronautical University during the academic year 1931-32, Coffey enrolled in this class as Robinson's student. This story seems to be borne out by the fact that Coffey's graduation certificate from the Curtiss-Wright Aeronautical University is dated July 26, 1932.[75]

In a different version, both Coffey and Robinson enrolled in the Curtis-Wright Aeronautical University at the same time.[76] Both had applied by mail and were accepted, but when they appeared in person, they were denied admission when school officials realized that they were African-Americans. Emil Mack, the white owner of the Chevrolet car dealership where they both worked, heard about their situation and threatened to either sue the school on their behalf or provide Robinson and Coffey the funds to do so. As a result, the school reversed its decision and admitted both Coffey and Robinson to avoid an expensive lawsuit and unpleasant publicity. [77,78] In this version of the story, Coffey and Robinson together trained the first class of African-American students at the Curtiss-Wright Aeronautical University in 1931-1932. This account is confirmed by Janet Bragg who in her biography stated that both Coffey and Robinson were her instructors in the first class.[79]

Regardless of the real story, after graduation from the Curtiss-Wright Aeronautical University, Coffey became the first African-American to become a certified airplane mechanic when he earned his Airplane and Engine (A&E) certificate (#11,598) on July 26, 1932. He later earned his pilot certificate, becoming the first African-American to hold both a pilot and a mechanic certificate. In August 1938 he also received his limited commercial certificate (#36,609).

Although at times their relationship was strained for various reasons, Coffey continued to work closely with Robinson until the latter departed for Ethiopia in 1935. After Robinson escaped Ethiopia shortly before its fall to the Italians in May 1936, Coffey even sold one of his airplanes to pay for Robinson's return trip to the United States.[80]

When Robinson opened his aviation school in 1936, Coffey

Willa Brown was the first African-American woman to be awarded her pilot certificate from the U.S. Department of Commerce.

served as an instructor, but in 1938 Coffey started his own flight training school, the Coffey School of Aeronautics, at Harlem Airport in Chicago.[81] This school directly competed with Robinson's school and later became the only non-university affiliated flight training center associated with the Civilian Pilot Training Program. Many of his students would go on to fly with the Tuskegee Airmen.

Willa Beatrice Brown

Willa Beatrice Brown (January 22, 1906 – July 18, 1992) was born in Glasgow, Kentucky but was raised in Indiana and graduated from Indiana State Teachers College (later renamed Indiana University) with a bachelor's degree in business and later from Northwestern University with a master's degree in business administration.

After briefly teaching high school in Indiana, Brown moved to Chicago to become a social worker but decided to learn to fly instead and enrolled in the first African-American class offered by Robinson at the Curtiss-Wright Aeronautical University from 1931-1932.

On June 22, 1938, she was awarded her private pilot certificate (#43,814) from the Department of Commerce, becoming the first African-American woman to earn her private pilot certificate in the

Janet Bragg was the first African-American to hold a commercial pilot's certificate.

a prominent African-American newspaper, and several other local black aviators, she was one of the founding members of the National Airmen's Association of America, an organization formed to advocate African-American participation in U.S. government pilot training programs.[87]

Janet Harmon Bragg

Jane Nettie "Janet" Bragg (nee Harmon, March 24, 1907 - April 11, 1993) was born in Griffin, Georgia and graduated from Spellman Seminary's (later renamed Spellman College) nursing program in Atlanta, Georgia.[88] In 1931 she moved to Chicago where she worked as a professional nurse. She was briefly married to Evans Waterford but enjoyed a long marriage to Sumner Bragg so in some references she is known alternatively as either Janet Waterford or Janet Bragg.

Bragg first became interested in aviation after noticing a billboard advertising flying lessons, so she enrolled in and graduated from John C. Robinson's first aviation class during the 1931-1932 academic year at the Curtiss-Wright Aeronautical University.

As the program provided only academic instruction, she decided to go out on her own to receive flight training. Coffey brought her to Acres Field where she took flight lessons from a white instructor, but the field was subsequently sold to a housing developer.[89,90]

As African-American aviators were typically banned from white flyers' airports, in 1931 Robinson managed to rent a field in Robbins, Illinois, a predominantly black suburb located about 15 miles south of Chicago.[91] Reserved for the exclusive use of black pilots, Bragg, Robinson, Coffey and other African-American aviators built their own airfield,

> We had to supply all the time, labor, and materials. The land had to be leveled, trees cut down, rocks moved, and ditches filled for a northeast-southwest runway. There wasn't room for more than one runway, and, anyway, the prevailing winds were mostly from the southwest. Every Saturday, Sunday, and holiday we met in Robbins to work.[92]

They also built a hangar, and the airfield was officially approved by the Department of Commerce, becoming the first accredited flying field operated solely by African-Americans.[93] Since the airport did not have an airplane for flight training, Bragg, who was doing quite well financially as a nurse, bought her own airplane sight unseen with Robinson and Coffey's help, an International model F-17.[94]

Gaining fame as "The Flying Nurse," the following spring Bragg started flight lessons under the tutelage of Robinson and Coffey and was soon ready for her private pilot certificate test,

> In a rented airplane, Johnny Robinson accompanied me

United States, Bessie Coleman having received her pilot certificate from the Fédération Aéronautique Internationale (FAI) in Paris.[82,83]

Brown also earned her mechanic certificate, becoming the first African-American woman to hold both a private pilot certificate and a mechanic certificate. On April 6, 1939 Brown became the first African-American woman to earn a limited commercial certificate. [84]

In 1937, Brown married Cornelius Coffey, and together they managed the Coffey School of Aeronautics.[85] She was also the first African-American female officer in the Civil Air Patrol, assigned to Illinois' 111th Flight Squadron.[86] In 1939, along with Coffey, Enoch Waters, editorial director of the Chicago Defender, to Pal-Waukee Airport, north of the city, where I took the test and passed with no problems. The federal examiner, a very nice white man, said 'It doesn't matter what color you are, just that you know what you are doing.' With the good instruction I had received, I did.[95]

Unfortunately, a violent windstorm in May 1933 tore through Robbins field, destroying the hangar and the airplanes inside.[96,97] The African-American pilots then relocated to Harlem Airport, located in Oak Lawn, Illinois, about 16 miles south of Chicago. There Bragg established her own flying school and taught both white and black flight students.[98]

In 1943 she traveled to the Tuskegee Institute to obtain her instrument and commercial certificates under the tutelage of African-American flight instructors Charles "Chief"Anderson and George Allen. Training complete, she flew her commercial check ride with T.K. Hudson, observers on the ground proudly watching as she executed each required maneuver flawlessly,

Hudson at last gave me the signal to land, and that, too was perfect, a three-point landing. My instructors and all the rest came to the plane. They were as happy as I was. 'How did she do, Mr. Hudson?' Allen asked.

With a long Southern drawl I'll never forget, he answered. 'Well, George, she gave me a good flight. I will put her up against any of your flight instructors. But I've never given a colored girl a commercial certificate, and I don't intend to now.' He threw his parachute in his car and drove off.

All of us were shocked, speechless. I looked at 'Chief,' and tears were in his eyes. Allen was nauseated. The others just walked away dejected. Finally, I came out of my shocked daze and said, 'Don't worry. We will find some way.' Every defeat was a challenge.[99]

Heartbroken, Bragg returned to Chicago and after only a few days of rest returned to familiar Pal-Waukee Airport for another attempt at the checkride,

I told the flight examiner, Mr. Ritter, a tall Texan, what had happened in Tuskegee. When he spoke with that Texas drawl, I thought, 'Oh my God, here we go again.'

He said, though, 'We shall see.' We went up and through some maneuvers like spins, chandelles, lazy eights, the same ones I had done in Alabama. Then he gave the signal to land. I had reached a saturation point. It didn't make any difference anymore if I passed or failed. But guess what? The man shook my hand, congratulated me, and told me to pick up my certificate on Wednesday at Chicago Municipal

Known as the "Father of Black Aviation," Charles A. "Chief" Anderson was the chief flight instructor at the Tuskegee Institute.

Airport, now Midway Airport. How about them apples![100]

Bragg was now the first African-American woman to hold a commercial pilot certificate. During World War II, as a highly qualified pilot with extensive experience, the owner of a flight school and several airplanes, she applied for service with the Women's Auxiliary Service Pilots (WASP) but was turned down by founder Jacqueline Cochran because of her race.[101] It is hard to imagine that someone as accomplished as Pensacola-born Jacqueline Cochran, who overcame tremendous obstacles to find a place for women in military aviation could be prejudiced, but regretfully even "interactions between black and white women were adversarial during this era."[102]

Charles Alfred Anderson

Charles Alfred "Chief" Anderson (February 9, 1907 – April 13, 1996) was born in Bridgeport, Pennsylvania and as a young boy became fascinated by airplanes, but as an African-American, he was unable to get even a passenger ride in one.[103]

So in 1928, he purchased his own airplane, a two-seat, high-wing Velie Monocoupe,

> It was impossible for blacks to fly then. They would just point-blank tell you, we don't take colored people up. So I bought a second-hand plane. Naturally, I had to learn, but nobody would teach me, so I taught myself. I became familiar with the feel of it and watched what other people were doing, and when it came time to solo, I just did what they did.[104]

On August 8, 1929, Anderson earned his private pilot certificate but being self-taught for routine take-offs and landings did not mean that he possessed the required skills to perform the advanced maneuvers necessary for his commercial pilot certificate.[105]

Providentially, a white pilot by the name of Russell Thaw asked to rent Anderson's airplane so that Thaw could fly to Atlantic City to visit his mother. While Thaw refused to provide flight instruction to Anderson, he offered to let Anderson accompany him to gain cross-country flight experience.[106] Anderson agreed, and while he did learn from Thaw, he continued to practice alone, but not necessarily with good results,

> He soon soloed his plane into a tree. Six decades later, you can still see the long scar that wanders across his forehead. 'All my scalp went back here behind my head,' says Anderson with his deep-bucket laugh. 'I remember reaching it forward and patting it down.' Seeing his wound, his mother, Janie, tried to chop up his plane with an ax.[107]

After a second accident, Anderson realized that he needed to find someone who would give him advanced flight instruction. Everyone turned him down except for one person, former German aviator Ernest H. Buehl Sr, the same Flying Dutchman who had taught Emory Malick to fly.

In February 1932 Anderson became the first African-American to earn his Department of Commerce air transport pilot certificate (#7,638).[108] But Buehl had to force the federal examiner to give Anderson his checkride,

> When the government agent came...he took me aside and he called me everything under the sun because I would even attempt to get that man into an airplane. I finally tell him, 'Look, I'm a foreigner. I'm a citizen by paper. That guy's born here.' And I threatened to make a little trouble for this guy. So he finally took him up and kept him up a considerable time longer than a white man. He really put him through the works.[109]

As will be discussed later, after completing a series of record-

William Powell, a visionary pioneer of black aviation who wrote the book Black Wings and formed the Bessie Coleman Aero Club.

setting transcontinental flights, Anderson was hired by Howard University in Washington, DC, to teach civilian pilot training courses. In 1940 he joined the Tuskegee Institute in Alabama as the school's chief flight instructor, a position in which he would gain everlasting fame as a mentor for the Tuskegee Airmen and also as the first African-American to fly a United States President's wife.

William J. Powell

William Jenifer Powell (July 27, 1897 to July 12, 1942) was born William Jenifer in Henderson, Kentucky. After his father died, his mother moved to Chicago, and she remarried to a man named Powell who adopted her children.[110] Powell was enrolled at the University of Illinois when World War I began, and he left school to serve in combat overseas as an officer with the segregated 365th Illinois Infantry Regiment. Severely injured in a poison gas attack on the last day of the war, he returned home to recuperate and finished his degree in electrical engineering.[111] He then opened several very successful automobile service stations and an automobile repair shop in Chicago.

In 1927 while attending an American Legion convention in France, Powell took the first flight of his life at Paris- Le Bourget Airport, the same airfield Charles Lindbergh landed at after completing the first solo, non-stop, transatlantic flight. Completely enamored with aviation, he was refused both civilian and military flight training in the United States because of his race. He well-documented that fact in a letter to the editor in response to magazine articles that stated there were no obstacles in the path of would-be African-American aviators and that the small number of black commercial pilots can only "be attributed to anything other than a lack of ability."[112]

Eventually, Powell did find a commercial aeronautical college in Los Angeles who would accept him. He sold his businesses, moved to California and successfully enrolled at the Warren School of Aeronautics in 1928, where he earned his pilot certificate.[113]

In 1929, he founded an African-American flying club, the Bessie Coleman Aero Club, named in honor of the famous black aviatrix, and to whom he dedicated his book *Black Wings,*

> To the memory of Bessie Coleman, the first Negro to fly an aeroplane successfully, who, although possessed of all the feminine charms that man admires in the opposite sex, also displayed courage equal to that of the most daring men.[114]

Established about the same time as Robinson's Challenger Aero Club, Los Angeles now emerged as a center of black aviation to rival Chicago's achievements. Unlike Robinson's Challenger Aero Club, which was a local venture, Powell hoped to establish a national network of Bessie Coleman Aero Clubs across the United States "to keep Coleman's dream alive by encouraging young African-Americans to become aviators."[115]

Powell also opened the Bessie Coleman School, an all-black flight school to train African-American male and female pilots and mechanics. Powell believed,

> That the demand for skilled fliers and mechanics would be so great that trained, competent blacks could overcome the racial barriers that had traditionally excluded them from responsible positions in other branches of the transportation industry. Yet scarcely a year after Powell began proselytizing young blacks, the organizers of the Air Line Pilots Association included a clause in the union's bylaws that restricted membership to whites only.[116]

In late 1929 Powell, along with his chief pilot James Banning,

unintentionally became the first African-Americans to fly across an international border.[117] Officials in Jackson, Mississippi had guaranteed them $2,500 to perform exhibition flights at the Mississippi State Fair. They purchased a Kinner Crown biplane and took off from Los Angeles intending to spend the night in San Diego before heading east. Depending on the version of the story, they were either the victims of a malfunctioning compass or made a significant error in visual navigation, but in any event, they became lost and eventually ran out of gas.

They made a successful emergency landing on an isolated sandy beach, believing that they were on the shores of the Salton Sea, a lake located about 130 miles northeast of San Diego. They were actually on the shores of Mexico's Gulf of California, approximately 420 miles southeast of San Diego. The downed aviators trekked across desolate terrain for four days before reaching the small village of San Felipe.[118] After recuperating for several days, they returned to their airplane, which they then refueled and returned home.

On Labor Day in September 1931, Powell and his Bessie Coleman Club produced the first air show in the United States featuring all-black performers. Held in Los Angeles and attended by an estimated 15,000 spectators, it was followed by an equally successful air circus a few months later in December 1931.

These air shows featured the first all-black flight demonstration teams, assembled by Powell and trained by Banning.[119,120] The first air show introduced a trio, Powell, Irvin Wells and William Aiken. The second air show added two more pilots, a woman by the name of Marie Dickerson Coker and the infamous Hubert Julian, billboards heralding the five pilots as the *Five Blackbirds*.[121] Their performance proved so successful that Powell announced plans for a 150-city tour to promote the formation of Bessie Coleman Clubs across the country, and added a second African-American female pilot to the team, Beatrice Reeves.[122,123] However, funding issues precluded the trip and the *Five Blackbirds*' saga ended with just the two performances.[124]

In 1932 Powell and his co-pilot Dick Wells became the first African-Americans to participate in a long-distance race when they flew in the Pacific division of the Cord Cup Transcontinental Handicap Derby.[125] Competing against 54 white pilots, they departed Los Angeles for Cleveland, a 2,369-mile trip, and were competitive through three days of racing until engine trouble near El Paso, Texas forced them to drop out of the race.[126]

A prolific writer, Powell formed the *Craftsmen of Black Wings*, a non-profit organization whose primary objective was to promote interest in aviation jobs for African-Americans and to disprove the idiotic idea that African-Americans could not fly.[127] He published a monthly trade journal called the *Craftsmen Aero-News* newsletter, and in 1934, he wrote a fictionalized autobiography titled *Black Wings* to inspire African-Americans to enter aviation, hoping "to fill the air with "Black Wings."[128] In the preface to the book Powell wrote,

Hubert Julian striking a historic pose astride his Packard-Bellanca. A controversial figure in black aviation history, Hubert Julian has been described as an inveterate self-promoter, a conqueror of the air, and a four-flusher. Yet he was always a crowd pleaser and enjoyed a healthy, if not checkered, career.

Stimulating interest in aviation among Negroes would not be such an arduous task were it not for stumbling blocks which seriously menace the Negro's entry into any line of commercial endeavor. Skepticism, superstition, mistrust, jealousy, lack of co-operation, lack of preparation, race prejudice, and lack of finance have caused many a young Negro to turn away from some field of commercial endeavor with disgust. These form the basis for my story, and I trust and sincerely hope that this book will serve as a guide to those of my race whose ambition it is to become the flyers of the future, in order that they may know what to expect and be ready for it.[129]

In 1935, Powell also prepared and distributed a 15-minute silent educational movie titled *Unemployment, the Negro and Aviation*, hoping to inspire young African-Americans into the field of aviation.[130]

Sadly, Powell passed away in 1942 at the age of 44, his premature death most likely caused by the severe lung damage he received from his World War I injuries. But he did live long enough to see his dreams of military aviation service by African-Americans fulfilled by the Tuskegee Airmen, whose first class convened in 1941.

Hubert Fauntleroy Julian

Any history of early black aviators would be incomplete without the mention of the *"Black Eagle of Harlem,"* Hubert Fauntleroy Julian (September 21, 1897 to February 19, 1982),

who was born in Trinidad as a British subject and emigrated to Canada in 1914. At his best, Julian can be described as a colorful, flamboyant, master of self-promotion. At his worst, a shyster who fleeced innocent people and profoundly offended fellow black aviators by his aggressive promotions for transatlantic flights to Africa and Europe, which never came to fruition, but gained him national notoriety, wealth and international celebrity.[131]

Julian immigrated to the United States in 1921 and claimed to have served as a Lieutenant in the Royal Canadian Air Force, although this was later disproved. He first specialized in parachute jumping displays over the city of New York, and his pilot for some of these trips was the famous aviator Clarence Chamberlin, who in June 1927 became the second person to fly across the Atlantic shortly after Charles Lindberg's May 1927 flight.

In his biography, Chamberlin recalled providing Julian flight training and also selling him a reconditioned Boeing seaplane that Julian intended to use for a highly publicized solo trans-Atlantic flight from the United States to Africa.[132] Julian's fund-raising drew the interest of the U.S. Department of Justice who suspected mail fraud and threatened prosecution if Julian did not attempt the flight. Chamberlin assisted Julian with his flight preparations and alongside thousands of spectators watched him make his takeoff from the Harlem River on July 4, 1924. Julian made a steep banking turn in an attempt to overfly the well-wishing crowd before beginning his journey but instead stalled and crashed into Flushing Bay. He was rescued unharmed, but the seaplane was destroyed.[133] He also promoted similar trips in 1926 and 1928, but they were never flown.[134]

In the early 1930s, Julian was invited by Emperor Selassie to serve in Ethiopia as his personal pilot.[135] His arrival preceded that of Robinson but the Emperor banished Julian when he crashed Selassie's sporty, brand-new de Havilland Gypsy Moth on an unauthorized flight and after he brawled with Robinson in a hotel lobby on August 8, 1935 in Addis Ababa after he had heard that Robinson had belittled his piloting skills.[136]

Julian continued his checkered career as a "mercenary, a gunrunner, a stunt pilot, and a diplomat, or whatever else the situation required," and to the end remained a controversial figure,[137]

> Julian's posturing, swaggering, and blustering reinforced white American's preconceived notion that blacks were at best inept pilots, seriously undermining the credibility of legitimate black aviators striving to prove that whites did not have a monopoly on flying aptitude. By the mid-1930's he had become an embarrassment to serious-minded blacks and he was soundly condemned by black editors.[138]

Albert Ernest Forsythe, M.D.

Albert Ernest "Bert" Forsythe (sometimes spelled Forsyth, February 25, 1897 to May 6, 1986) was born in Nassau, Bahamas. After finishing secondary schooling in the Bahamas in 1911, he immigrated to the United States to study architecture at the Tuskegee Institute in Alabama but transferred to the University of Illinois and the University of Toledo in Ohio to complete his pre-medical school studies.[139] He graduated on June 14, 1923 and after being refused acceptance at American medical schools due to his race, he enrolled at McGill University Medical School in Canada where he earned his Doctor of Medicine (M.D.) in May 1930.

Forsythe then moved to Atlantic City, New Jersey where he established his medical practice. In 1932 after taking several passenger rides with local barnstormers he decided to take flying lessons, but he was unable to find a flight instructor due to his race,

Dr. Albert E. Forsythe purchased his own airplane and received flight training from Charles A. Anderson and Ernest H. Buehl Sr.

> In this land known as the home of the free and the brave, a land of opportunity, but also a land of discrimination and segregation, nothing was simple. Bert was a man who had the intellect to be admitted to and graduate with honors from one of the top medical schools on the continents and a man who the financial means to take flying lessons. But he was a man who had the handicap of being the wrong color.[140]

Forsythe refused to be denied, and like Charles Anderson before him, decided to buy his own airplane. He traveled to Maryland hoping to purchase a single-wing, enclosed cabin 95-horsepower Fairchild 24, but again could not find a single flight instructor who would teach him to fly. Coincidently, the husband of his medical partner's daughter had heard of an African-American pilot who was flying newspapers between Philadelphia and Atlantic City. Forsythe traveled to the airfield to meet none other than Charles Anderson himself, who immediately offered to provide him flight instruction along with Anderson's good friend, German-born Ernest H. Buehl Sr.[141] Flying from Buehl's field in Somerton, Pennsylvania, Forsythe quickly earned his pilot certificate and even purchased an airplane from Buehl.

As will be seen in the next chapter, with his new private pilot certificate safely in hand, Forsythe's next goal was to partner with Anderson to garner international publicity on the aeronautical skills of African-American aviators by completing a series of long-distance cross-country flights.

James Lincoln Holt Peck

James Lincoln Holt Peck (September 8, 1912 to February 6, 1996), was born in Stoops Ferry, Pennsylvania and became interested in aviation after seeing several Curtiss JN-4 *Jenny's* barnstorm in his hometown. He briefly attended the University of Pittsburgh but left to enroll at a Curtiss-Wright flight school in Pennsylvania to pursue a career in aviation. Warned that local Civil Aeronautics Authority flight examiners refused to issue pilot certificates to black aviators, the school's director recommended he transfer to the Cleveland Institute of Aeronautics in Ohio, where he would be "judged solely on his flying ability." [142]

Peck agreed and successfully earned his pilot certificate, but he was unable to find a flying job in military or commercial aviation in the United States due to his race. He toured the nation for several years as a musician, but after the outbreak of the Spanish Civil War, he was recruited by the Spanish government to serve as a combat pilot.[143] Peck enlisted in the Spanish Republican Air Force, fighting on the side of the elected Loyalist Republicans against the rebel Nationalists led by General Francisco Franco.[144]

He departed the United States aboard the RMS *Queen Mary* and after a hike across the Pyrenees Mountains eventually arrived at Santiago de la Ribera, a Spanish military air base located on Spain's Mediterranean coast. Along with other volunteers, Peck completed an intensive three-week aerial combat training program under Russian military advisors and Spanish flight instructors that included aerobatics, gunnery and formation work.[145] Upon completion of training in September 1937 Peck was commissioned a lieutenant, and he primarily flew two Russian-built fighters, the Polikarpov I-15, a biplane nicknamed *Chato* (snub-nose) by the Republican pilots and the Polikarpov I-16, a revolutionary low-wing, monoplane fighter known as the *Mosca* (house fly).[146]

Initially assigned coastal patrol missions from Santiago de la Ribera, Peck wrote about his first air-to-air combat engagement in a 1938 magazine article, describing how his flight of ten Republican *Chato's* battled nine Nationalist Italian-designed Fiat CR.32 biplane fighters over the sea. [147] Peck described his rollicking dogfight in great detail, with each fighter damaging the other before the engagement was broken off.

He wrote additional articles about his Spanish dogfighting experiences, including an article that appeared in *The New York Times Magazine*.[148] In a spirited story in his book *Armies with Wings*, Peck described flying a Polikarpov I-16 *Mosca* in a night engagement against Italian-built Caproni bombers where he was "undoubtedly closer to death that night than ever before, or since."[149]

Peck continued to fly, conducting day and night bomber escort and interception missions as well as ground support bombing

James L. H. Peck flew for the Spanish Republican Air Force during the Spanish Civil War. He is shown in his U.S. Merchant Marine uniform.

and ground strafing sorties, until all international volunteers were ordered out of the country in November 1937.[150] Nearly six years would pass before the next African-American pilot attacked an enemy airplane, a Tuskegee airman flying from North Africa in July 1943 against the German Luftwaffe.

Peck claimed to have shot down five aircraft, two single-seat Heinkel He-51 biplane fighters, and three Fiat CR 32 fighters, all while flying the Polikarpov I-15 *Chato*, which would make him the first African-American ace.[151] However, he never claimed the victories in his book or articles, and aviation historians have not been able to corroborate these claims.[152]

Upon returning to the United States in December 1937 Peck was once again unsuccessful in finding employment as a pilot, so he instead joined the United States Merchant Marine as a commissioned officer. He wrote numerous magazine articles about his combat experiences in Spain and soon established himself as a journalistic expert in aviation. He became a well-recognized author and published two books and wrote an extraordinary number of articles for several magazines, including *Scientific American, New York Times Magazine, and Harper's*.[153,154,155] ∎

Chapter Two
The Great Transcontinental Flights

In 1932 James H. Banning and Thomas C. Allen made the first transcontinental flight of the United States in history by African-American aviators.

J. Herman Banning
Pilot

Thomas C. Allen.
Mec.

FIRST TRANS-CONTINENTAL FLIGHT

Seeking to draw attention to the skills of black aviators and shatter racial stereotypes, several record-breaking long-distance and publicity-seeking flights were made by prominent African-American aviators. Designed to demonstrate their aeronautical skills, these black pilots hoped that successful completion of these dangerous flights would inspire fellow African-Americans to view these "black aviation triumphs as a stride toward equality,"

Since flying involved skills beyond most Americans, if blacks could pilot these 'wondrous machines' they would shatter the myth of black inferiority. How could white America not see that black equality in the air should lead to black equality on the ground?[1]

1932 Banning and Allen's One-Way Transcontinental Flight

In 1932, the first attention-drawing flight was made by James Herman Banning and his mechanic Thomas Cox Allen (April 2, 1937 to September 11, 1989). Allen was born in Quitman, Texas and as a young boy watched an airplane make an emergency landing on his family's farm, which ignited his interest inflight.[2] His family moved to Oklahoma City, and an owner of a nearby airfield let him work with the engine mechanics. After chasing various aviation maintenance jobs around the country, Allen eventually landed a position at William J. Powell's Bessie Coleman Aero Club in Los Angeles, where he met Banning.

Banning became interested in making a transcontinental flight when he heard that there was a $1,000 prize for the first African-Americans to fly across the United States, a sizeable amount of money at the height of the Great Depression.[3] Banning recruited Allen to accompany him on the trip not for his co-piloting abilities, but rather for Allen's expert aviation mechanic skills. With minimal funds, they rebuilt an ancient Alexander Aircraft Company *Eagle Rock,* a rugged, open-cockpit biplane described by the press as a "rickety airplane with a wheezing motor that most fliers wouldn't take off the ground."[4,5]

They departed Los Angeles in late September on a "leisurely tour with frequent stops," which included several emergency landings due to engine problems.[6] They affectionately became known as the "The Flying Hobos," because they launched with absolutely no sponsorship and less than $25 in cash in their pockets[7] Every time they stopped, whether it be for fuel, repairs or rest, they had to raise money for gasoline, oil, spare parts, emergency repairs, hangar rent, food, drink, and lodging.

Every person who made a donation or contribution signed their name on the lower left wing tip of their airplane, which they dubbed the "Gold Book."[8] By the time they landed on Sunday morning, October 9, 1932 at the Valley Stream Airport on Long Island, New York they had visited 24 communities and had 65 names inscribed in their Gold Book.[9]

Banning and Allen thus became the first African-Americans to fly transcontinental across the United States, traveling the 3,300 miles from Los Angeles to New York in 41 hours and 27 minutes, although the trip actually required nearly three weeks to complete.

Still, it was an improvement upon the first transcontinental flight in the history of the United States, flown by Calbraith P. Rodgers in 1911, who flew east to west in a Wright biplane that took him 49 days and 82 hours and 4 minutes to complete.[10] In comparison, in 1930 famed aviator Frank Hawkes set a transcontinental record by flying from Los Angeles to Valley Stream in 12 hours and 25 minutes.[11] Today, a flight from Boston to Los Angeles takes less than 7 hours.

Banning and Allen never were able to track down the $1,000 prize and after being feted in New York began their return journey home on November 11, 1932.[12] Their *Eagle Rock* airplane, now christened *The Spirit of the Pittsburgh Courier* by Banning and Allen in grateful appreciation for the newspaper's support, was destined never to return to Los Angeles. Badly damaged in an emergency landing due to engine failure near Blairsville, Pennsylvania, the biplane was repaired but grounded by a mechanic's lien.

Affectionately known as the Flying Hobos, Allen and Banning launched on their transcontinental flight with no sponsorship and less than $25 between them.

Uninjured in the crash, Banning and Allen were not able to raise the funds necessary to pay the repair bill and returned home by bus, their airplane eventually sold and broken up for parts.[13]

1933 Forsythe and Anderson's Roundtrip Transcontinental Flight

The next sensational transcontinental flight was made a year later in 1933 by Charles A. Anderson and Dr. Albert E. Forsythe, who partnered to become the first African-Americans to pilot an airplane from coast to coast and then return. Forsythe proposed the trip, explaining that the reason for the flight was not to top Banning and Allen's record,

It was something that had to be done to break down all the restrictions. We did it because we wanted to open up avenues for blacks in aviation.[14]

They intended to make as many publicity stops as possible to maximize national awareness of their efforts. Unlike Banning and Allen, Forsythe also intended for their trip to be flown in a reliable airplane and to be well-funded. Toward that end, Forsythe decided their flight should originate from Atlantic City, where he maintained his medical practice. Forsythe also volunteered the use of his personal airplane, an enclosed cockpit Fairchild monoplane, which he christened the *Pride of Atlantic City.* He was very successful in garnering financial support from local businesses and professional organizations, including the Atlantic City Board

Atlantic City to Los Angeles and Return - 67 Hours - July, 1933

In July, 1933, Dr. Albert E. Forsythe and Charles A. Anderson became the first African-Americans to complete a round-trip transcontinental flight.

of Trade and the newly formed National Negro Aeronautical Society and even carried a letter from Atlantic City Mayor Harry Bacharach addressed to his counterpart Los Angeles Mayor Frank Shaw.[15,16,17]

Anderson and Forsythe departed Atlantic City at 3:00 a.m. on July 17, 1933 and using only a road map and a compass for navigation landed uneventfully at Glendale, California two days later on July 19, 1933. A celebratory crowd of an estimated 2,000 African-Americans organized by William J. Powell and his Bessie Coleman Aero Club greeted them.[18] Their total flight time was 33 hours and 15 minutes.[19]

They then departed California on July 21, 1933 and after a series of planned stops and weather delays returned to Atlantic City on July 29, 1933, completing their round-trip transcontinental flight in 12 days and 67 flight hours.[20] A crowd of well-wishers welcomed them home, including Mayor Bacharach who presented them with a commemorative medal celebrating their achievement.[21] A major celebration was held a month later on September 23, 1933 when Anderson and Forsythe flew the *Pride of Atlantic City* to Newark, New Jersey. They met with the governor of New Jersey and were

honored with a parade attended by an estimated 15,000 spectators.[22]

In November 1933 the two intrepid airmen flew to Montreal, Canada, purportedly making them the first African-American aviators to cross an international border intentionally, Powell and Banning's unplanned flight across the Mexican border in 1929 notwithstanding.[23]

1934 Forsythe and Anderson's Pan-American Goodwill Tour

Buoyed by the success of these two cross-country flights, Anderson and Forsythe next started planning for a flight to the Caribbean Islands and South America to promote better interracial and international relations and to gain prestige for African-American aviators.[24] Their idea was to launch from Atlantic City, fly down the eastern coast to Miami, and then leap across the Atlantic Ocean to their first scheduled destination, Nassau, Bahamas, the birthplace of Dr. Forsythe. In all, Anderson and Forsythe intended to travel 12,000 miles in about 35 days. They planned to visit 25

Forsythe and Anderson enjoy a quiet moment as they review their planned flight route.

Pan-American countries, including Cuba, Jamaica, Haiti, Dominican Republic, Puerto Rico, Virgin Islands, Grenada, Trinidad, British Guiana, Brazil, Venezuela, Colombia, Panama, Nicaragua, El Salvador, Honduras, Guatemala, and Mexico.[25]

Forsythe again wanted to ensure that the trip was well-financed and turned to the Inter-Racial Goodwill Aviation Committee for support, which had replaced the National Negro Aeronautical Society, sponsor of Anderson and Forsythe's first two cross-country flights.[26] Planning, fundraising, and publicity for the trip was extensive and proved extremely successful with both the U.S. State Department and the U.S. Department of Commerce pledging support and all countries promising elaborate welcomes.[27]

A new airplane with increased fuel efficiency was also needed as Forsythe's Fairchild did not have the range to fly over large expanses of water. Forsythe decided to purchase a stylish black and orange, two-seat, enclosed-cabin Monocoupe, built by the Lambert Aircraft Corporation of St. Louis, Missouri and equipped with auxiliary fuel tanks to give it a cruising range of 1,000 miles.[28] On August 23, 1934 when Anderson and Forsythe flew to Missouri to exchange the Fairchild for the Lambert Monocoupe, they were introduced to Charles Lindbergh, who happened to be there at the same time to purchase his own Monocoupe.[29] Lindbergh shared his own experiences with long overwater flights and his visits to various Caribbean and South American airfields.

Forsythe decided to name his new airplane *Booker T. Washington*, in honor of his mentor at the Tuskegee Institute, and he traveled to Tuskegee on September 15, 1934 with Anderson for an official christening with Dr. Robert Moton, the current President of the Tuskegee Institute. In attendance for the ceremony was Col. Benjamin Oliver Davis Sr., U.S. Army, the head of the military department at the Tuskegee Institute, and whose son, Benjamin

Oliver Davis Jr., would enroll in the first Tuskegee Airmen class nearly seven years later.[30]

Anderson and Forsythe officially departed Atlantic City on their Pan-American Goodwill Tour on November 8, 1934 and during the next 51 days garnered international attention as they traveled 689 miles and visited ten countries. Many years later Anderson recalled Forsythe's delight in emphasizing their race,

> 'When I was flying over the Caribbean with Dr. Forsythe, we were passing over this ocean liner,' he recalls. 'Dr. Forsythe says, 'Get down close to the boat so they can see that blacks are flying this airplane.' So I swung right down by it, almost at deck level. That crew was positively surprised.' A big chuckle. 'Gave them something to think about.'[31]

Their trip ended prematurely, however, in Port-of-Spain, Trinidad on December 14, 1934 when the *Booker T. Washington* crashed shortly after takeoff upon encountering a severe downdraft. Neither Forsythe nor Anderson was hurt, but the airplane was severely damaged, and the decision was made to end the tour. Both aviators, along with a disassembled *Booker T. Washington,* returned to the United States aboard a steamship liner.

Forsythe later related that the real goal of the trip had been to,

> Demonstrate to all concerned that blacks were able to navigate and fly aeroplanes under the most hazardous situations and thus demonstrate that the myths about blacks, myths held up by the U.S. military and others, were irresponsible and a threat to racial harmony in the United States.[32]

While Anderson went on to fame as a flight instructor for the

Tuskegee Airmen, Forsythe returned to his medical practice and without regret never piloted an airplane again after 1935.[33] Forsythe noted,

> My main business was medicine, surgery. I was not interested in becoming involved much in aviation. We just made a series of flights for the sole purpose of opening the road for blacks who wanted to fly.[34]

The Future

Despite the impressive achievements of these heroic, record-setting black pilots, not a single African-American aviator flew for an American airline or served in the aviation branches of the armed forces of the United States. In his 1934 book, *Black Wings,* Powell noted,

> Out of 18,041 active pilot licenses in the US, only 12 are held by Negroes. Out of 8,651 mechanics' licenses only 2 are held by Negroes. I bow my head in shame.[35]

The aeronautical skills and exceptional competence of African-American aviators were rarely reported upon by the mainstream white American press, and even coverage by predominantly black newspapers is best described as spotty.

So the three-pronged horns of racism, perceived lack of aeronautical adaptability, and ignominy denied African-Americans knowledge of the bright potential of careers in aviation or for those who wanted to fly, even the most basic opportunity to take flight training. What few prospects existed for African-Americans in aviation remained little known outside the small black aviation community. As one reporter noted,

> Aviation has tremendous and dramatic possibilities to help the race in its fight for world-wide respect. The Lindberghs and Earharts, the Eckners and Byrds have fired the imagination of the whole civilized world, whether flying alone into the heart of a people, sitting at the controls of a passenger Zeppelin or risking death in icy isolation at 'the bottom of the world.' Negro youth needs that kind of inspiration, not only from a Lindbergh whose rich military experiences are barred to the black flyer, but from an Anderson or a Forsythe who has plodded the hard way from one slight achievement to another and who has gone forward on the encouragement of his fellow men.[36]

It seemed like nothing could change a national policy of exclusion of African-Americans from aviation. But a novel program envisioned by an enlightened member of the newly created Civil Aeronautics Authority just might. It was named the Civilian Pilot Training Program (CPTP), and the inclusion of African-Americans in this program required another long, dangerous cross-country flight by daring black pilots. ■

ATLANTIC CITY IS AIR-MINDED TOO—CITY OFFICIALS AND CITIZENS BIDDING AVIATORS ANDERSON AND FORSYTHE GOD-SPEED AT THEIR TAKE-OFF ON THE HISTORY MAKING PAN-AMERICAN GOOD-WILL FLIGHT, NOVEMBER 8, 1932—THE MONOPLANE BOOKER T. WASHINGTON IN THE BACKGROUND.

Dr. Albert E. Forsythe and Charles Anderson preparing to depart Atlantic City, New Jersey for a round-robin trip around the Caribbean Islands and South America.

"If I have seen further than others, it is by standing on the shoulders of giants." Tuskegee Institute president Dr. Robert Moton is flanked by Dr. Albert Forsythe (left) and Charles Anderson.

Chapter Three Civilian Pilot Training Program and Public Law 18

I n 1939 the U.S. Army Air Corps, the aviation component of the U.S. Army, was commanded by then Maj. Gen. Henry A. "Hap" Arnold, who reported to the War Department, headed by the Secretary of War Harry H. Woodring, a civilian cabinet-level position responsible for the operation of the U.S. Army. In 1940 Henry L. Stimson replaced Woodring as Secretary of War.

It may be hard to believe today, but during the first half of the 20th century, the conventional military wisdom was that African-Americans were mentally and physically incapable of flying an airplane. To rationalize their decision to bar African-Americans from military flight training, the U.S. Army Air Corps used a 1925 study prepared by the faculty and students of the U.S. Army War College.[1] This study's contrived unscientific and racist findings deemed African-Americans more suited for assignment to segregated noncombatant labor and service units than combat units due to their general lack of intelligence, insufficient technical education, and illiteracy.[2]

So the official policy of the War Department and the U.S. Army Air Corps was that African-Americans were barred from military flight training. All black applicants were rejected, leaving African-Americans no other means of proving their aptitude for flight.

This situation began to change beginning in 1939 when Congress passed the first of four significant pieces of aeronautical-related legislation.

Civil Aeronautics Act and the Civilian Pilot Training Program

The first legislation was the passage of the Civil Aeronautics Act of 1938.[3] Its premise was simple: create a five-member Civil Aeronautics Authority whose members were tasked with promoting the safe and orderly development of the fledgling American airline industry.

While the Civil Aeronautics Authority exercised broad powers over the development of non-military civil aeronautics and air commerce, "no such beneficence was offered to the other section of aviation, called then private flying."[4] Private flying consisted of two elements; the first was small fixed-based operators (FBOs) offering flight training and airplane rentals; the second was light airplane manufacturers. Both were suffering severe financial hard-

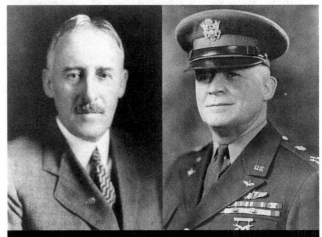

Henry L. Stimson (left) served as Secretary of War and later five-star Gen. Henry H. "Hap" Arnold served as Chief of the U.S. Army Air Corps during the era of Tuskegee military flight training.

ships during the Great Depression.

One charter member of the Civil Aeronautics Authority, Robert H. Hinckley, was a former fixed-based operator, and he conceived a program that would attract young people into careers in aviation, benefiting both light airplane manufacturers and small fixed-based operators.[5] Entitled the Civilian Pilot Training Program (CPTP), he planned to use vocational tax dollars to teach up to 20,000 college students a year to fly. With the winds of war sweeping the European continent and the entry of the United States into the conflict inevitable, the Civilian Pilot Training Program's value in creating a pool of qualified pilots for military service did not go unnoticed.

As it would turn out, no single government initiative served to advance the cause of African-American aviators more than this Civil Aeronautics Authority-sponsored Civilian Pilot Training Program. Although segregated in its initial implementation, the program eventually opened the doors to government-sponsored flight training for African-Americans and allowed them to demonstrate their aerodynamic adaptability for complex commercial and military flight operations.

The Civilian Pilot Training Program did not use military

Orville Wright (left) with Robert H. Hinckley, who as a member of the Civil Aeronautics Authority, originated the concept of the Civilian Pilot Training Program, which by law provided that participation could not be denied on account of race, creed, or gender.

instructors, aircraft or facilities. Instead, the intention was to train new pilots using the faculty and classrooms of private and public colleges or universities who already had established courses in aeronautics and who also had an independent fixed-based operator willing to provide flight training located within 10 miles of their campus. Merging flight training curricula used by military and civilian pilot-training programs, the Civil Aeronautics Authority developed its own extremely detailed standardized curriculum.[6]

Initially, the program provided only an Elementary flight course, which included a 72-hour ground school course and a 35 to 50 flight hour course that culminated with a flight test for a private pilot certificate. Participating students were charged only a small fee to cover the costs of a flight physical and a life insurance policy; the government paid the remainder of all costs, including $20 to the college and $290 to its fixed-based operator partner for each student.[7]

President Franklin D. Roosevelt approved the plan on December 27, 1938 and 13 colleges were selected for a trial program that began in February 1939. No African-American students from historically black colleges and universities (HBCUs) were enrolled, although women were encouraged to participate and about 2,500 women eventually completed the program, 40 percent of whom later became Women Airforce Service Pilots (WASPs).[8,9] With a budget of $100,000, 330 college students began the program, and 313 participants subsequently passed their ground and flight tests, a most impressive achievement.

With the proof of concept course an unparalleled success, the next step for President Roosevelt was to gain congressional approval for successive appropriations, which would occur only if the Civilian Pilot Training Program was enacted into law. This happened on June 27, 1939 with the passage of the Civilian Pilot Training Act.[10]

Before this legislation passed, however, African-American leaders, unwilling to accept that black student aviators would be excluded from the Civilian Pilot Training Program again, began to mount a hard-hitting lobbying effort for equal opportunity.

1939 White and Spencer's Cross-Country Ten-City Goodwill Flight

In Chicago, the Challenger Air Pilots' Association, created by John Robinson, Cornelius Coffey, Janet Bragg, Willa Brown and other colleagues, formed a new organization, the National Airmen's Association of America (NAAA), "to aggressively advocate for black participation in the all-white Civilian Pilot Training Program."[11]

The NAAA's first president was Cornelius Coffey, and the membership proposed that two members of the NAAA fly cross-country from Chicago to Washington, DC to petition in person for the inclusion of historically black colleges and universities (HBCUs) in the new fiscal year's Civilian Pilot Training Program. Chauncey E. Spencer, who co-piloted the trip noted, "that was the birth of what surely must have been one of the most unusual flights ever made by pilots anywhere."[12]

Dale L. White, Sr. (1899 to 1977) was chosen to be the pilot. White was born in Minden, Louisiana and moved to Chicago to attend the Curtiss Wright Aeronautical University, earning his private pilot certificate in June 1936 and later his maintenance certificate.[13]

Chauncey E. Spencer (November 5, 1906 to August 21, 2002) was selected to be the second pilot and navigator. Spencer was born in Lynchburg, Virginia and after graduating from college he tried to enroll in an aviation school in Virginia, but none would admit him because of his race.[14] Spencer moved to Chicago in 1934 and enrolled into the all-white Aeronautical University. White students objected to his presence, and the school's administrator struck a deal that if Spencer could obtain flight instruction from black instructors at the Coffey School of Aviation, they would award him an Aeronautical University certificate, which is what happened.

After graduation, Chauncey recalled just how hopeless the job situation was for black aviators,

> I couldn't be entirely optimistic, though; past experience with racial discrimination wouldn't allow too much hope. I knew that the public's attitude was extremely hostile to Negro flyers. Repeatedly, I heard, "You'll never get a job flying," and this was said with good reason. The Negro flyers I knew were all supporting themselves with other kinds of jobs. Nobody wanted a Negro pilot, including the armed services. Negroes were not allowed in the training program

INTREPID CHICAGO AVIATORS PILOT 'OLD FAITHFUL' IN CROSS COUNTRY GOODWILL TOUR

Chauncey "Clark Gable" Spencer, left, and Dale White, Chicago aviators and representatives of the National Airmen's Association, with the airplane "Old Faithful," which they are piloting to eastern cities in behalf of the Air Show to be held in Chicago in August. From Pittsburgh where they arrived Friday, they flew to New York, landing Saturday morning. In Washington they will be greeted by several members of Congress and by Edgar G. Brown, valiant crusader for racial rights, who has conducted a successful fight for recognition of the Negro aviator in the nation's law.—Photo by Taylor.

In May, 1939 Chauncey E. Spencer and Dale L. White flew from Chicago to Washington, D.C. to lobby for African-American participation in the new Civilian Pilot Training Program. Their airplane, *Old Faithful*, did not live up to its name but still completed the 3,000 mile journey.

for the Army Air Corps...but there was hope in the wind.[15]

Both men took positions with the Works Progress Administration (WPA), a national work relief program established by the United States government during the Great Depression. The selection by NAAA of White and Spencer to make the flight turned out to be an ideal fit,

> Dale was the conservative type, while Chauncey was just the opposite, an outgoing personality. They made a perfect team. We were proud of them and glad to have them represent us.[16]

While the straight line distance from Chicago to Washington, DC is less than 600 miles, the pair intended to travel more than 3,000 miles, visiting ten cities along their planned route to provide air shows and give airplane rides to draw attention to their cause. The stops included Cleveland, Pittsburgh, Washington, Philadelphia, New York City, Baltimore, West Virginia State College, Dayton, Ohio and Fort Wayne, Indiana.[17]

Unfortunately, the NAAA was unable to obtain any financial assistance by local organizations, except for a $1,000 donation from the "celebrated Jones brothers of Chicago" who apparently had made a lot of money from a local numbers game.[18] To show their appreciation, two months after their return White and Spencer flew low over the Jones brothers' estate and dropped a "bouquet of white flowers and a note of thanks right at their front porch."[19]

Boosted by an additional $500 Spencer had saved, they rented a dual-cockpit Lincoln-Paige LP-3 biplane equipped with only two flight instruments: oil pressure and airspeed.[20] They named their cream and red-striped airplane *Old Faithful*, which proved to be anything but as they were forced to make several emergency land-

ings due to mechanical problems.

They departed on their planned 3,000 miles, round-trip, Ten-City Goodwill Flight on May 8, 1939. As Spencer recalled,

> A day of high winds and even higher hopes. Convinced we were about to make history, co-pilot Dale White and I had taken off at about six a.m. from Chicago. The plane's top speed was near one hundred ten miles an hour, and whenever we met a heavy wind we'd literally start flying backwards. But that didn't seem important. All that mattered to us was that we were two Negroes flying an airplane in a day and age when many white people believed we couldn't, either because of incompetence, ignorance, or a combination of both. We were bound for Washington, D.C. where we planned to urge Congress to include black pilots in the proposed Civilian Pilot Training Program for the Army Air Corps, the predecessor of the Air Force.[21]

After only four hours of flight, *Old Faithful* threw a crankshaft and started bucking like a bronco. The pair landed immediately, and upon touchdown, the airplane swerved, skidded and finally came to a stop in a cloud of dust,

> We landed in a corn field in Sherwood, Ohio, descending on the land like a giant locust. A farmer, in plaid shirt and overalls, ran across the field towards us. I don't think he'd seen more than one or two Negroes in his entire life. Now here were two in his backyard in an old, two-wing airplane that seemed to be falling apart.[22]

The white farmer proved to be very gracious, arranging hotel accommodations and lending his barn as a temporary repair han-

Left to Right: Representative from the noted Jones Brothers, (unidentified), Corneilius R. Coffey, President of National Airmen's Association, 1938; and Horace C. Kayton (far right) greet Dale L. White and Chauncey on their return to Chicago after their National Goodwill flight to Washington, May 18, 1939.

Dale L. White (center) and Chauncey E. Spencer (second from right) are greeted by Cornelius R. Coffey (second from left) after completion of their trip.

gar. Townspeople rushed to the farm to see the airplane and kindly paid all of White and Spencer's expenses while they waited for parts. Several days later White and Spencer resumed their journey but to show their gratitude they returned a few months later to spend an entire day with the townspeople providing free airplane rides.[23]

At other stops, whites were not quite so accommodating. Due to their race, they were often denied gas, food, and accommodations. Caught in the dark after being refused overnight hangar space at one airport, and trying to make Pittsburgh where they would be more warmly welcomed, they followed a Pennsylvania-Central Airlines airliner in for a safe landing, where they were greeted by among other dignitaries, James Peck, who wrote a newspaper article on their adventures.[24]

They were also met by a Civil Aeronautics Authority inspector, who promptly grounded them because he thought they had flown too close to the airliner and that they had also violated regulations by landing after dark without airplane lights. After the publisher of the *Pittsburgh Courier* interceded on their behalf, White and Spencer were cleared to leave the next morning.[25] They landed at Hoover Field directly across the Potomac River from Washington

D.C. on Sunday, May 14, 1939, six days after departing Chicago.[26]

Meetings with Congressmen and Senators

They were welcomed by the National Airmen's Association of America's lobbyist, Edgar Brown, who served as the powerful head of the Negro Federal Workers Employees Union. Brown escorted White and Spencer to several scheduled meetings the next day with Congressman William B. Bankhead, Speaker of the House of Representatives, and critical members of the Senate and House military affairs committees.[27]

One of the meetings was with Illinois Congressman Everett M. Dirksen who befriended the group and promised his unqualified support in inserting an "amendment guaranteeing equal benefits to all flyers regardless of race, creed or color" in the next fiscal year's Civilian Pilot Training Program.[28]

But many believe that it was a chance encounter with Missouri Senator Harry S. Truman that provided the tipping point. As Spencer recalled,

He [Brown] took us on the underground train connecting the

Capitol and Congressional offices. As we were getting off the electric car, Harry S. Truman, then a Senator from Missouri, came walking down the corridor. Brown intercepted him to introduce us and explain our mission to Washington. Truman was interested and in his customarily direct, blunt way asked many questions.

'What do you do?' he questioned. We explained that we were both working for the WPA. 'So what are you doing here? Why aren't you working today?' We told him we had taken time off because we felt we had to dramatize the need for the inclusion of the Negro in the Army Air Corps. 'Why aren't you in the Air Corps? Can't you get in?' He seemed genuinely surprised. Edgar Brown explained to him that Negroes were not accepted.

'Have you tried?' 'No, sir, but others have tried and have just been embarrassed. They've been turned away without regard for their training or ability. Only the color of their skin mattered.' 'Well, I think you should try.' 'We'd like to try but we'd also like for you to help us open the door. We haven't been able to break down the barriers ourselves. Mr. Truman, you don't know what it means to be embarrassed. I've tried these things before. There's just no use.'[29]

They explained to Senator Truman that African-American aviators were not allowed to participate in the Civilian Pilot Training Program. Senator Truman asked to see the plane they flew in from Chicago and visited the airport that afternoon. As Spencer recalled,

He was full of questions and as he climbed up on the wing and looked into the cockpit. 'How much gas can this carry? How much did it cost to rent? Do you have insurance?' He was enthusiastic, though he didn't want a plane ride. We had our flight suits on, ready to take him up if he wanted a ride. They were khaki jumpsuits of our own design. He said that if we had guts enough to fly this thing to Washington, he'd have enough guts to back us. And he did just that.[30]

During their return trip, White and Spencer completed several scheduled stops at various cities to stimulate interest in aviation by African-Americans and landed in Chicago to a hero's welcome.

CROSS-COUNTRY FLIERS GREETED BY EDITOR

Dale White and Chauncey Spencer, Chicago aviators, are greeted by Robert L. Vann, editor of The Courier, upon the occasion of their arrival in Pittsburgh from Cleveland. Left to right: Lieut. Jimmie Peck, Pittsburgh airman; Chauncey Spencer, Dale White and Mr. Vann. The editor of The Courier has shown a pioneer interest in aviation and a chance for Negro aviators. The Pittsburgh Courier, under his direction, initiated and promoted the fight to force Congress to recognize black flyers.—Photo-by John G. Taylor.

White and Spencer are greeted by Robert L. Vann, editor of the *Pittsburgh Courier*, an African-American newspaper that provided national coverage of early black aviation achievements.

Civilian Pilot Training Program Includes African-Americans

As a result of this and other efforts, language was inserted in the Civilian Pilot Training Act of 1939 that stated, "None of the benefits of training or programs shall be denied on account of race, creed, or color."[31] The Civilian Pilot Training Act was signed by President Franklin D. Roosevelt on June 27, 1939, and with a stroke of a pen, African-Americans could no longer be denied entry into U.S. government-sponsored flight training programs, although training was segregated and the U.S. Army Air Corps continued to bar black applicants.

For fiscal year 1940, the Civilian Pilot Training Program arranged for ground courses at 33 colleges and flight instruction at 33 nearby airports.

Six historically black colleges and universities (HBCUs) were also selected to participate, including:

Provided, That in the administration of this Act, none of the benefits of training or programs shall be denied on account of race, creed, or color.

This single sentence inserted into the Civilian Pilot Training Act of 1939 opened for the first time in history military flight training for African-Americans.

Thousands of lightplane-trained pilots have been graduated by the CPTP in one year.

by *Virginia Withington*

Is the pet program of the CAA about to be curtailed or possibly discontinued entirely? There are indications in Washington that drastic changes are coming.

BY the time this appears, the Civilian Pilot Training Program, launched not quite two years ago and now a familiar part of aviation, may have been changed beyond recognition. Under the impact of the Army Air Corps expansion and present national policy, the CPTP is being turned from its original purpose of encouraging civilian flying toward service primarily as a feeder of pilots to the Army and Navy.

Last spring, in an effort to adjust itself to the times, the Civil Aeronautics Board introduced an advanced training course designed to fit students for the armed services' secondary courses. This process of adaptation is another step with the budget for 1941-42, in which CPTP funds are cut sharply. Under this budget, only $18,000,000 is to be spent on civilian pilot training, reducing the number of elementary pilots graduated from 45,000 to 30,000, the advanced, from 9,000 to 6,000. With this, it is agreed in Washington, will come changes in the nature of the program itself.

Civilian pilot training at Government expense was begun on an experimental basis in the spring of 1939 with National Youth Administration funds to see whether the Government could fill what aviation had long felt to be a grievous need. Some way had to be found to bring together young men and women

Favored above lightplanes are military-type secondary trainers like this Waco.

with enthusiasm for flying and the planes they could not afford.

At first it was thought that the answer lay in the establishment of seven great training centers. Robert H. Hinckley, now Assistant Secretary of Commerce in charge of aeronautics, and then a member of the CAA, countered with the suggestion that the program be dispersed as widely as possible. He urged that advantage be taken of existing facilities, *(Continued on page 58)*

The Civilian Pilot Training Program opened the door for government-sponsored flight training for black student pilots. Its replacement after Pearl Harbor, the War Training Program, barred African-Americans and women, as discussed in this *Flying and Popular Aviation* magazine article.

1. Delaware State College, Dover, Delaware
2. Hampton Institute, Hampton, VA
3. Howard University, Washington, DC
4. North Carolina Agricultural and Technical State University, Greensboro, NC
5. Tuskegee Institute, Tuskegee, AL
6. West Virginia State College, Institute, WV

One prerequisite for participation in the Civilian Pilot Training Program was two years of college, which matched the U.S. Army Air Corps requirement for its aviation cadets.[32] The law also specified that at least 5% "of the students selected for training shall be selected from applicants other than college students," so two additional non-college affiliated black schools were also selected:

1. Coffey School of Aeronautics,16 miles southeast of Chicago in Oak Lawn, IL
2. Chicago School of Aeronautics, 18 miles northwest of Chicago in Wheeling, IL

The Coffey School of Aeronautics was managed by two married pioneering black aviators, Cornelius Coffey and Willa Brown. The Chicago School of Aeronautics was operated by Harold S. Darr, a white former U.S. Army Air Corps pilot who was a good friend of John C. Robinson.

It is interesting to note that the Coffey School of Aeronautics and the Chicago School of Aeronautics were the only two Civilian Pilot Training Programs in the same city. As previously mentioned, Chicago was considered the grand epicenter of black aviation in the 1930s, rivaled only by Los Angeles. Southern African-Americans who wanted to fly flocked to these and other northern cities for flight training, concentrating pioneering black aviators into small, tight-knit communities.

In fact, Chicago emerged as the Tuskegee Institute's chief competitor for U.S. Army Air Corps military flight training, almost to the point where we might instead be discussing the Chicago Airmen instead of the Tuskegee Airmen. Yet despite being host to world-famous black aviators, the first black air shows, and ground-breaking black aviation organizations, most books on the history of aviation in Chicago fail to mention even a single black aviator.[33]

Buoyed by the Civilian Pilot Training Program's trial experiment success in 1939, $4 million was allocated for fiscal year 1940 training, and 9,885 private pilots were trained. With Hitler's invasion of Poland on September 1, 1939 setting in motion World War II, the appropriation was increased to $37 million for fiscal year 1941 to create a larger pool of potential military pilot candidates.

The program also expanded from 1939's single Elementary flight course, which culminated in a private pilot certificate, to a Secondary flight course, which concluded in a commercial pilot certificate. Flight instructor, cross country, and instrument courses with applicable ratings were also added. Recording nearly 12 million flying hours, the Civilian Pilot Training Program eventually operated at 1,132 colleges and 1,460 flight schools. 435,165 civilian pilots were trained from 1939 to 1944, including approximately 2,000 black pilots and 2,500 women.[34]

But the December 7, 1941 Japanese attack on Pearl Harbor and the subsequent declaration of war on Japan and Germany caused the Civilian Pilot Training Program to lose its civilian identity. By executive order of President Roosevelt, all civilian pilot training resources were devoted exclusively to the needs of the military. So after operating during the fiscal years ending June 30, 1940, 1941, and 1942 under the title of Civilian Pilot Training Program, the program's name was eventually changed to the War Training Service.

Now strictly a military training program, women and African-Americans were ineligible for participation since both demographics were barred from U.S. Army Air Corps flight training.[35]

But the myth that African-Americans were incapable of flying complex aircraft had been dispelled.

Public Law 18

Signed within months of the Civilian Pilot Training Act on April 3, 1939, Public Law 18 was an appropriations bill enacted to provide $300 million for the expansion of the U.S. Army Air Corps in preparation for the United States certain entry into the war in Europe. [36]

The statute also authorized the U.S. Army Air Corps to detail military flight students to civilian flight schools as needed. This provision was requested by Maj. Gen. Henry H. Arnold, Chief of the U.S. Army Air Corps, who planned to increase U.S. Army Air Corps' pilot training capacity by transferring Primary flight training, the first phase of military flight training, to civilian contract primary flight schools under U.S. Army supervision.[37]

It is important to note that although both the Civil Aeronautics Authority-sponsored Civilian Pilot Training Program and the U.S. Army Air Corps-sponsored civilian contract primary flight school program used civilian flight schools and operated concurrently, they were wholly distinct and independent programs.

Section 4 of Public Law 18 also contained a provision that expressly authorized the Secretary of War to lend aircraft and aeronautical equipment to,

> Accredited civilian aviation schools, one or more of which shall be designated by the Civil Aeronautics Authority for the training of any Negro air pilot, at which personnel of the Military Establishment are pursuing a course of education and training pursuant to detail thereto under competent orders of the War Department.[38]

The purpose and intention of this provision was for the first time in history to allow African-Americans to enroll in U.S. Army Air Corps flight training, since aviation cadets assigned to contract primary flight schools were enlisted in the U.S. Army Air Corps.

But U.S. Army Air Corps leadership purposely misinterpreted

the intention of this provision, deeming that nothing in the legislation's wording mandated the training of African-Americans by the U.S. Army Air Corps as military aviators. Maj. Gen Arnold, Chief of the Army Air Corps, "stood firmly adamant in his stand of excluding blacks because he could foresee the absolute unsavory situation of having black officers on the same base as white enlisted men, a hopeless and dangerous powder keg combination to his way of thinking."[39] His superior, Secretary of War Henry L. Stimson, also held low regard of the military aviation abilities of African-Americans and he "predicted that Negroes would fail as pilots."[40]

They believed the legislation simply authorized the U.S. Army Air Corps to lend equipment to a civilian school designated by the Civil Aeronautics Authority to provide a Civilian Pilot Training Program course to African-Americans.[41] When the Civil Aeronautics Authority designated the Chicago School of Aeronautics at Glenview, Illinois as such a school, the U.S. Army Air Corps felt that its obligation was complete.[42] This was confirmed by the U.S. Army's own Judge Advocate General who agreed that nothing in Public Law 18 compelled the U.S. Army Air Corps "to enlist Negro flying cadets."[43]

Thus, the U.S. Army Air Corps never trained any African-American military pilots at the Chicago School of Aeronautics. This convenient lack of action later embroiled the U.S. Army Air Corps in controversy when in 1940, under pressure from black advocates to admit African-Americans into military flight training, they announced that the U.S. Army Air Corps was already sponsoring such training at civilian institutions. [44]

It didn't take long to figure out the truth, that not a single African-American had been admitted to U.S. Army Air Corps flight training. This dishonesty on the part of U.S. Army officers only served to increase African-American activists resolve to break this untenable deadlock.

Selective Service and Training Act

The fourth piece of legislation that influenced the enrollment of African-Americans in military flight training, while not directly aeronautically related, was the passage on September 16, 1940 of the Selective Service and Training Act, which enacted the first peacetime conscription in the history of the United States.

This law included two separate provisions prohibiting discrimination, Sec.4.(a) specifically noting,

> That in the selection and training of men under this Act, and in the interpretation and execution of the provisions of this Act, there shall be no discrimination against any person on account of race or color.[45]

The wording was unequivocal, insisted upon by African-American activists whose "past experience made it necessary to write

such 'legislative safeguards' into law." [46] A clear and unambiguous message had been sent to the War Department and the U.S. Army Air Corps regarding the admittance of African-Americans into military flight training.

To their discredit, U.S. Army Air Corps leadership continued to fight against admitting African-Americans into military flight training. Later, when ordered to do so by President Roosevelt, the War Department still insisted upon segregation of training, which was not prohibited by any federal statute.[47]

Unprecedented Opportunities for African-American Aviators

Each of these four pieces of legislation served to build momentum for the acceptance of African-Americans into U.S. Army Air Corps military flight training. The creation of the Civil Aeronautics Authority and the Civilian Pilot Training Program gave black student pilots the extraordinary opportunity of government-sponsored, no-cost flight training to prove their aeronautical adaptability and increase public awareness of their skills. Public Law 18 and the Selective Service and Training Act provided African-American activists and their Congressional supporters a legal basis to challenge the U.S. Army Air Corps refusal to admit African-Americans into military flight training. As will be discussed, the final piece of the puzzle fell into place on July 18, 1940 when President Franklin D. Roosevelt, a Democrat, was nominated for an unprecedented third term against Republican opponent Wendell Wilkie. Roosevelt desperately needed black voter support to remain in office.[48]

Thus, a door was partly opened for black aviators, and it would be at the Tuskegee Institute that the most significant accomplishment of all would be made: African-Americans would enter U.S. Army Air Corps military flight training. ■

Chapter Four Tuskegee Institute and the Civilian Pilot Training Program

The first three presidents of Tuskegee University, from the left, Booker T. Washington, Robert R. Moton, and Dr. Frederick D. Patterson. Under Patterson's guidance, the Tuskegee Institute's civilian aviation training program blossomed into a full military flight training program.

The Tuskegee Institute, as it was known during the time of the Tuskegee Airmen, is located near the town of Tuskegee, Alabama, approximately 40 miles east of Montgomery, Alabama. Initially established in 1881 by the Alabama legislature as a normal school, or teacher-training institution, for African-Americans, the school's name was changed in 1892 to the Tuskegee Normal and Industrial Institution to reflect additional instruction in agricultural and mechanical arts. In 1937 the school was renamed Tuskegee Institute and in 1985 assumed its current name of Tuskegee University.

The first president of the school was Booker T. Washington, who was born a slave on a plantation in Virginia.[1] Freed at the end of the Civil War and longing for an education, after a series of dangerous, menial jobs, he enrolled and graduated from the Hampton Normal and Agricultural Institute in Virginia, where he returned to teach.

In 1881 Washington accepted an invitation to be Tuskegee's first administrator and upon his arrival in Tuskegee, the 23-year old teacher's primary task was to find a location for the new school,

> After looking the town over with some care, the most suitable place that could be secured seemed to be a rather dilapidated shanty near the coloured Methodist church, together with the church itself as a sort of assembly-room. Both the church and the shanty were in about as bad condition as was possible. I recall that during the first months of school that I taught in this building it was in such poor repair that, whenever it rained, one of the older students would very kindly leave his lessons and hold an umbrella over me while I heard the recitations of the others.[2]

Washington set July 4, 1881, as the first day of school. He was the only teacher, and he had 30 students, although he was joined afterward by a second teacher, Olivia A. Davidson, who proved to be an invaluable fundraiser and whom he would later marry. Approximately three months later, Washington arranged for the purchase of an old, abandoned 100-acre plantation located about a mile from the town of Tuskegee as a new home for the school, the nucleus of the present campus of the university.

Washington served as Tuskegee's president until his death in 1915. During the 34 years of his tenure, he increased the school's enrollment to nearly 3,000 students, 200 professors, more than 2,300 acres of land and 100 buildings.[3]

Robert R. Moton

Washington's successor was Robert R. Moton, the son of a slave and also a Hampton Institute graduate, who served until his retirement in 1935. During World War I, he was extremely active in advising President Woodrow Wilson and Secretary of War Newton Baker on issues associated with African-American participation in the war, including a visit to France to dispel rumors that fighting units commanded by black officers had been a failure,

> On the 2nd of December, 1918 at the request of President Wilson and Secretary of War Newton D. Baker, I went to France to look into conditions affecting Negro soldiers, many of whom were undergoing hardships of one kind and another. Secretary Baker said that he and President Wilson felt that my going to France would be encouraging to the men, and that the presence and words of a member of their own race would be particularly helpful, in view of all the circumstances under which they were serving the nation, at the same time inviting me to make any suggestions that might in my judgment help the situation. In spite of pressing matters in connection with the Institute, I felt that it was the school's duty to do anything possible to help our Negro soldiers, and decided to make the trip.

> While in France, I visited nearly every point where Negro soldiers were stationed. At most of them I spoke to the men, and at each place I was most cordially welcomed by the officers and men. I also had the privilege of conferring with Col. E. M. House; Bishop Brent, senior chaplain of the American Expeditionary Forces; General Pershing, and many other high officials of the American and French governments, all of whom I consulted with reference to the record which had been made by Negro troops, and received only words of very highest praise and commendation on their character and conduct in all branches of the service.[4]

Robinson Visits the Tuskegee Institute

On May 22, 1934 John C. Robinson, one of the most famous and most experienced African-American aviators in the world, flew from his home in Chicago to the Tuskegee Institute in an attempt to interest President Moton in establishing an aviation program.[5] An alumni of the Tuskegee Institute, he timed his flight to arrive during commencement activities and his own 10th class reunion.

African-American flight training was prospering in Chicago and Los Angeles but similar aviation programs in the deep South were non-existent. Robinson believed that the Tuskegee Institute's automobile mechanics and welding programs would provide a solid foundation for airplane mechanic training. The school also owned enough land to establish an airport for flight training.[6]

Robinson and his close friend Cornelius Coffey flew in a two-seat *International* equipped with extra fuel tanks for the long journey. They were accompanied by one of Robinson's former students, Grover Nash, who flew in his own brand-new, single-seat Buhl *Pup*. Almost exactly four years later, on May 19, 1938, Nash earned his own place in African-American aviation history when he became the first black pilot to fly airmail during a National Air Mail Week celebration.[7]

The nearly 700-mile trip was long and dangerous and if successful would become the third-longest cross-country flight ever embarked upon by African-American aviators, exceeded only by

The two airplanes flown by John C. Robinson on his 1934 trip from Chicago to Tuskegee. On the left is the OX-6 powered *International*, a 3-seat, open cockpit, wood and fabric biplane. On the right is the Buhl *Pup*, a single seat, open cockpit, mid-wing, wire-braced monoplane.

On May 25, 1934 *The Montgomery Advertiser* featured a photograph of John C. Robinson at Tuskegee in his Buhl *Pup*.

Banning and Allen's 1932 flight and Anderson and Forsythe's 1933 flight.[8]

About 160 miles from Tuskegee, Robinson and Coffey crashed their *International* after a forced landing at Decatur, Alabama,

> The landing was well done, but the takeoff was made with great difficulty. The air was light and there was very little lift. Just as he was about to take off something happened and the plane crashed into the chimney of a nearby farmhouse and floundered down into a cotton field. The damage was considerable and this ended the flight to Tuskegee in the big plane. Johnny flew Nash's plane the rest of the journey while Coffey and Nash finished the trip to Tuskegee in a bus.[9]

Since the Tuskegee Institute had no aviation facilities, Robinson landed the Buhl *Pup* on a nearby oat field prearranged by Captain Alvin J. Neely, a school official. It was the first airplane to ever land at the Tuskegee Institute, and he was given a celebratory welcome by an "assembled crowd of spectators, students, teachers, and officials,"[10]

> This was the first time that these young African American students, mostly from the rural South, had ever seen an aircraft flown by a black pilot. To many black southerners, the sight of a black flyer must have seemed miraculous. [11]

Despite the cheering crowds, Robinson was not successful in convincing President Moton of the value of aviation training. While the reasons are not entirely known, pragmatically some have assumed that purchasing airplanes, constructing an airport, and building classrooms and other aviation training facilities were much too expensive for the money-short Tuskegee Institute.[12]

Others have speculated that Moton and his staff were too "cautious in their adoption of modern vocational training, especially vocations that were considered highly technical, nonagricultural, and within the domain of "white men.""[13]

Charles A. Anderson and Dr. Albert E. Forsythe Visit Tuskegee

But the seed had been planted. It was further nurtured on September 15, 1934 when Charles A. Anderson and Dr. Albert E. Forsythe flew to the Tuskegee Institute shortly before their Pan-American Goodwill Tour seeking support from President Moton.[14] Morton agreed and his wife, Jennie Dee Moton, was given the honor of christening their Lambert Monocoupe with the name *Booker T Washington* by "splintering over the end of the plane a bottle in which mingled water from the River Jordan and from the artesian wells of Tuskegee Institute."[15]

In the deep South, it was highly unlikely that anyone had ever seen even a single African-American pilot. Within four months, five black aviators had flown two different airplanes to the Tuskegee Institute.

Dr. Frederick D. Patterson

Upon Moton's retirement in 1935 he was replaced as President of the Tuskegee Institute by Dr. Frederick D. Patterson, who served until 1953. Patterson was orphaned at age two and subsequently raised by his oldest sister. He received a Doctor of Veterinary Medicine (D.V.M.) from Iowa State and a Ph.D. in Veterinary Medicine from Cornell University. He joined the faculty of the Tuskegee Institute in 1928, first serving as head of the veterinary division, and next as Director for the School of Agriculture before being appointed to the presidency.

While President Moton may have been reluctant about embracing aviation, Dr. Patterson proved to be more receptive, and he eventually guided the establishment of both civilian and military training programs at the Tuskegee Institute.

In June 1936, less than a month after his return from Ethiopia and almost exactly two years since his previous visit to the campus, Robinson flew back again to Tuskegee to attempt to convince officials to establish an aviation program.[16] Greeted warmly by President Patterson, Robinson addressed the students and faculty, and he was enthusiastically received. Privately, however, Robinson was informed that due to the severe economic downturn caused by the Great Depression, the school lacked the financial resources to support an aviation program. [17]

Nonetheless, George L. Washington, the head of the Department of Mechanical Industries, offered Robinson the opportunity to teach aviation at the Tuskegee Institute. After careful consideration, and weighing the fact that school officials would provide no financial support, leaving him alone to raise funds, Robinson declined. Throughout the years, however, Washington and Robinson remained in contact and in the spring of 1941 Robinson even

In preparation for their 1934 Pan-American Goodwill Tour, at Tuskegee on September 15, 1934, Jennie Dee Moton, spouse of Tuskegee Institute President Robert R. Moton, christened Charles Anderson's and Dr. Albert Forsythe's Lambert Monocoupe, the *Booker T Washington*. From the left, President Moton, Charles Anderson, Mrs. Moton, and Dr. Forsythe.

assisted Washington with locating training airplanes.[18]

President Patterson recognized the potential of new job opportunities in commercial aviation, although he was well aware that African-Americans were excluded from flying. Establishing an aviation program was just too expensive, although he soon became aware of a government program that might subsidize its start at the Tuskegee Institute.

In his autobiography, he noted,

> An aviation program was expensive. There was no way in which Tuskegee Institute or practically any other college, black or white, could have started a program on its own. But aviation was one of those fields of promise that the federal government wanted to advance. The U.S. government has opened up most of the industrial areas of large potential, such as railroading. Most major developments had to be started with money which only the government could afford to risk.

When we learned that West Virginia State College, a black school in Institute, West Virginia, had been awarded an aviation program because of certain existing relationships with the Department of Defense (sic), it became apparent to us at Tuskegee that we too should attempt to provide training in aviation. When we began to investigate the possibility of offering an officially endorsed and government-funded civilian pilot training program, we discovered that it operated on a contract basis. If we could supply the students and locate qualified instructors, the government would pay for everything else.[19]

George Leward Washington

Patterson decided to commit to an aviation program, and he had just the person in mind to run it. He selected George L. Washington, Director of Mechanical Industries at the Tuskegee Institute, to head the new aviation program with the title of Director of Aviation Training. Washington, who had no aviation background, was an engineer by trade and had earned his bachelor's and master's degree from the Massachusetts Institute of Technology.[20]

Washington proved to be a brilliant choice, and he performed Herculean feats in ensuring the success of the aviation program at the Tuskegee Institute, expertly laying the foundation for the subsequent military aviation training of the famed Tuskegee Airmen.

Washington's first task was to prepare the necessary application paperwork for the Tuskegee Institute to join the Civilian Pilot Training Program.

Tuskegee Institute's Civilian Pilot Training Program Application

In August 1939 Washington submitted the Tuskegee Institute's application for participation in the 1939 to 1940 Civilian Pilot Training Program to the Civil Aeronautics Authority.[21] Washington anticipated that Tuskegee's submission would be approved relatively quickly, so he immediately began publicizing the new program among the student body. He received 66 applicants for 20 student slots, and he also arranged for an aviation medical examiner to administer their first flight physicals. [22]

By October 1939, nothing had been heard from the Civil Aeronautics Authority. A phone call to them inquiring about Tuskegee's status revealed an unpleasant truth. Tuskegee Institute's application to participate in the Civilian Pilot Training Program was about to be turned down due to noncompliance with contract requirements.[23]

One of the conditions of the Civilian Pilot Training Program to minimize student transportation costs was that the associated independent flying school must be located within a 10-mile radius from the university or college providing the ground instruction. The Tuskegee Institute did not have an airfield, nor was there one located within 10 miles of the school.

So Washington counter-proposed to contract flight training with the Alabama Air Service, owned by a white pilot named Joseph W. Allen, who operated from Montgomery Municipal Airport, located about 40 miles west of Tuskegee.[24] Washington immediately drove to Washington, D.C. and petitioned Civil Aeronautics Authority representative Leslie A. Walker, an Alabama native, to make an exception for the Tuskegee Institute.[25]

Elementary Flight Course Approved

Walker agreed and on October 13, 1939 the Tuskegee Institute was officially approved for a waiver to participate in the Civilian Pilot Training Program and to offer the Elementary flight course ground and flight courses during academic year 1939 to 1940.

Due to the Civil Aeronautics Authority waiver, a joint certifi-

George L. Washington served as the Tuskegee Institute's first Director of Aviation Training and was the driving force in establishing civilian pilot training programs at the Tuskegee Institute, paving the way for the military flight training of the famed Tuskegee Airmen.

cate was issued. The Tuskegee Institute was certificated to provide ground instruction while the Alabama Air Service was certificated to provide flight training.[26]

Initially, Washington proposed using two Tuskegee Institute teachers as ground school instructors, neither of whom had flight experience. But he had second thoughts when he considered that at the end of the school year the Civil Aeronautics Authority would administer formal examinations to evaluate student knowledge. Wanting his students to excel, he searched instead for ground instructors with aviation backgrounds.

He obtained the services of two white Alabama Polytechnic Institute (now known as Auburn University) professors. Bloomfield M. Cornell, a former U.S. Navy pilot, and Robert G. Pitts, a certified aviation mechanic with a master's degree in aeronautical engineering.[27] They agreed to teach two nights a week, three hours each night, on the Tuskegee Institute campus.[28] Ground instruction began on December 1, 1939 with 20 students enrolled, including two women, Mildred Hanson and Mildred Hemmons, who would go on to earn their private pilot certificates.[29]

Washington's intuition was well-rewarded. On March 25, 1940 end of course examinations were administered in person by a Civil Aeronautics Authority examiner to the Tuskegee Institute's students and graded the same day,

> Everyone gathered around the inspector as he graded the exams. The excitement heightened as, in the case of each

Flight students are introduced to their flight instructors at the Tuskegee Institute's Kennedy Field. Behind them, a lineup of Piper J-3 *Cub's* and Taylor Tandem Trainers await their young charges. Both aircraft were described by students as a delight to fly, although they could be chilly during an Alabama winter.

subject (Civil Air Regulations, Meteorology and Air Navigation), he finished paper by paper and put down the grade. It was a moment beyond description when at the very end of the scoring every student had passed every subject![30]

It was an unprecedented achievement and one that was well-rewarded with complimentary publicity in several national magazines and multiple newspapers. The Tuskegee Institute was the first school, which included some impressive white colleges and universities, among the seven participating Southern states to achieve a 100% pass rate on the examinations. [31]

Flight instruction began on January 1, 1940 and was standardized by a Civil Pilot Training Manual issued by the Civil Aeronautics Administration that provided detailed step-by-step guidance for every flight maneuver.[32] The only airplane requirement was that it have more than 50 horsepower and the Piper J-3 *Cub* was an ideal fit. As a result, nearly three-quarters of all pilots in the Elementary flight course of the Civilian Pilot Training Program were trained in the Piper J-3 *Cub,*

The J-3 was an easily maneuverable, two-place, single engine, high-wing monoplane, the student in front, the instructor in the rear. It was an essentially simple airplane, light but rugged, cost little to repair and could be repaired in a hurry. If a student wrecked the landing gear on a bad approach, and many did, it could be replaced within the hour.[33]

It soon became evident that the Civil Aeronautics Authority's concern about the 40-mile distance between the Tuskegee Institute and the Alabama Air Services flight line at Montgomery was justified. Student academic schedules were disrupted, and the university's transportation costs far exceeded Civil Aeronautics Authority reimbursements.

Overall, though, administrators and students were elated with the program.[34] It was time, however, for the Tuskegee Institute to locate an airfield a little closer to home. ■

5

Chapter Five Tuskegee Airfields and U.S. Army Primary Flight Training

CPTP students at Tuskegee, under the direction of a lone carpenter, built this two-plane hangar themselves. This was one of the requirements of the CAA before granting a training unit to the school.

Tuskegee Institute's aviation facilities at Kennedy Field. The hangar was built by students to support their Civilian Pilot Training Program and it could house three Piper J-3 *Cubs*.

Kennedy Field, AKA Airport Number One and Mother Field

Seeking to relocate the flight training portion of the Tuskegee Institute's Civilian Pilot Training Program Elementary flight course closer to the school, on February 1, 1940 George L. Washington, Tuskegee's official coordinator of civilian pilot training, hosted a meeting with federal, state, and local officials to assist with the selection of a suitable site.[1]

The best option agreed upon was Kennedy Field, a grass airstrip located about five miles from the school.[2] John Connor owned the property but leased it to three white pilots, one of whom was named Stanley Kennedy, the presumed namesake of the field. Dale E. Altman, the Civil Aeronautics Authority's General Inspector of Flying Fields from the Atlanta regional office, carefully inspected the landing area on foot and conducted several takeoffs

and landings.[3] He deemed Kennedy Field suitable for Civilian Pilot Training Program flight training, pending some required improvements.

Kennedy agreed to sublease the field to the Tuskegee Institue, and Tuskegee's aviation students provided the labor to cut down trees and fill in various holes and low spots. Additionally, the Tuskegee Institute invested $1,000 in the building of a wooden hangar that could accommodate three Piper J-3 *Cubs* as well as fuel storage, lavatory, and record-keeping facilities.[4,5,6]

While the name Kennedy Field was retained, it was seldom used by Tuskegee Institute students and staff who referred to it as Airfield Number One, or more affectionately, Mother Field.[7] The 1945 U.S. Army Air Forces airfield directory described the airfield as,

A 55-acre L-shaped property having 3 sod runways, the longest being 1,900' north/south. The field was said to have

1943 view of Kennedy Field, a grass strip with several hangars visible in the lower right. All of the Tuskegee Institute's Piper J-3 *Cubs must be flying.*

4 wood & metal hangars, the largest being 88' wide, and to be owned & operated by private interests.[8]

Upon notification of the completion of the required improvements, the Civil Aeronautics Authority officially approved the field for Civilian Pilot Training Program training use in late February 1940. Almost immediately, the Tuskegee Institute's Elementary flight course flight instruction was transferred officially from Montgomery to Tuskegee, with the Alabama Air Service still providing all flight instruction.

In May 1940, Tuskegee's flight students underwent their Civil Aeronautics Authority flight tests, and everyone earned their private pilot certificate.[9] One student, Charles Foxx, whose average on the ground examinations set a national record, was selected as one of only seven Civilian Pilot Training Program trained private pilots, and the only African-American, to represent the southeastern region in an Institute of Aeronautical Sciences contest.[10]

All of these achievements resulted in national publicity, a congratulatory note from the Civil Aeronautics Authority on the excellence of the Tuskegee program, and a flood of letters from African-American students interested in enrolling in Tuskegee's flight program.[11]

This student excellence in flight and ground training continued, and the subsequent impressive successes of African-American students enrolled in the Tuskegee Institute's Civilian Pilot Training Program accomplished what no single program or adventure had been able to do since Emory C. Malick first flew in 1912. It put the faces of hundreds of bright, successful young black pilots in front of white America. No one could deny the fact that African-Americans were excelling in the demanding, fast-paced flight training environment.

Tuskegee Awarded Civilian Pilot Training Program Secondary Flight Course

Anticipating expansion of the program in the 1940 to 1941 academic year, Washington immediately set his sights on building a new airport to be located on Tuskegee Institute-owned property. Additionally, on May 20, 1940 Washington submitted a proposal

THE NEGRO IS FLYING

No gasoline pumps are available at Tuskegee's "temporary" airport. This makeshift platform is the refueling site.

by Manning Austin

Air-minded Negro youths have fought their way into aviation despite great odds. Theirs is a story of perseverance.

WITH four phases of the CAA's Civilian Pilot Training Program in operation and courses in private flying and aviation mechanics practically assured for the fall term, Tuskegee Institute at Tuskegee, Ala., is becoming a center of Negro aviation.

Tuskegee—the world's largest Negro college—is located in the warm, flat country of the Deep South, the earliest home of the Negro in this country, where ideal flying conditions prevail the year around. The school's aviation program, under the direction of President Fred L. Patterson and Director of Mechanical Industries George L. Washington, began the year very favorably. The Institute has:

1. Increased its fleet by two Wacos and two *Cubs*, bringing the total to four Wacos and eight *Cubs*.

2. Completed the training of eight apprentice instructors from Tuskegee and four other colleges and contracted with the CAA to give a refresher course to five other qualifying Negro instructors.

3. Pushed to completion an alumni drive to raise $3,000 toward building an airport and aviation mechanics building on its own spacious campus.

4. Enlarged its primary training program from groups of 15 and 20 to three annual groups of 30 students and trebled its secondary program to include 30 students from seven Negro colleges.

Without even an airport, the Institute began its aviation program December 1, 1939, when the CAA awarded it a unit of the Civilian Pilot Training Program. Initial flight training was given at the Montgomery airport, 40 miles away. Ground school training was given at Tuskegee.

Because it had not a landing field within the required 10 miles, Tuskegee at first faced the prospect of being denied the primary training program which the CAA had awarded to 400 other colleges. Director Washington went to Washington

to appear before CAA officials with a special plea for Tuskegee's aviation future. He explained that should the CPT program be denied Tuskegee, aviation training would be lost to the Negro race in an area where there is the heaviest Negro population in the United States. The CAA granted Tuskegee an exception and its aviation program was assured of a start.

After December, 1939, the program expanded rapidly. Tuskegee students set a record among colleges in the south by passing 20 out of 20 students in the ground school of the first (1939-40) class, then sending a quota of 20 through the flight tests to receive private pilot certificates. Last summer's class of 15 students and a quota of 20 for the fall class were graduated and a new class of 30 began its training in January, 1941.

Tuskegee was the first Negro school to be selected by the CAA for a secondary aviation program at which students from

The docile Piper J-3 *Cub* (left) was used for the Elementary flight course of the Civilian Pilot Training Program while the more powerful WACO YPT-14 was use for the advanced flying maneuvers of the Secondary flight course.

to the Civil Aeronautics Authority for the Tuskegee Institute's participation in the newest addition to the Civilian Pilot Training Program, an advanced flight training program known as the Secondary flight course.[12] The Secondary flight course involved advanced aerobatics and precision maneuvers, including snap rolls, Cuban 8's, Split S's, Immelmann's, cross country and night flying. The course concluded with the commercial pilot certificate flight test.[13]

On June 2, 1940 Washington traveled to Chicago to address the Tuskegee Alumni club and seek donations for the new airfield. Demonstrating the small circle within which black aviators flew, he visited Willa Brown at her flying school and was flown over the city by her.[14]

The new airfield project assumed additional importance when the Civil Aeronautics Authority announced in July 1940 that the Tuskegee Institute had indeed been selected to conduct the Civilian Pilot Training Program's Secondary flight course.[15] Three classes of ten students were enrolled in the Secondary flight course with the completion of the Elementary flight course a prerequisite for participation.

While the Elementary flight course used the smaller Piper J-3 *Cub*, the Secondary flight course required the use of a heavier, higher-powered training aircraft that could not be easily accommodated by Kennedy Field. Uniquely, this Secondary flight course aircraft was expected to have both a military designation for use in U.S. Army Air Corps flight training and a Civil Aeronautics Authority approved type rating for use in the Civilian Pilot Training Program.[16]

The aircraft that met this specification was the WACO YPT-14 trainer, manufactured by the WACO Aircraft Company of Troy, Ohio. The WACO YPT-14 trainer was a WACO UPF-7 variant adopted explicitly for the Civilian Pilot Training Program, and more than 600 of these aircraft were eventually built. This fabric-covered, tandem-seating, open cockpit biplane offered a 220 horsepower engine and a cruise speed of about 120 miles per hour. Per military requirements, it was a dual-controlled trainer, although with the stick removed for civilian use two passengers could be accommodated in the front seat.[17] The Tuskegee Institute was responsible for purchasing all WACO YPT-14's needed for their Secondary flight course.

1,000 national scholarships were awarded by the Civil Aeronautics Authority for attendance at the 8-week long Secondary flight course.[18] Trainees were selected individually by the Civil Aeronautics Authority, who assigned them to training schools throughout the country. These trainees, who had already passed a civilian flight physical, were also required to complete a military flight physical and wear a uniform, which strongly implied qualification for possible follow-on military flight training with the U.S. Army Air Corps.

The Secondary flight course was segregated for African-Americans, and the Tuskegee Institute offered the only Secondary flight course in the entire nation for black flight students. They came from several historically black colleges and universities (HBCUs), including Howard University, Hampton Institute, West Virginia State College, and the Agricultural and Technical College of North Carolina. Trainees and flight instructors were housed in their own residence hall on the grounds of the Tuskegee Institute.

Borrowing Alabama Polytechnic Institute's Airfield

During informal discussions with the Civil Aeronautics Authority before it was officially announced that the Tuskegee Institute had been awarded the Secondary flight course, two contingencies were placed upon Washington and the Tuskegee Institute.

The first was that Kennedy Field must be improved or a more suitable airfield obtained for Secondary flight course operations. The second contingency was that the Tuskegee Institute must assume responsibility for Elementary flight training, rather than contracting it out to the Alabama Air Service, which was the present situation.[19] Washington agreed to both conditions.

As an interim fix, while waiting for the construction of a new Tuskegee-owned airfield, the Tuskegee Institute approached the Alabama Polytechnic Institute (now known as Auburn University) about temporarily utilizing their landing field for Tuskegee's Secondary flight course. Located about 20 miles distant from Tuskegee, Alabama Polytechnic Institute (API) had its own small aviation program, currently the second oldest collegiate flight training program in the United States following only Embry-Riddle Aeronautical University.

Uneasy about letting black student aviators fly from the school's field, Alabama Polytechnic Institute's president, Luther N. Duncan, put the decision to a vote among the Alabama Polytechnic Institute's white aviation students, who unanimously agreed to the proposal.[20] Of interest, Alabama Polytechnic Institute would not get their own Secondary flight course approval until the 1941 spring session.

Alabama Polytechnic Institute also graciously made available a shed, apparently the only structure at the field, for the Tuskegee Institute to store various aviation equipment.[21] Absent hangars, the Tuskegee Institute's only WACO YPT-14 trainer would have to be tied down outside, unprotected from the elements or trespassers.

Once flight training started, whites from Auburn and the surrounding rural areas gathered at Alabama Polytechnic Institute's airfield to watch the black student pilots fly. Observed Dr. Frederick D. Patterson, the Tuskegee Institute's President,

> Not a single unpleasant experience was reported by the trainees. I think they enjoyed be [sic] at the center of the stage before large audiences, particularly Sundays. When you come to think about it, Tuskegee Institute must have had a good store of goodwill among the whites. With the Waco staked out an occasion could have been found to set fire to the Waco or otherwise damage it, regardless of watchman service.[22]

Tuskegee Institute's First Flight Instructor Charles A. "Chief" Anderson

The selection and hiring of the Tuskegee Institute's first flight instructor was equally straightforward. A year before, in the spring of 1939, Charles A. Anderson, the first African-American to earn a commercial pilot certificate, had flown Richard Robert Wright, Sr. of Philadelphia, a prominent African-American educator, civil rights advocate and banker, to the Tuskegee Institute for a visit.

Anderson ended up staying "several days, taking students on flights and talking to groups about flying and aviation in general."[23] Anderson had previously visited the Tuskegee Institute in 1934 when he and Dr. Albert E. Forsythe brought their airplane the *Booker T. Washington* to be christened by then President Morton's wife before their Pan-American Goodwill Tour.

Anderson must have made quite a favorable impression because in July 1940 Dr. Patterson personally visited Anderson to offer him the chief flight instructor position at Tuskegee.[24] At this time Anderson was living near Washington, DC and employed by the Hybla Valley Flying Service.[25] Anderson had helped start Howard University's own Civilian Pilot Training Program and was currently serving as a Civilian Pilot Training Program flight instructor.[26]

Anderson eagerly accepted the position, but before moving to

This photograph appeared in the March 1941 issue of *Popular Aviation*. Tuskegee Institute's first flight instructor Charles A. Anderson, shows off the school's brand-new WACO YPT-14 to George L. Washington, director of aviation activities, and Dr. F. L. Patterson, the Tuskegee Institute's president.

Tuskegee, he was asked to attend a Civil Aeronautics Authority mandated refresher course in aerobatics in the WACO YPT-14. This aerobatics course was required by the Civil Aeronautics Authority before a flight instructor could teach the advanced aerial maneuvers performed in the Civilian Pilot Training Program's Secondary flight course.

The Civil Aeronautics Authority authorized Anderson's aerobatic training to be conducted at the Chicago School of Aeronautics at Glenview Field. This school was one of two flight schools in Chicago approved by the Civil Aeronautics Authority for Civilian Pilot Training Program training, and they had also received a primary flight training contract from the U.S. Army Air Corps. The school was owned by Harold S. Darr, a former U.S. Army Air Corps pilot who flew in France during World War I and was a close friend of John C. Robinson.[27] During his stay in Chicago, Anderson was the guest of John C. Robinson, who insisted that Anderson stay at his apartment during his several weeks of training.[28]

Anderson was one of the most experienced black aviators in the world, but he inexplicably failed his Civil Aeronautics Authority aerobatics checkride. Sitting in the front seat of a Stearman PT-13 with the inspector in the rear seat, "Anderson experienced difficulty in executing slow rolls, though the instructor in the rear seat performed them flawlessly."[29]

Slow rolls were simple aerial maneuvers for Anderson, and he suspected malfeasance. He waited until the inspector had left and then he,

> Took the ship up, flying from the rear seat, and performed the maneuver properly as he knew he could. He discovered that the front controls had been rigged so that some maneuvers could not be performed properly. Someone purposely wanted him washed out of the course. This was a period when America did not afford equal opportunity to all her citizens."[30]

Now wise to the situation, Anderson subsequently passed his checkride, and the WACO company was directed to deliver the Tuskegee Institute's brand-new WACO YPT-14, tail number NC 20970, to Anderson in Chicago for him to ferry to Tuskegee. Anderson took custody of the WACO and wired Washington that he would land at Kennedy Field on the afternoon of July 29, 1940.

Nearly everyone at the Tuskegee Institute went to the field to witness his arrival. Anderson did not disappoint. The WACO YPT-14, painted in the U.S. Army Air Corps blue and yellow, soon appeared over the horizon. Anderson came in low and fast and in the words of Washington, "zoomed over the institute…the heaviest and fastest plane the area had ever claimed, and it sounded to us like a bomber."[31] It must have been a magical moment for everyone as the WACO YPT-14 gently touched down on Kennedy Field.

The aircraft was subsequently repositioned to Alabama Polytechnic Institute's airfield in preparation for the commencement of the Tuskegee Institute's Civilian Pilot Training Program Secondary flight course. Washington flew with Anderson on the 19-mile trip from Tuskegee to Auburn, Alabama,

> Finally, it came time to fly the plane to the airfield at A.P.I., and it fell to my lot to ride with Anderson, to show him the way. I didn't realize the speed of the plane and was too excited to navigate accurately. So we wound up over Columbus, Georgia {about 35 miles east of Auburn} in no time at all. With apologies to Anderson I pointed to Auburn where we landed in a few minutes.[32]

Anderson went on to endear himself to nearly every Tuskegee Airman with his professionalism, expertise, and high expectations. Affectionately called "Chief" in recognition of his position as Chief Flight Instructor, one author noted that "like the widening circles that emanate from a pebble tossed into a still pond, Chief Anderson has touched the lives of an untold number."[33]

In his memoirs, Washington paid high compliments to Anderson, acknowledging that he was the "Daddy of Flying Training" on Tuskegee's training fields; just as President Patterson acknowledged that Director Washington was the "Daddy of Aviation" for the entire Tuskegee Institute.

> No one could expect greater loyalty, cooperation, and hard work of an employee than that which Anderson gave willingly and without being asked…I shall always be grateful to the Chief for the inspiration, comfort and encouragement given in difficult situations, not to mention loyalty and outstanding services.[34]

Washington also had high praise for Anderson's wife, Gertrude Anderson, who became Washington's assistant and assumed responsibility for the heavy burden associated with Civil Aeronautics Authority and U.S. Army Air Corps paperwork.

Secondary Flight Course Begins at the Tuskegee Institute

In the Elementary flight course, the Tuskegee Institute provided ground training while the Alabama Air Service conducted flight training.[35] Less than a month later on July 22, 1940, a second significant milestone for the Tuskegee Institute under the Civilian Pilot Training Program occurred when the ground training portion of the Secondary flight course officially began, followed by the initiation of flight training on July 30, 1940 at Alabama Polytechnic Institute's airfield.[36] The entire program of instruction included 126 hours of ground instruction and 50 hours of flight training in the powerful Waco YPT-14.[37]

In the Elementary flight course, the Tuskegee Institute provided the ground training while the Alabama Air Service provided the flight training. But for the Secondary flight course, the Tuskegee Institute conducted both ground and flight instruction, which was unprecedented in all of the Civil Aeronautic Authority's Civilian Pilot Training Programs. Anderson served as the sole flight instructor while there were three ground instructors.

On October 10, 1940 all of the Tuskegee Institute's Secondary flight course students were administered ground school examinations by a Civil Aeronautics Authority and once again 100% of the students passed. As a reward, the students were treated to a tour of U.S. Army Air Corps training at Maxwell Field as well as a tour of U.S Navy training facilities at NAS Pensacola.[38]

For the fall 1940 session of the Secondary flight course, the Civil Aeronautics Authority tightened the required flight instructor to student ratio. Under Civil Aeronautics Authority regulations for the Elementary flight course, one flight instructor and one airplane were required for every ten students, so class size was limited to ten students.[39] For the Secondary flight course, however, the ratio was decreased to one flight instructor for every five students, which required the Tuskegee Institute to hire an additional flight instructor.

Anderson recommended Lewis A. Jackson of Marion, Indiana, an African-American who had earned his transport pilot certificate and instructor pilot certificate and was working as a flight instructor at Willa Brown's school in Chicago.[40] Jackson was hired in November 1940 and completed his required Civil Aeronautics Authority aerobatic training at the Chicago School of Aeronautics.

The Tuskegee Institute ordered a second WACO YPT-14 for Jackson's use in the Secondary flight course and that aircraft was delivered to Tuskegee in January 1941.[41] In addition, the Civil Aeronautics Authority now required that all flight instructors be specifically trained before they could be certified to teach in the Civilian Pilot Training Program Elementary flight course.[42] Since a new Civil Aeronautics Authority Elementary flight instructor course was also scheduled to start at Tuskegee, two additional Piper J-3 Cubs were also ordered for their use.[43]

One specific area that was not clear was whether African-

Photograph of the Tuskegee Institute's first Civilian Pilot Training Program Secondary flight course class that appeared in the magazine *Popular Aviation* in March 1941, as well as many other publications. The fact that the students were in military uniforms led many to believe that African-Americans were enrolled in U.S. Army Air Corps flight training, which they were not.

American flight students who participated in the Secondary flight course were eligible to enter U.S. Army Air Corps flight training. Hope springs eternal and a magazine article on the Tuskegee Institute program reported that the Civil Aeronautics Authority had recently announced,

> All Negro students now receiving flight instruction are required to pledge their willingness to enter military service, if qualified and will be called upon the same as white students in the CPT program. The method of selection of these Negro flyers will be determined by the War Department. Thus far no plan has been announced.[44]

And no plan would ever be announced because the U.S. Army Air Corps had no intention of admitting successful African-American graduates of the Tuskegee Institute's Secondary flight course into military flight training.

Challenges of Assembling an All African-American Staff

Washington wanted to employ an all African-American flight training and ground support staff, but there simply were not enough qualified black pilots and mechanics in the United States to fill the needed positions. So by necessity, Washington integrated his aviation workforce. In the fall of 1940, he hired three additional personnel, George Allen, a black pilot who later rose to chief flight instructor; Joseph T. Camilleri, a white pilot with U.S. Navy experience; and Frank Rosenberg, a white pilot with a commercial pilot certificate who was also dual qualified as an airplane mechanic.[45] Washington hoped that in the future he could train and source only African-American flight instructors through Tuskegee's Civilian Pilot Training Program.[46]

President Patterson recalled the challenge of finding qualified African-American pilots and mechanics,

> Because of the general situation of pilot procurement, and particularly in regard to Negro pilots, it was fairly clear that we would have to employ pilots or mechanics regardless of race and look forward to the young men we were training under the CPT program as a major source of flight instructor supply. It did turn out this was our principal source. However, at the peak we had to search the country for Negro pilots with a view to further training them as instructors... Negro pilots were few and far between.[47]

The challenge, though, was to find enough people to run the program. With Anderson's help, we searched the country to find people who could fly and were willing to come. Eventually, we assembled a staff of instructors and an allocation of aircraft, mechanics, and the other things we needed at the onset. In fact, I was somewhat surprised when black aviators proved willing to join us. Their numbers were not legion, and they were scattered around the country."[48]

Kennedy Field Certified for Secondary Flight Course Operations

Although the distance from the Tuskegee Institute to Alabama Polytechnic Institute's airfield was less than 20 miles, the same scheduling and transportation problems occurred for students as it did with the use of the Montgomery airport.

Still waiting to purchase their own airfield, as an interim solution, Anderson felt that Kennedy Field might be feasible for use in the Secondary flight course. So Washington contacted the Civil Aeronautics Authority and requested a reevaluation of Kennedy Field for Secondary flight course operations.[49] A Civil Aeronautics Authority inspector flew test flights at the field and provided a list of required improvements, which included runway markers and field lighting for night operations.

These improvements were completed, and in January 1941 the Civil Aeronautics Authority approved Kennedy Field for both Elementary and Secondary flight course operations, the official certificate issued on February 1, 1941.[50] At the beginning of the 1941 summer session, the Tuskegee Institute also assumed responsibility for the flight training portion of the Elementary flight course. In turn, Washington hired Forrest Shelton, a white pilot who had been employed by the Alabama Air Service, to teach at Kennedy Field.[51]

The decision to get Kennedy Field certified for the advanced Secondary flight course and to seek a second airfield on Tuskegee Institute property proved to be prescient timing by Washington. The U.S. Army Air Corps was about to ask the Tuskegee Institute to sign a civilian primary flight school contract, and this certificate, as well as a new airfield, were two of the requirements to execute this new contract.[52]

U.S. Army Air Corps Subcontracts Primary Military Flight Training

At the same time that the Civil Aeronautics Authority was conducting the Civilian Pilot Training Program, a purely civilian flight training program designed to attract college students to aviation and establish a pool of qualified pilots for possible military service, the U.S. Army Air Corps had been conducting since 1939 its own purely military flight training program that was contracted to civilian flight schools.[53]

Known as the civilian contract primary flying school program, the U.S. Army Air Corps initiative was to contract out the first phase of the official U.S. Army Air Corps flight training program, known as Primary flight training, in anticipation of increased flight training requirements in preparation for the United States entry into World War II. Maj. Gen. Henry H. Arnold, Chief of the U.S. Army Air Corps, hoped that,

> By turning over the responsibility for primary training to other agencies, he could free the Air Corps to concentrate its full resources on later phases of training, and thus in effect expand the capacity of its own training establishment.[54]

The civilian contract primary flight schools were well-compensated for their efforts. Per the provisions of their contract, each school agreed to furnish flight and ground instructors, flying fields and classroom facilities for training.[55] In turn, the U.S. Army Air Corps provided all training aircraft, parts, fuel, oil, curriculum, and student pilot and instructor equipment.

To ensure quality control, a small detachment of U.S. Army Air Corps personnel, under the command of an officer known as the U.S. Army Air Corps Supervisor of the Primary Flying School, was stationed at each civilian contract school.[56] The responsibility of this detachment was "to supervise the military aspects of aviation cadet training and to act in a liaison capacity with training center and other AAF stations.[57] Accordingly, all aviation cadets wore uniforms.

U.S. Army Air Corps Southeast Training Center Activated

To accommodate such a significant expansion of aviation training programs, on July 8, 1940 the U.S. Army Air Corps reorganized its flight training organization structure and divided the United States into three geographical zones. All flying schools located east of the 92nd meridian, where the Tuskegee Institute was located, were placed under the jurisdiction of the Southeast Air Corps Training Center, headquartered at Maxwell Field, Alabama, located about 40 miles west of Tuskegee.[58]

By August 1940 some 18 civilian contract primary flight schools were in operation. Yet not a single one of these schools accepted black student aviators due to the U.S. Army Air Corps policy of denying military flight training to African-Americans.

To the surprise of Tuskegee officials, this situation was about to change when U.S. Army Air Corps officers from Maxwell Army Air Field visited the Tuskegee Institute and asked Dr. Patterson to take the lead in an unprecedented initiative. ■

Chapter Six
Breakthrough

Despite the success of black aviators in the Civilian Pilot Training Program, U.S. Army Air Corps leadership remained steadfast in their determination to deny military flight training to all African-Americans. This included Maj. Gen. Henry H. Arnold, Chief of Air Corps, who was on record as stating that he was against the training of African-American pilots, even if conducted in segregated units.[1,2] Therefore, every request by African-Americans for flight training was denied with the terse statement, "It is regretted that the nonexistence of a colored Air Corps unit to which you could be assigned in the event of completion of flying training, precludes your training to become a military pilot at this time."[3]

It was a classic Catch-22: there were no black squadrons, so there was no need for black pilots; there were no black pilots, so there was no need for black squadrons.[4] Two events unfolded, however, that changed this conundrum.

The first was the tight reelection campaign in the fall of 1940 that Democratic President Franklin D. Roosevelt faced against Republican candidate Wendell Wilkie. One critical key to a Roosevelt victory was his need to court African-American Democratic voters and black leaders, and this could only be achieved in part by removing barriers to African-American participation in combat units.

The second element was Roosevelt's preparations for the inevitable entry of the United States into World War II. On September 16, 1940 Roosevelt signed into law the Selective Training and Service Act, which established the nation's first peacetime compulsory draft and specifically prohibited discrimination against any person on account of race or color.[5]

Nothing in this act precluded segregation of training, however, and this was affirmed in an October 9, 1940 press release by the White House which rubber-stamped the War Department's 7-point policy regarding the use of African-Americans in the national defense,

1. Strength of Negro personnel of the Army of the United States will be maintained on the general basis of the proportion of the Negro population of the country.
2. Negro organizations will be established in each major branch of the service, combatant as well as noncombatant.
3. Negro reserve officers eligible for active duty will be assigned to Negro units officered by colored personnel.
4. When officer candidate schools are established, opportunity will be given to Negroes to qualify for reserve commissions.
5. Negroes are being given aviation training as pilots, mechanics, and technical specialists. This training will be accelerated.
6. At arsenals and army posts, Negro civilians are accorded an equal opportunity for employment at work for which they are qualified by ability, education, and experience.
7. The policy of the War Department is not to intermingle colored and white enlisted personnel in the same regimental organizations. This policy has been proven satisfactory over a long period of years, and to make changes now would produce situations destructive to morale and detrimental to

EXAMINING BOARD FOR AIR CORPS FLYING CADETS
Maxwell Field, Alabama

31/rb

October 11, 1940

Mr. Garland Fort Pinkston,
Cardova, Tennessee.

Dear Sir:

Through the most unfortunate circumstances, your application was allowed to be completed because of our ignorance of your race. At the present time the United States Army is not training any except members of the White race for duty as pilots of military aircraft. Such training may be begun during this present national emergency and it is suggested that all papers being returned to you herewith, be held in readiness so that in event the above mentioned training becomes an actuality, your application may be reopened.

Please accept our sincerest apologies for allowing you to go to so much trouble through our oversight in connection with your original letter to this Board.

Very truly yours,

(Signed) HERBERT M. WEST, JR.,
1st Lieutenant, Air Corps,
Recorder.

Example of a rejection letter sent to a potential African-American aviation cadet who had applied to join the U.S. Army Air Corps.

FOR WHITES ONLY—A U. S. Army air corps training plane over the "West Point of the air"—Randolph Field, Texas. Negroes are not being accepted and trained by the Army air corps at any field in the nation, despite all the talk of national unity and of the urgency of every group serving in national defense.

WHEN DO <u>WE</u> FLY?

JAMES L. H. PECK

In December, 1940 James Peck wrote a magazine article that detailed how the War Department was misleading the public into thinking that black student pilots were enrolled in U.S. Army Air Corps flight and aviation maintenance training.

preparation for national defense. For similar reasons, the department does not contemplate assigning colored reserve officers other than those of the Medical Corps and chaplains to existing Negro combat units of the Regular Army. These regular units are going concerns, accustomed through many years to the present system. Their morale is splendid, their rate of reenlistment is exceptionally high, and their field training is well advanced. It is the opinion of the War Department that no experiments should be tried with the organizational set-up of these units at this critical time.[6]

Point 7 simply reinforced the War Department's insistence on segregation. The order of the day was "separate-but-equal rights," and the U.S. Army would go through extreme efforts and much expense to ensure separation between white and black personnel.

Point 5, however, was a half-truth and a deliberate attempt by the U.S. Army Air Corps to mislead civil rights activists. Point 5 referred to aviation training underway at the Chicago School of Aeronautics. While it was true that pilot training for African-Americans was offered through the Civilian Pilot Training Program at this site, the U.S. Army Air Corps was only providing airplanes and equipment as required by Public Law 18 for the

all-white contract primary flying school operating there. Not a single African-American aviation cadet at the Chicago School of Aeronautics had been admitted to the U.S. Army Air Corps civilian contract primary flying school program.

Pressure to Open U.S. Army Air Corps to African-American Flight Students

On November 5, 1940, President Franklin D. Roosevelt was re-elected President of the United States for an unprecedented third term. Holding him to his campaign promises, black leaders, civil rights activists and the black press collectively pressured Roosevelt to open the U.S. Army Air Corps to African-Americans.

Also, the influence and support of the First Lady, Eleanor Roosevelt, cannot be ignored. As one general described the U.S. Army Air Corps chain of command,

> General Arnold got his orders from General Marshall, and he got his from Secretary of War Stimson, and he got his from Mrs. Roosevelt.[7]

President Roosevelt was left with no choice but to direct the War Department and the U.S. Army Air Corps to accept African-Americans into military pilot training.

The first step began in November 1940 when officers from nearby Maxwell Field quite unexpectedly approached Dr. Patterson asking for assistance in locating a military airfield near the Tuskegee Institute for the possible training of U.S. Army Air Corps African-American military pilots.[8]

Beyond pressure from the White House, the reasons for this dramatic change of policy by U.S. Army Air Corps leadership to admit African-Americans into their military flight training program are myriad and somewhat complicated but are perhaps best captured by George L. Washington's private analysis,

> In short, developments against the Army were snowballing on a course heading towards the courts. So I believe the Army saw the handwriting on the wall and didn't feel confident it could win in the courts or on the basis of merit. Thus I believe that by the early Fall 1940 it decided it would have to admit Negroes to the Air Corps, and also that it would be better to plan their entrance on terms of the Army, rather than the courts. To avoid integration in training and combat units, it would establish separate training facilities and activate an all-Negro fighter group, where the pilot flies alone. This policy was in line with Army practice, but the economics of it might operate in court in favor of integrated training at least, and any integration must not take place. But how to proceed and beat legal action to the draw was the question?[9]

War Department Announced Formation of All African-American Pursuit Squadron

In January, 1941 the War Department learned that Yancey Williams, a successful graduate of Tuskegee's Secondary flight course who had been rejected by the U.S. Army Air Corps for flight training due to his race, was planning to file a lawsuit in United States District Court with the support of the National Association for the Advancement of Colored People's (NAACP) legal department. [10,11] With additional lawsuits probable, avoiding legal action was no longer an option for the U.S. Army Air Corps, and the courts would most certainly order not only the enlistment of Williams but even more distastefully, direct that all flight training be integrated.

The War Department's solution to their problem on how to avoid court-ordered integration of flight training occurred on January 16, 1941 when Undersecretary of War Robert P. Patterson held a press conference that announced the formation of an all African-American pursuit squadron.[12] The squadron, to be comprised of 33 pilots, was to be formed and trained at the Tuskegee Institute, the U.S. Army Air Corps successfully preempting any legal attempts to deter its policy of segregation, which they intended to extend even to the complexities and high costs of flight training. Of interest, Yancey Williams did eventually become a Tuskegee Airman, graduating in 1944.

Several prominent African-American activists and nearly all major African-American professional organizations were immediately critical of this decision by the U.S. Army Air Corps to segregate flight training. The black press was particularly harsh,

> According to our interpretation, this is in line with a policy of excluding colored persons from every branch of the Army, except a few Jim Crow set-ups and it is high time for the Negro people to rise as one man in protest against the chains that are surely tightening around our feet, this time in the guise of 33 pairs of wings.[13]

Another vocal critic was African-American Judge William H. Hastie, who was serving in a senior advisory position in the Roosevelt administration. In 1940 Hastie had been appointed by President Roosevelt to the War Department to serve as a civilian advisor on "all policy decisions or projects that had a racial significance" for Secretary of War Henry L. Stimson and Undersecretary of War Robert P. Patterson.[14] Before Patterson's announcement, he was asked for his opinion about U.S. Army Air Corps intentions to form a single black combat pursuit squadron. Hastie advocated the integration of flight training and "pointed out that there were Air Force Centers where this could be accomplished, as well as contract Primary Flying Schools in non-southern or segregated areas." [15]

In a December 1940 memorandum to Patterson expressing his

Franklin Delano Roosevelt, 32nd President of the United States, who served from 1933 until his death in office in 1945. Bowing to political pressure, he ordered the U.S. Army Air Corps to accept African-Americans for flight training.

views, Hastie was highly critical of U.S. Army Air Corps intentions to segregate flight training at an isolated southern military post,

> In brief, the plan as submitted creates problems and aggravates difficulties without offering any compensating advantages. If the Army will only begin the training of Negroes for the Air Corps in a normal manner, I am confident that immediate and long-range results will be gratifying. Specifically, it seems to me that the places for the training of Negro flying personnel should be the three existing training centers. Technical personnel should be trained in the regular course at the Air Corps Technical School at Chanute Field and such other institutions as are being used for such training.[16]

But Hastie was a pragmatist, and after consultations with Robert A. Lovett, special assistant for air affairs to Secretary of War Stimson, he realized that he was in a zero-sum situation: segregated flight training or none at all. So Hastie withdrew his formal objections, giving the U.S. Army Air Corps freedom to proceed with their plans, but he remained on record as stating that he did

On Clipped Wings

THE STORY OF
JIM CROW IN THE
ARMY AIR CORPS

by William H. Hastie

Judge William Hastie, the War Department's civilian advisor on racial policies, opposed the segregation of U.S. Army Air Corps flight training and later published this pamphlet detailing his opinions.

not agree with segregated flight training.[17] Hastie later resigned from his position in a very public protest over the discriminatory practices of the U.S. Army Air Corps and in October 1943 published *On Clipped Wings, The Story of Jim Crow in the Army Air Corps.*[18] In this 27 page pamphlet, he outlined that the U.S. Army Air Corps enlisted African-Americans only when compelled to do so by the White House and that "there is not now and never has been any good reason for the segregated training of Negro pilots."[19]

In advance of Undersecretary of War Patterson's press conference, Maj. Gen. Henry H. Arnold, Chief of Air Corps, sent a telegram to Dr. Frederick Patterson, president of the Tuskegee

Institute, providing him details on the new program,

Under Secretary of War will announce substantially as follows at a press conference at three P.M. 'The War Department will establish a Negro pursuit squadron. The plan will begin by the enlistment of approximately four hundred thirty Negro high school graduates to undertake technical training and other specialized instruction at Chanute Field, Rantoul, Illinois, in courses varying from twelve to thirty weeks. Approximately six months after training is begun at Chanute Field a nucleus of trained technicians will be available for transfer to Tuskegee, Alabama to start organization of squadron. A site for installations at Tuskegee already has been selected.

Pilot trainees will be obtained from those completing civil pilot training program secondary course and will be enlisted as flying cadets subject to present standards. They will be sent to Tuskegee for basic and advanced flying training and unit training in pursuit types of aircraft. The squadron will be organized at Tuskegee as soon as fully trained pilots become available. Instruction will proceed as soon as funds are made available for this purpose by the Congress.[20]

Tuskegee Institute Prepares for Military Training

This telegram from Maj. Gen. Arnold did not come as a complete surprise to President Patterson as he was already involved in assisting U.S. Army Air Corps officers from nearby Maxwell Field in the selection of a suitable site for the new Tuskegee Army Air Field.[21]

But Dr. Patterson had his suspicions about the U.S. Army Air Corps' intentions for African-American military flight training. He recalled,

When I heard about the plans to include blacks in the new Air Corps, I was anxious to learn more. The argument against establishing a segregated corps and segregated training was sound, but I wanted to learn whether the rumored integration of the corps was based on fact.

My concern was genuine. If the U.S. government was at long last ready to integrate the military well and good. With desegregation of the military, there would be no reason for starting any new program under the banner of segregation! I made a thorough investigation to discover what course the military was about to take, specifically whether the new recruits to the Air Corps would be integrated.

In Washington, I consulted the office of the secretary of

war, Henry L. Stimson. I met with Robert Patterson, the assistant secretary of war. He knew and I knew, as did others, that William Hastie, a black man who worked for Stimson as assistant secretary in charge of Negro affairs, and Walter White, the head of the National Association for the Advancement of Colored People, were publicly promoting integration. I told the assistant secretary of war, 'Tuskegee Institute is available if flying is going to be offered on a segregated basis. We do not want it if there's a chance of immediate integration.'

If integration was not part of the initial picture of U.S. military aviation, we saw Tuskegee as an ideal place for training black flyers. We were only fifty miles from Maxwell Field, the military air base in Montgomery, and the Alabama climate facilitated year-round flying. In our opinion, aviation was another important area of technical education consistent with the direction in which Tuskegee was oriented. It would have been difficult to find a better place than Tuskegee for setting up a program such as military flying. The fact that we already had both student military training [Reserve Officer Training Corps program under the command of then-Colonel Benjamin O. Davis, Sr.] and civilian aviation at Tuskegee put us a few steps ahead of other institutions because we had experience to build on.

Patterson told me in unequivocal terms that military flying would not be integrated. I was told the same thing by some of the leading officers of the Air Corps. I believed that Tuskegee would by no means be needed if the Air Corps was to be integrated. But if young black men could serve their country in the Air Corps only in segregated units like those maintained by the army, then Tuskegee would make its resources available.[22]

Dr. Patterson's agreement to host segregated U.S. Army Air Corps flight training at the Tuskegee Institute was not well received by all African-American activists.

Facilitating Failure or Supporting Success

A question often arises on why the first African-Americans in the history of the U.S. Army Air Corps were assigned to single-seat fighters, certainly the most challenging type of combat flying of all the air arms. In addition to mastering complex air-to-air combat tactics, fighter pilots must also become skilled at air-to-ground strafing and bombing procedures, often in close proximity to friendly ground troops. Three opinions have emerged.

The most generally-accepted belief is that U.S. Army Air Corps leadership wanted the Tuskegee Airmen program to fail.

It was an experiment bound for failure! Senior leaders of the U.S. Army Air Corps were simply unable to believe that blacks could learn to fly or to perform in combat. Their training, their experience, and their ultra-conservative attitude prevented it. They had never heard of Eugene Bullard, or Bessie Coleman, or Cornelius Coffey, or Willa Brown, and they had never seen a black pilot in the U.S. Army Air Corps!. They didn't read the black press, so they never read of the Banning-Allen or Anderson-Forsythe flights. What they believed was the prevailing attitude in the United States and, at least partially, the outgrowth of a 1925 Army War College 'study' that argued vehemently that blacks were unfit to fly.[23]

The exact opposite reason may also be true, that is, fighter pilot training was selected because it is so demanding. If the Tuskegee Airmen excelled during flight training and in actual combat, the myth of black aeronautical ineptitude would be shattered, paving the way for future generations of African-Americans to serve in the military and commercial aviation.

Of course, the simplest explanation may be that the U.S. Army Air Corps just wanted to limit the number of African-Americans aviators and support personnel in its ranks.[24] A fighter required only a single pilot. A B-17 or B-24 bomber, however, necessitated an average crew size of about ten men, including pilot, co-pilot, navigator, bombardier, radio operator and various gunners. Also, bombers required a much larger maintenance team and ground echelon support staff.[25]

Use of the Term "Experiment"

It is important to note that by July 1941, when the 99th Pursuit Squadron, Tuskegee's first U.S. Army Air Corps pursuit squadron, was activated, more than 300 African-Americans had been trained as pilots under the Civilian Pilot Training Program.[26] Yet to prove just how out of touch with reality the U.S. Army Air Corps leadership was regarding the achievements of these young African-American aviators, as well as the accomplishments of other expert black pilots across the country, both the U.S. Army Air Corps and the white press used the term "experiment" to describe this first African-American fighter squadron.

Of interest, this expression was never used to describe African-American participation in the Civilian Pilot Training Program. In his memoirs, Washington noted,

Because the Civilian Pilot Training program placed sole emphasis upon individual performance there seemed no basis for looking upon the programs at Negro colleges as experimental. Thus there was never the suggestion of experimentation. Also, right from the beginning of this program the Tuskegee students had excelled in ground school instruction

Tuskegee Institute mechanics, including two women, perform a 100-hour inspection on a Fairchild PT-19A *Cornell* trainer at Moton Field. In many ways, maintenance training for the first cadre of support personnel for the 99th Fighter Squadron was more intensive that the pilot course of instruction.

and had done well, if not better than white students on the average in flight instruction. There is no doubt that on an individual basis Negro students equaled the performance of whites.[27]

Tuskegee CPTP Secondary Course Substituted for U.S. Army Primary Flight Training

In December 1940 the U.S. Army Air Corps advised George L. Washington that Tuskegee's Civilian Pilot Training Program Secondary flight course would be substituted for U.S. Army Air Corps primary flight training. This was a much different approach than how white U.S. Army Air Corps aviation cadets were trained and confirmed for Washington that this was a strategy by the U.S. Army Air Corps to avoid integrating training at existing civilian

contract primary flying schools.[28, 29]

To accommodate this new initiative, the Tuskegee Institute's Civilian Pilot Training Program Secondary flight course curriculum was modified to include additional U.S. Army Air Corps primary flight training requirements. These changes resulted in a one-of-a-kind hybrid Civil Aeronautics Authority - U.S. Army Air Corps (CAA-Army) Secondary flight course that was offered only at the Tuskegee Institute.

To prepare civilian flight instructors to conduct the military primary flight curriculum, the U.S. Army Air Corps provided a specialized military flight instructor course. So in mid-summer 1941, Charles A. "Chief" Anderson and three Tuskegee Institute flight instructors, Milton P. Crenshaw, Forrest Shelton, and Charles R. Foxx went through the Primary Instructor Training Course, administered by U.S. Army Air Corps flight instructors at Tuskegee's Kennedy Field.[30] Two additional Waco YPT-14 trainers were provided to the Tuskegee Institute by the U.S. Army Air Corps for use in the new CAA-Army Secondary flight course.

The CAA-Army Secondary flight course also required an administrative reorganization in the Tuskegee Institute's flight training structure to separate the Tuskegee Institute's Civilian Pilot Training Program Elementary flight course from the U.S. Army's civilian contract primary flying school training. Anderson was designated chief pilot of the U.S. Army Air Corps program while George Allen assumed responsibility as chief pilot of the Civilian Pilot Training Program Elementary flight course.

In January 1941 the Tuskegee Institute's unique CAA-Army Secondary flight course started at the Tuskegee Institute with 30 aviation cadets, all of whom had passed military flight physicals and were graduates of the Civilian Pilot Training Program Elementary flight course at various historically black colleges and universities (HBCUs) from across the United States.[31] Successful graduates were then supposed to be fed directly into U.S. Army Air Corps Basic flight training, the next phase on the prescribed training track towards earning U.S. Army Air Corps silver wings. Basic flight training would be conducted at Tuskegee Army Air Field (TAAF), a new airfield to be constructed at Tuskegee.

Decision Reversed

But on February 15, 1941, while the first CAA-Army Secondary flight course was still in session, the U.S. Army Air Corps notified the Tuskegee Institute that it had changed its mind. Students who successfully completed the current CAA-Army Secondary flight course would not be sent directly to U.S. Army Air Corps Basic flight training.

Instead, the U.S. Army Air Corps issued a new contract to the Tuskegee Institute that canceled the CAA-Army Secondary flight course and established a civilian contract primary flying school at Tuskegee to equalize the black flight training pipeline with the white flight training pipeline, although this training would remain segregated.[32,33]

As to what happened to the poor 30 students who were enrolled in the CAA-Army Secondary flight course? Director Washington recalled,

> Apparently Air Corps headquarters forgot or wrote off the 30 students who took and passed that secondary course. On the other hand one of the students who passed that course was among the first class of cadets that began training in Primary August 25, 1941. I have reference to Cadet George S. Roberts, who must have sailed through primary flight with the greatest of ease and received the same training at the Government's expense.[34]

Cadet Roberts did, in fact, excel in flight training,

He enjoyed extra privileges extended to him by his primary instructor, Charles Foxx, with whom he had taken his CPTP training. Foxx would allow him to perform any maneuver he desired (when off by themselves), most of which were never tried even in advanced training, much less in a PT-13A. In fact, Mr. Foxx learned a little from the unauthorized flights himself, often wondering who was the instructor.[35]

Roberts went on to serve as the very first Commanding Officer of the 99th Fighter Squadron, the number assigned to the first African-American pursuit squadron, and eventually, most of his fellow CPTP classmates were inducted into the U.S. Army Air Corps.[36]

Enlisted Training

As contrary as it may seem, training pilots is a relatively quick and easy process. Either you can fly an airplane, or you cannot. If not, you are attrited. It is much harder and takes a great deal longer to train enlisted personnel to service, maintain, repair and arm aircraft, particularly for operations in combat field conditions. During World War II the average ratio of total ground personnel to flying personnel was seven to one.[37] The 99th Fighter Squadron's proposed complement was 27 airplanes, 33 pilots and 276 ground personnel, a ratio of 8.4 to one.[38]

Due to its segregationist policies, the U.S. Army Air Corps was faced with the formidable challenge of building the 99th Pursuit Squadron's maintenance department from scratch. As a result, raw recruits were used for the squadron's mechanics and crew chiefs instead of transferring into the 99th Fighter Squadron experienced white maintenance personnel from other U.S. Army Air Corps squadrons.

Fortunately, the U.S. Army Air Corps had the good sense to request the assistance of the Tuskegee Institute in recruiting and selecting officers and enlisted men to staff the ground echelon of the 99th Pursuit Squadron. Director Washington traveled to Washington, DC and met with U.S. Army Air Corps manning specialists to identify the specific qualifications needed for each position. He then created his own application form, which he circulated to various historically black colleges and universities (HBCUs) for candidates. As one would imagine, the response was tremendous, and from these applicants, the first cadre of personnel for the ground echelon of the 99th Pursuit Squadron was built.[39]

While these might have been well-qualified recruits, with each selected due to their mechanical backgrounds, college education, and aptitude tests results, nothing can substitute for real-world aircraft type experience.[40] An established squadron's maintenance department possesses a broad range of maintenance experience. From senior personnel with extensive knowledge about a specific airplane's nuances and peculiarities; to middle-grade personnel with some experience; to junior personnel without any experience at all, who require a tremendous amount of initial training. War Department officials noted,

> It is desired to strongly emphasize the fact that a much longer period of time will be required for key enlisted personnel to absorb the requisite technical skill and experience that is indispensable to the proper functioning of tactical air units. A period of at least from three to five years is normally required before enlisted personnel are qualified as competent crew chiefs, line chiefs, and hangar chiefs.[41]

Additionally, other support personnel are also needed to outfit a new squadron, including administrative staff, medical personnel, cooks, supply clerks, parachute riggers and more specialized personnel like meteorologists, intelligence specialists, and flight surgeons.[42]

While on-the-job training might compensate for lack of experience, it is not prudent to do so while conducting combat

66TH AAFFTD MOTON FIELD
Tuskegee, Alabama

Ground crew formed to the side of their PT-17's on this cover of a booklet on the 66th Army Air Force Flying Training Detachment (AAFFTD) at Tuskegee.

operations.[43] Fortunately, or unfortunately, depending on one's perspective, it took so long for the War Department to deploy the 99th Pursuit Squadron overseas to a combat zone that its maintenance personnel had more than enough time to become experts on their assigned aircraft before they departed the United States.

Activation of the 99th Pursuit Squadron

To preserve its inviolate policy of segregation, the U.S. Army Air Corps intended to establish what was for all intents and purposes an independent black air force. But while it could effortlessly segregate black fighter pilot training at Tuskegee, it was impractical to do so for enlisted training with the nearly 13 separate courses of instruction required. So U.S. Army Air Corps leadership pragmatically decided to concentrate most enlisted and some non-pilot officer training at Chanute Field, Illinois, where nearly all of the technical training in the U.S. Army Air Corps was centralized.[44]

Since this initial enlisted technical training would take much longer than pilot training, on March 22, 1941 the War Department activated the segregated 99th Pursuit Squadron at Chanute Field with Capt. Harold R. Maddux, a white officer, serving as the squadron's first commanding officer.[45] This event occurred more than three months before the first pilot training class was scheduled to convene. The plan was for these personnel to undergo initial training at Chanute Field, then transfer en masse to Maxwell Field for additional training before finally reporting to Tuskegee for squadron duty.

Fourteen black enlisted men from two U.S. Army infantry regiments were ordered to Chanute Field to provide core support for the newly reporting enlisted members of the new squadron. Mostly cooks, supply, and administrative personnel, they are considered to be the first African-Americans to serve in a U.S. Army Air Corps squadron.[46]

66th Army Air Corps Primary Flying School Established

On May 30, 1941 the Tuskegee Institute and the U.S. Army Air Corps officially signed a contract for the Tuskegee Institute to provide facilities and personnel to operate the 66th Air Corps Primary Flying School (later renamed 66th Army Air Force Flying Training Detachment).[47] The number "66" merely reflected the 66th such contract entered into by the U.S. Army Air Corps since it had started subcontracting out primary flight training to civilian flight schools.[48]

In June 1941 Capt. Noel F. Parrish, a white officer who later rose to the rank of Brig. Gen., reported to the Tuskegee Institute to serve as the first U.S. Army Air Corps Supervisor of the Primary Flying School at Tuskegee.[49] Parrish had previously served as the assistant supervisor of the primary flying school at the Chicago School of Aeronautics, where he worked closely with Cornelius Coffey and Willa Brown, so he was very familiar with the program.[50]

Parrish officially assumed command of the 66th Air Corps Primary Flying School on July 19, 1941 and served in this position until December 1, 1941 when he transferred to the Tuskegee Army Air Field as Director of Training. In December 1942, after promotion to Lt. Col., Parish assumed command of Tuskegee Army Air Field, remaining until 1946.[51]

The new contract also required the Tuskegee Institute to conduct a Preflight School. Preflight was a recent addition to the U.S. Army Air Corps pilot training curriculum designed to provide initial administrative processing and military indoctrination to aviation cadets before they started actual flight training.[52] Preflight School, which eventually transferred to the Tuskegee Army Air Field, was to precede the official start of Primary flight training for the first class of African-American flight students, hard-scheduled to begin on July 19, 1941.[53]

Seeking Funds for a Second Tuskegee Institute Airfield

Despite the modifications made to Kennedy Field to make it suitable for the civilian Secondary flight course, it was still leased property and unsuitable to accommodate planned increases in both the civilian Elementary flight course, the civilian Secondary flight course, and the U.S. Army Air Corps subcontracted primary flight course.

Tuskegee Institute officials wanted their own airfield on school-owned property. After touring several locations and consulting with U.S. Army Air Corps personnel, an ideal site was selected about 4 miles northeast from the Tuskegee Institute. The property was owned by S. M. Eich, who agreed to sell some 650 acres at $50 per acre.[54,55]

Financing of the land purchase and airfield construction was Tuskegee's responsibility, and initially, President Patterson and Di-

First Lady Eleanor Roosevelt takes a ride at Tuskegee in a Piper J-3 *Cub*. Chief Flight Instructor Charles Anderson is at the controls with Director of Training Lewis Jackson off to the side.

rector Washington estimated the total cost to be between $300,000 and $400,000, the total investment to be adjusted depending on U.S. Army Air Corps training requirements.[56]

Despite Patterson's and Washington's best efforts, they were unable to secure funding. In a last-ditch effort, they approached the Julius Rosenwald Fund, a philanthropic organization principally dedicated towards building schools for African-American children in the rural South. Although preliminary inquiries with executives of the Rosenwald Fund were discouraging, President Patterson shrewdly invited the organization to hold their annual board of trustees meeting in March 1941 at the Tuskegee Institute.

"Chief" Anderson Takes First Lady Eleanor Roosevelt For a Flight

One of the Julius Rosenwald Fund's Board of Trustee members was First Lady Eleanor Roosevelt, who spent three nights at

Front gate of Moton Field with a bust of Robert R. Moton, the second president of the Tuskegee Institute, set in a brick gate in the right background.

Moton Field's flight line packed with Fairchild PT-19A *Cornell* trainers, used during Primary flight training.

Boeing-Stearman PT-17 biplanes in front of Moton Field's hangar, which today's houses the National Park Service's Tuskegee Airmen National Historic Site.

Key administrative personnel in the Division of Aeronautics. The General Manager is responsible directly to the President of Tuskegee Institute for efficient operation of Tuskegee Institute's Pilot Training School. Assembled are supervisors and heads of Flying, Ground School, Aircraft Maintenance, physical plant and business departments, covering Airport "Number One" and Moton Field.

George L. Washington meeting with key members of his staff. From a one-person, part-time operation, Washington expanded Tuskegee Institute's pilot training program to include flight, maintenance, and business operations at Kennedy Field and Moton Field. The person seated immediately to Washington's left is most likely Gertrude Anderson, administrative assistant to Washington and spouse of Chief Flight Instructor Charles Anderson, who is the third person seated to Washington's right

Tuskegee, attending board meetings in the morning and touring during the afternoon.

President Patterson took this opportunity to acquaint Mrs. Roosevelt with the new airfield project and on Saturday afternoon, March 29, 1941, he escorted her to Kennedy Field to observe flight operations. To the surprise of everyone, she took a spontaneous flight with Tuskegee's Chief Flight Instructor "Chief" Anderson aboard a Piper J-3 *Cub*. One author noted that "her willingness to fly with a black instructor....carried great symbolic value."[57]

Anderson later recalled meeting the First Lady,

First thing she said was, 'I always heard colored people couldn't fly airplanes,' says Anderson. 'She was amazed.' Anderson invited the First Lady for a spin in his Piper Cub, and over the objections of her aides, she accepted, leaving her entourage dithering on the ground. 'While we were up there,' says Anderson, 'she told me she had planned to take flying lessons herself with Amelia Earhart.'[58]

Roosevelt herself recalled the flight in her daily newspaper column *My Day*,

Finally we went out to the aviation field, where a Civil Aeronautics unit for the teaching of colored pilots is in full swing. They have advanced training here, and some of the students went up and did acrobatic flying for us. These boys are good pilots. I had the fun of going up in one of the tiny training planes with the head instructor, and seeing this interesting countryside from the air.[59]

Mrs. Roosevelt's flight and influence proved fruitful, the Rosenwald Fund Board of Trustees voted to loan the Tuskegee Institute $200,000 of the $300,000 needed to build the new airfield. The funding problem for the new landing site was permanently solved when the scale of the field was subsequently reduced based on projected decreased pilot training demands by the U.S. Army Air Corps.[60]

Second Tuskegee Institute Airfield Built and Dedicated as Moton Field

Since the new airfield was to be used for U.S. Army Air Corps primary flight training, construction plans required approval by the U.S. Army Air Corps Headquarters in Washington, DC. Yet Director Washington experienced difficulties in obtaining exact specifications for the flying field and necessary buildings. So he invited African-American engineer Archie A. Alexander to visit Tuskegee and consult on the new airfield design. [61] Alexander

A group of the Division of Aeronautics Flying Instructors at Moton Field. All Negro Aviation Cadets receive their fundamental and first Army flying training at the hands of these men.

Flight instructors of the 66th Army Air Force Flying Training Detachment at Moton Field. Hired and supervised by the Tuskegee Institute, they taught the primary phase of U.S. Army Air Corps flight training, which had been subcontracted across the country by the U.S. Army Air Corps to expand training capacity.

and his white partner Maurice A. Repass operated Alexander and Repass, an Iowa-based construction company.

Together Washington and Alexander visited other U.S. Army Air Corps civilian contract primary flying schools to tour their facilities, with Washington photographing and sketching buildings for his own plans and Alexander providing an estimate of costs.[62]

Pilot training quotas drove the size and scale of the new airfield but continuously changing numbers provided by the U.S. Army Air Corps threw Washington into an interminable do-loop. On April 7, 1941 Washington submitted the first of three separate blueprints he eventually produced for the new airfield's design to the U.S. Army Air Corps.[63] Finally approved on June 1, 1941, construction began immediately.

Since the Tuskegee Institute was financially responsible for construction, President Patterson hired Alexander and Repass to build the new airfield with a scheduled completion date of July 19, 1941 for preflight classrooms and August 23, 1941 for the construction of runways so that actual primary flight training could commence.[64]

Initially, the complex included a 2,800-foot square sod landing area, a concrete ramp, an adjoining hangar, all roadways and utilities, and various offices and workshops.[65] Alexander and Repass subcontracted the heavy construction work to a local white contractor, J. H. LaMar, who was tasked with completing the "rough and finish grading of the flying field, roadwork, well digging, and sewer and storm water lines."[66]

Heavy summer rains, however, delayed construction and the flying field was not available for flight operations by the desired

date of August 23, 1941. Instead, Kennedy Field was used as a temporary substitute.[67]

The new airfield was officially dedicated as Moton Field in honor of Robert R. Moton, the second president of the Tuskegee Institute, on Founder's Day, 1943. [68] A niche was built in the brick entrance to the field to hold a bust of Moton to honor him.[69]

Moton Field was the only contract primary flight school available to U.S. Army Air Corps African-American aviation cadets during World War II. Of interest, Moton Field closed on November 30, 1945 and the National Park Service acquired the land and structures in 1998, where it is currently home to the Tuskegee Airmen National Historic Site.

U.S. Army Air Corps Redesignated U.S. Army Air Forces

In a June 1941 reorganization to facilitate greater autonomy in command and control, the War Department officially formed the U.S. Army Air Forces to succeed the U.S. Army Air Corps. This sometimes causes confusion as the press, and various writers, continued to use the older title "Air Corps." For the remainder of this book, the author will strive to use only the phrase "U.S. Army Air Forces" as appropriate.

With enlisted technical training firmly underway, the timing was right to begin pilot training at Tuskegee. ■

Chapter Seven
Tuskegee U.S. Army Pilot Training

T he training plan for the initial cadre of Tuskegee student pilots was to convene classes at five-week intervals with the flight students progressing through a standardized five-phase U.S. Army Air Forces flight training program.

In the first phase, known as Preflight, the flight students, both aviation cadets and previously commissioned officers, underwent administrative processing, military indoctrination, physical conditioning, medical screening and academic training, with a particular emphasis on mathematics and physics as experience proved that most flight students were deficient in these areas.[1] As no actual flying occurred during this phase of flight training, Preflight aviation cadets were affectionately known as Dodos "because that extinct breed of bird was incapable of flight."[2]

In the second phase, known as Primary flight training, flight students began their actual flight instruction with the Tuskegee Institute's civilian flight instructors under the direction of "Chief" Anderson at Moton Field. The first primary trainer (PT) aircraft flown by most Tuskegee Airmen was the Fairchild PT-19A *Cornell* followed by the Boeing PT-13 or PT-17 *Kaydet,* the specific variant for each aircraft depending on the installed engine.

The Fairchild PT-19 *Cornell* was a two-seat, fabric-covered, low-wing monoplane built around a steel tube fuselage equipped with fixed landing gear. The use of a single wing instead of a traditional biplane was unique as Fairchild executives recognized the need for a military training airplane whose performance characteristics more closely resembled those of front-line operational aircraft.

The Boeing PT-13 *Kaydet* was a rugged all-fabric, two-seat, fixed landing gear traditional biplane relatively forgiving of any student pilot mistakes. The *Kaydet* was built initially by the Stearman Aircraft Corporation until 1934 when the Boeing Aircraft Company absorbed the company, but all aircraft remain universally known as Stearman's.[3] Students accumulated about sixty-five flying hours during this phase of training.[4]

In the third phase of flight training, known as Basic training, flight students transferred to the newly constructed Tuskegee Army Air Field to receive basic flight training from U.S. Army Air Forces flight instructors, which also included ground school courses such as meteorology, radio communication, and navigation.[5] They flew the faster single-wing Vultee BT -13 *Valiant* airplane,

FLYING TRAINING: Pilots

PREFLIGHT SCHOOL—10 weeks' course: sea and air recognition, 30 hours; code, 48 hours; physics, 24 hours; math, 20 hours; maps and charts, 18 hours; daily physical and military training.

PRIMARY FLYING SCHOOL—10 weeks' course: 70 hours in 125 to 225 horsepower open cockpit biplanes or low-wing monoplanes; 94 hours academic work in ground school; 54 hours military training.

BASIC FLYING SCHOOL—10 weeks' course: 70 hours in a 450 horsepower basic trainer; 94 hours in ground school; 47 hours military training. By the end of basic school trainees have learned to fly a plane competently. Further training will teach them to fly a warplane the AAF way. Before the end of basic, trainees are classified—on the basis of choice and instructors' reports—for single-engine training (fighter pilot) or 2-engine training (bomber, transport or 2-engine fighter pilot).

ADVANCED FLYING TRAINING—10 weeks' course (single-engine and 2-engine): 70 hours of flying; 60 hours of ground school; 19 hours military training. Single-engine trainees fly 600 horsepower AT-6s and take a course in fixed gunnery. Two-engine trainees fly AT-24s, AT-17s, AT-9s, or AT-10s. Based on performance and choice, they are earmarked for heavy or medium bombardment, transport, troop-carrier or 2-engine fighter. At the end of advanced training the graduates, single- and 2-engine, are awarded the silver pilot's wings of the AAF and appointed flight officers or commissioned 2nd lieutenants.

Detailed description of U.S. Army Air Force academic and flight training. Upon completion of Advanced flying training, aviation cadets were winged and commissioned as 2nd Lt.'s. They then transferred to Transition training for qualification in operational aircraft.

where BT stood for basic trainer. Nicknamed the "Vibrator," it was often accused by flight instructors of being "too easy to fly."[6] The two-seat BT-13 *Valiant* lacked retractable landing gear but was equipped with the flight instruments necessary to train new pilots in the basics of flying on instruments in poor weather. At this point, the average flight student had typically accumulated 10 flight hours in a Piper J-3 *Cub,* 65 hours in a Fairchild PT-19 *Cornell* and Boeing PT-17 *Kaydet,* and 70 hours in a BT-13 *Valiant.*[7]

In the fourth phase of flight training, known as Advanced training, flight students finished their flight training in the North American AT-6 *Texan,* AT standing for advanced trainer, the ubiquitous Allied advanced military pilot trainer of World War II. The two-seat, single-wing AT-6 *Texan* was equipped with retractable landing gear and a powerful 650 horsepower engine. Ground school courses included advanced navigation, gunnery,

Outstanding line-up of four of the six training airplanes flown by the Tuskegee Airmen. From the top, Boeing PT-17 *Kaydet*, Vultee BT-13 *Valiant*, North American AT-6 *Texan*, and Curtiss P-40 *Warhawk*. Not shown is the Fairchild PT-19 *Cornell* and the Bell P-39 *Airacobra*, which was also flown in the United States before deploying overseas.

and air combat tactics.[8] Upon successful completion of advanced flight training, all graduates were awarded their silver U.S. Army Air Forces pilot wings and all aviation cadets commissioned as 2nd Lieutenants or Flight Officers in the U.S. Army.

The non-commissioned Flight Officer rank, equivalent to a warrant officer, was created in July 1942.[9] All current enlisted pilots, commonly known as flight sergeants, were promoted to Flight Officer and a flight student's performance during training determined whether he was commisioned as a 2nd Lieutenant or a Flight Officer.[10]

The fifth and final phase of flight training, known as Transition training, was conducted after graduation and during this phase of flight training, the newly-rated pilots were taught to fly and fight in a frontline combat fighter and ground attack aircraft. In the Tuskegee Airmen's case, they flew the single-seat, Curtiss P-40 *Warhawk,* and the single-seat Bell P-39 *Airacobra,* both of which were flown in combat by the Tuskegee Airmen at different times in North Africa, Sicily, and the Italian mainland. To learn and practice gunnery tactics, the Tuskegee Airmen flew to ranges located at Eglin Army Air Field in Fort Walton Beach, FL and Dale Mabry Army Air Field in Tallahassee, FL.

Upon completion of Advanced training, the next logical step was an overseas combat assignment. As we shall see, however,

despite having successfully completed all required training in air-to-air and air-to-ground combat operations, overseas active duty combat assignments were initially withheld from the 99th Pursuit Squadron.

The planned completion time for each phase of training was: Preflight (5 weeks); Primary training (10 weeks); Basic training (10 weeks); and Advanced training (10 weeks).[11]

History Made: First African-American Flight Students in the U.S. Army Air Forces

The War Department established July 19, 1941 as the official start date for the first class of African-American student pilots in the history of the U.S. Army Air Forces. The intention was for the students to first attend Preflight and Primary flight training at the Tuskegee Institute under civilian flight instructors before being handed off to military flight instructors at the Tuskegee Army Air Field on August 23, 1941 for Basic, Advanced, and Transition flight training.[12]

A formal ceremony was held on July 19, 1941 on the campus of Tuskegee Institute in front of the Booker T. Washington Monument to commemorate the moment. The guest speaker was Maj. Gen. Walter R. Weaver, commander of the Southeast Air Corps Training Center at Maxwell Field, Montgomery, AL, who addressed the assembled group,

Today we inaugurate the organization of a new flying school in the Southeast Air Corps Training Center. This training school is one of forty-two schools which make up the Southeast Air Corps Training Center. This particular school is unique because it is the first flying school started by the U.S. Army for Cadets of the Negro race. It therefore becomes a most important duty for the officers and the cadets to do their utmost because not only are the people of your country, but also the people of your own race are turned in your direction.

If you knew all the planning that has gone into making this opportunity possible you would more fully realize the significance and the weight of your responsibility. Dr. Patterson, your president, has fittingly referred to the significance of having this ceremony in front of the monument dedicated to the illustrious founder, Booker T. Washington. What Booker T. Washington stood for--the principle of work, attention to duty, loyalty to cause--these especially, with these in front of you, you cadets can but be inspired.[13]

Class 42-C and Benjamin O. Davis Jr.

The first class to enter training was designated Class 42-C, the

On July 19, 1941 before the Booker T. Washington Monument on the campus of the Tuskegee Institute, Maj. Gen. Walter R. Weaver, Commander of the Southeast Air Corps Training Center, formally inaugurated the start of flight training for the first class of African-American student pilots in the history of the U.S. Army Air Forces.

number 42 signifying the year of their expected graduation (1942) and the letter C indicating their graduation month (A signifying January, B for February, C for March, and so on).[14] Class 42-C's initial complement was 12 aviation cadets and one officer.

The sole officer was Capt. Benjamin O. Davis Jr., son of a career soldier and one of the most influential figures in the entire history of the Tuskegee Airmen. Davis' father, Brig. Gen Benjamin O. Davis Sr. had risen from the enlisted ranks to become the first African-American soldier ever to be promoted to general in the U.S. Army.

Young Davis received an appointment to the U.S. Military Academy at West Point and reported in 1932 where he roomed alone and was "silenced" by his classmates. Except in the line of duty, no one spoke with him for his entire four-year stay at West Point,

> I was silenced solely because cadets did not want blacks at West Point. Their only purpose was to freeze me out. What they did not realize was that I was stubborn enough to put

up with their treatment to reach the goal I had come to attain.[15]

Davis achieved his goal when he graduated from West Point in 1936 and was commissioned a 2nd Lt. in the U.S. Army. He was the first African-American to graduate from West Point in the 20th century, preceded by only three other black graduates who had graduated in the late 1800's. The U.S. Army now had a total of two black line officers, Davis, and his father.

Davis applied for pilot training with the U.S. Army Air Corps the fall before his graduation but was turned down due to his race. Instead, his initial assignment was the 24th Infantry Regiment at Fort Benning, Georgia, followed by a tour at the Tuskegee Institute as a Reserve Officers' Training Corps (ROTC) instructor. In 1939 he was promoted to 2nd Lt. and in 1940 to Captain. In 1941, he was assigned as an aide to his father who was currently serving as commanding general of the 4th Cavalry Brigade of the 2nd Cavalry Division at Fort Riley, Kansas.

Capt. Davis was in this assignment for only a few weeks when

Sidebar: Curtiss P-40 *Warhawk*

The Curtiss P-40 *Warhawk* was the first of two combat fighters flown by 1st Lt. James R. Polkinghorne Jr., the second being the Bell P-39 *Airacobra*. Sadly, aviation historians have not been kind to either airplane. Although they fought courageously in the low altitude attack role, both have been severely criticized for their lack of high altitude performance against contemporary German and Japanese fighters, a mission for which they were not originally designed.

A lineup of Curtiss P-40's *Warhawks* with North American AT-6 *Texans* in the background at Tuskegee Army Air Field.

The origin of the P-40 *Kittyhawk* is traced to a 1938 proposal by the Curtiss-Wright Corporation to the U.S. Army Air Corps to modify a P-36A airframe to accommodate an Allison V-1710 engine rated at 1,160 horsepower, estimating that the airplane would be capable of attaining a 350 mph speed.[1] The U.S. Army Air Corps agreed, and on July 30, 1938 issued Curtiss-Wright a contract, designating this airplane the XP-40 (XP representing an experimental pursuit fighter).[2]

The XP-40 flew for the first time on October 14, 1938 and as designed was a single-seat, single-engine, retractable gear, low-wing tail-dragger of all-metal construction, except fabric-covered but metal framed flight control surfaces, including electrically operated flaps. 3 After several improvements, the XP-40 entered and won the January 1939 fighter competition, eventually reaching a top speed of 366 mph at the specified 15,000-ft altitude.4

On April 26, 1939 Curtiss-Wright was awarded the first of many U.S. Army Air Corps production contracts for P-40s, at that time breaking a record for the largest order ever made for an American-built fighter.5 During an airplane's production life modifications that significantly change an airplane's design are identified by unique variant letters, for example, the P-40B or P-40C. In the case of the Curtiss P-40 *Warhawk*, there were more than 15 variants, including export versions to various foreign countries in different configurations.

As the U.S. Army Air Corps did not officially confer nicknames upon airplanes, the manufacturer's trade name was usually adopted.[6] Since nearly all earlier Curtiss biplane fighters had been called some derivative of "Hawk," the Curtiss P-40 continued the tradition and was christened the *Warhawk*. Export versions to Great Britain's Royal Air Force (RAF) were known as *Tomahawk*'s and *Kittyhawk*'s depending on the exact configuration.[7]

The majority of Curtiss P-40 *Warhawks* were powered by a supercharged, 12-cylinder Allison V-1710 series liquid-cooled inline engine, the supercharging system delivering compressed combustion air for high altitude combat operations.[8] While the Allison's performance below 15,000 feet was excellent, the supercharger was not very effective at higher altitudes and power decreased significantly.[9] As a result, the Curtiss P-40 *Warhawk* was outmatched at high altitudes by the Messerschmitt Bf-109's, Focke-Wulf-190's and Mitsubishi A6M Zero's it faced in air-to-air combat, a serious shortcoming that discredited the Curtiss P-40 *Warhawk* throughout its service.

The exact Curtiss P-40 *Warhawk* weapons capability depended on the U.S. variant and export version. The Curtiss P-40C *Warhawk* is usually considered the first genuinely combat-ready production variant, and it was equipped with two .50-caliber machine guns nose-mounted on the fuselage and synchronized to fire through the propeller arc with two .30-caliber machine guns in each wing.[10] The Curtiss P-40D *Warhawk* deleted the nose machine guns but increased the four wing

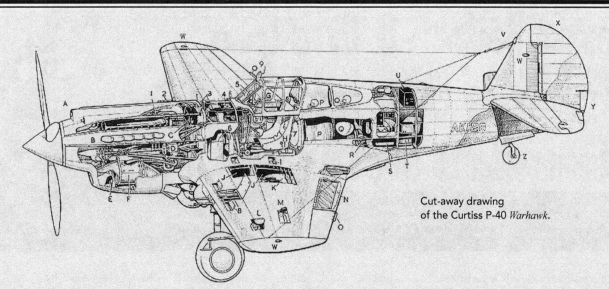

Cut-away drawing
of the Curtiss P-40 *Warhawk*.

machine guns to .50-caliber. Subsequent variants increased the number of .50-caliber machine guns to three on each side while providing the capability of carrying both centerline bombs and wing-mounted bombs and rockets.[11]

It was while flying with the 1st American Volunteer Group (AVG) of the Chinese Air Force, however, that the Curtiss P-40 *Warhawk* gained immortal fame. Nicknamed the Flying Tigers and composed of volunteer U.S. Army, U.S. Navy and U.S. Marine Corps pilots, three squadrons were covertly formed in July 1941 with the approval of President Franklin D. Roosevelt to help protect Chinese supply routes through Burma.[12] In seven months of combat, they shot down 286 Japanese airplanes and produced 39 aces until absorbed into the U.S. Army Air Forces on July 4, 1942.[13,14]

The Flying Tigers painted their Curtiss P-40's with a ferocious shark-mouth nose art that "remains among the most recognizable image of any individual combat airplane or combat unit of World War II."[15] The Curtiss P-40 airframe was particularly well-suited for the shark-mouth design as the massive engine air scoop at the front of the airplane naturally formed a large jaw.[16] The shark-mouth design itself, however, was not unique to the AVG, having been painted on various British and German airplanes since World War I.[17]

This has led to some confusion whether for their advanced training the Tuskegee Airmen were assigned Curtiss P-40 Tomahawks or P-40E

Warhawks previously flown by the AVG. While the Tuskegee Airmen indeed flew older, wearier, hand-me-down Curtiss P-40 *Warhawk's* at the Tuskegee Army Air Field, most aviation historians agree that they were not from the AVG but rather passed down from other squadrons who had also adopted the shark-mouth logo.

At the height of production, Curtiss was producing some 250 P-40 *Warhawk's* a month, at one point producing 463 P-40L's in a single month.[18,19] But by 1944 the availability of higher performance fighters such as the Republic P-47 Thunderbolt and North American P-51 Mustang had made the Curtiss P-40 *Warhawk* obsolete. When the Curtiss P-40 *Warhawk* production line was finally closed in November 1944, a total of 13,768 P-40 *Warhawks* of all variants had been built. [20]

A formation of Tuskegee Airmen P-40's *Warhawks*, including one sporting a shark-mouth design, fly near Selfridge Army Air Field, Michigan.

Captain Benjamin O. Davis Under Training As Flying Cadet; To Be Commander Of Negro Air Squadron

The leader of the Tuskegee Airmen in war and peace, then Capt. Benjamin O. Davis Jr. was assigned to the first class at Tuskegee and slated to be the first commanding officer of the newly formed 99th Pursuit Squadron. After an illustrious career, Davis retired as a four-star general.

his father received an utterly unexpected letter. Headquarters, U.S. Army Air Forces asked that Capt. Davis be released to join the initial African-American flight training class at the Tuskegee Institute.

The first step was a flight physical,

> I regarded the examination as a mere formality because I had passed easily at West Point. The flight surgeon at Fort Riley, however, did not know that the Air Corps had changed its policy of not accepting black applicants and unhesitatingly failed me by reporting a falsified history of epilepsy. Considering that Air Corps Headquarters was in no way mystified or deterred by this report, it is reasonable to assume that the corps had told flight surgeons to fail black applicants for pilot training.
>
> Headquarters immediately understood why I had failed the physical and flew me to Maxwell Field in Montgomery, Alabama, for another, which I passed with no difficulty, my epilepsy having miraculously disappeared in a few days. The failure of a good many other black pilot training applicants to qualify must have been based on similar policy directives to examining flight surgeons, who manufactured phony 'deficiencies.'[16]

Tuskegee Army Air Field

At nearly the same time Moton Field was being planned and built by the Tuskegee Institute, the U.S. Army Air Forces were constructing their own military air base, to be designated Tuskegee Army Air Field. This third and largest of the airfields built near the Tuskegee Institute comprised 1,650 acres and was used for Basic and Advanced flight training. Unlike Kennedy and Moton Fields, which were leased or owned by the Tuskegee Institute, this

military base was purchased, built and operated directly by the U.S. Army Air Forces.

The U.S. Army Air Forces asked the Tuskegee Institute for assistance in choosing a site, selection of which was hampered by the objections of the white citizens of Tuskegee who were opposed to an airfield used by African-Americans being located too close to their town.[17]

After evaluating several sites, the final choice was located seven miles northwest of the Tuskegee Institute near the town of Chehaw. President Patterson recalled the location,

> We had a spot in Chehaw in mind for building an airfield. Chehaw, Alabama, is on the mainline of the Southern Railroad. Because of Tuskegee Institute's national reputation, Chehaw was a scheduled stop on the Crescent Limited, a train running from New York to New Orleans. For many years a little spur railroad ran from Chehaw up to the campus of our school. The spur was used mainly to bring coal when Tuskegee burned coal as a major fuel, but also carried a passenger car. One could purchase a ticket from New York to the campus of Tuskegee Institute, changing at Chehaw. There was even a little store at the Chehaw stop that sold knick-knacks and sundries. The Tuskegee students used to laugh at the railroad because the trail was so slow that you could walk to Tuskegee faster than you could travel by railroad from Chehaw.[18]

By the end of May 1941, U.S. Army Air Forces officials approved the site and directed the quartermaster general to obtain title to the property. Acquisition of approximately 1,650 acres of land from eight property owners was completed by the end of July 1941.[19]

African-American architect Hilyard Robinson from Washington, DC was selected to design the airfield. Although he had never

Overhead view of Tuskegee Army Air Field where the Tuskegee Airmen received all their military flight training.

planned an airfield before, all of the facilities were standard U.S. Army Air Forces structures, and the design process was eased by the assistance of Maxwell Field officers.[20] Plans also called for segregated barracks and dining halls for both officers and enlisted men. It was a major irritant to every African-American stationed at Tuskegee Army Airfield that a base built intentionally to segregate the training of black fighter pilots itself had segregated facilities.

McKissack and McKissack, Inc., of Nashville, TN was awarded the $1.1 million construction contract to build the airfield, including four runways, three hangars, numerous offices, and other support facilities.[21] Said to be the most massive government contract ever granted to an African-American owned firm at that time, the project eventually ended up costing an estimated $3 million

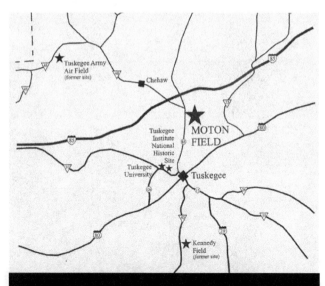

The three primary airfields associated with the training of the Tuskegee Airmen: Kennedy Field to the south of the Tuskegee Institute, Moton Field 2 ½ miles to the northeast, and the Tuskegee Army Air Field 6 ½ miles to the northwest.

due to extra grading and draining requirements.[22]

As with Alexander and Repass on the Moton Field project, McKissack and McKissack subcontracted the earthwork to two white subcontractors, the C. G. Kershaw Contracting Company and the Daugette-Millican Company[23,24]

Construction started on July 23, 1941 with a scheduled completion date of November 8, 1941, just in time for the transfer of the first class from the Tuskegee Institute's Primary flight training to the U.S. Army Air Forces' Basic flight course.[25,26]

In mid-August, however, it became apparent that the new base would not be completed on time as "clearing, grading, and drainage costs at the Chehaw site were significantly higher than cost estimates," which were based on a previous site selection.[27] Funds were not available to overcome an estimated $1.2 million shortfall or to pay overtime to accelerate the schedule.[28] Nonetheless, U.S. Army Air Forces leadership remained adamant that actual flight training start on time.

One stop-gap measure proposed was to have Class 42-C start Basic flight training at another U.S. Army Air Forces field and then return to Tuskegee Army Air Field when construction was complete. But that suggestion was resoundingly rejected by U.S. Army Air Forces leadership due to integration concerns. Instead, $3,000 was allocated to construct a "temporary tent camp and temporary sanitary facilities to accommodate troops" near the only runway nearing completion.[29]

As a result, the first African-Americans ever to enroll in U.S. Army Air Forces Basic flight training began their course of instruction on November 8, 1941, precisely on time. Initially, all went well in tent city,

Although crude, these arrangements 'were not particularly uncomfortable during the mild weather of November 1941, but when the weather became more severe in December and the winter rains set in they were a real trial to the pioneer class.'

When the rains came, they transformed the partially completed field, still undergoing grading and excavation and lacking an adequate drainage system, into a 'bottomless morass.' Indeed, the mud became such a problem that the men often joked that soon the commander would be forced to furnish all personnel 'long poles with flags at the top so that when they disappeared the rescue squad would know where to dig.'[30]

Auxiliary Fields

Two known auxiliary fields were used near the Tuskegee complex to support flight training and relieve congestion from the main airfields.

Tuskegee Army Air Field had its own auxiliary field "on the Tallapoose River just north of Milstead, Alabama nearly due west from Tuskegee."[31,32] Known as Griel Field after its owner, it was described as a "320-acre irregularly-shaped field having a 5,689' x 3,368' all-way turf landing area." [33] There were no facilities at the field, although in 1943 this site was temporarily used for the training of liaison pilots, the first African-American aviators assigned to U.S. Army ground forces as aerial field artillery observers.[34]

The Tuskegee Institute maintained its own auxiliary field at Hardaway, Alabama which was leased in late 1942 or early 1943 and located southwest from Tuskegee.[35,36,37] Known as Shorter Field, it was described as a "241-acre irregularly-shaped field having a 3,560' x 3,270' all-way turf landing area."[38] This field also did not have any facilities.

Class 42-C Flight Training

Davis and his classmates finished the 5-week long Preflight course and transferred to Primary flight training on August 23, 1941. In Primary, Davis flew the Boeing PT-17 *Kaydet* which he found to be,

A complete, unadulterated joy. It was summer in Alabama, and flying over the green trees, the streams, and the orderly plots of brown farmland below was more exhilarating than anything I could have imagined.[39]

Davis soloed on September 2, 1941 with about six flight hours of dual instruction. Upon completion of Primary flight training, his class transferred to the Tuskegee Army Air Field on November 8, 1941 for Basic flight training. At Basic flight training, Davis was introduced to the Vultee BT-13 *Valiant* and more advanced flight training maneuvers,

> A rather lumbering airplane that was much less maneuverable than the PT-17, although more powerful. The BT-13 did have landing flaps, but its landing gear was no more retractable than that of the PT-17, and the pilot had to crank down the flaps. I loved it all, stalls, practice landings, forced landings, pins, inverted flight, loops, slow rolls, snap rolls, and vertical reverses. We also did chandelles, abrupt, steep, climbing turns that had to be smoothly executed to gain maximum altitude and change of direction at the expense of airspeed. It is a beautiful and satisfying maneuver, requiring precision flying. In basic we were also introduced to formation and night flying.[40]

Together at Last

All throughout this period, enlisted personnel had been undergoing technical training at Chanute Field. It was not until November 10, 1941 that the first ground crews of the 99th Pursuit Squadron began to arrive at the Tuskegee Army Air Field. With all the separate technical training classes at Chanute Field, the enlisted personnel hardly knew each other, and they certainly did not know any of their pilots who were still undergoing flight training. It would take a dynamic and forceful commanding officer to unite this disjointed gaggle of personnel into a first-class, close-knit fighting team.

United States Entry into World War II

World War II began on September 1, 1939 when Germany invaded Poland, prompting Great Britain and France to declare war on Germany to honor their alliance with Poland. Nothing could stop the German blitzkrieg and by the spring of 1940 Hitler's armies had smashed their way across Europe, eventually trapping the British army at Dunkirk and forcing its evacuation from continental Europe. The Germans entered Paris in June 1940, compelling France to sign an armistice on June 22, 1940.

In North Africa, the Italians invaded British-controlled Egypt in September 1940 but in early 1941 an Allied counteroffensive destroyed the Italian 10th Army, and the Germans dispatched the Afrika Korps commanded by Gen. Erwin Rommel to North Africa to reinforce the faltering Italians.

Meanwhile, the United States government attempted to remain neutral, although it was inevitable that the country would soon be embroiled in what had become a worldwide conflict. The surprise Japanese attack on Pearl Harbor on December 7, 1941, resulted in a declaration of war by the United States on Japan on December 8, 1941 and on Germany and Italy on December 11, 1941 after both

An aviation cadet's solo approach and landing is closely evaluated by a watchful flight instructor, fully equipped with a clipboard and grade sheet, as this PT-17 *Kaydet* crosses the fence at Moton Field.

countries had declared war on the United States. War in Europe and the Pacific would last for nearly four deadly years.

Tuskegee Class Sizes

Initially, U.S. Army Air Forces strategic planning did not extend beyond the establishment of a single African-American pursuit squadron with a full complement of 33 rated pilots.[41] Headquarters, U.S. Army Air Forces was directly responsible for establishing pilot class sizes at Tuskegee and needed to factor in several variables for class loading, including expected attrition rates during pilot training, probable pilot combat losses overseas, and the projected number of replacement pilots needed to support routine squadron pilot rotation. Confusion, however, existed within the headquarters staff itself on whether there was a need to load additional cadets beyond those necessary to staff the 99th Fighter Squadron to man additional African-American pursuit squadrons.[42]

Much to the surprise of everyone at Tuskegee, the first contract executed between the War Department and the Tuskegee Institute in 1941 called for the loading of only ten aviation cadets per class, a suspiciously small number even if only a single pursuit squadron was to be manned in a reasonable amount of time.[43] To place this class size in perspective, in 1941 the U.S. Army Air Forces expected overall graduation rate for white aviation cadets was approximately 56%.[44] When one considers that classes convened at five-week intervals at Tuskegee and that it would take about nine months for a student pilot to complete all training, the 99th Pursuit Squadron would not reach its full complement of pilots for more than a year.

READY TO MEET THE ENEMY ... FIRST TO GET U.S. ARMY "WINGS"

Shown in the picture are Col. Frederick V. H. Kimble, commanding officer of the Air Corps Advance Flying school, pinning "wings" on the breast of Captain Benjamin O. Davis Jr., son of Brigadier-General Benjamin O. Davis of the U.S. Army, among the group of the first members of the race to be awarded the insignia of the U.S. Army Air Corps, while Major Noel F. Parrish, extreme left, holds the "wings." Reading from left to right in addition to Captain Davis are: Lt. Lemuel Rodney Curtis, Hartford, Conn.; Lt. Charles DeBow, Indianapolis, Ind.; Lt. George Spencer Roberts, Fairmont, W. Va., and Lt. Mac Ross, Dayton, Ohio. The graduating exercises were held at the Post theatre and were attended by military personnel of the army, officers of Tuskegee institute and the Veterans' Administration, and relatives and friends of the members of the graduating class.—P. H. Polk, Tuskegee Institute Photo. **Other Pictures, Pages 5 and 10.**

Class 42-C receives their wings with Captain Davis the first to have his pinned on.

African-American activists were alerted to this lack of urgency, and the War Department received heavy criticism for intentionally restricting the number of black aviation cadets in the U.S. Army Air Forces while the demand for white aviation cadets was nearly insatiable for a nation at war. The waiting list of qualified black aviation cadet applicants surpassed 200 candidates but U.S. Army Air Forces leadership,

Resisted efforts to modify the selection process or enlarge quotas, just as they had opposed the establishment of the first segregated squadron a year earlier. They insisted that the Tuskegee project was an 'experimental' program and therefore could not be enlarged until the results were evaluated.[45]

As increased political pressure was brought to bear, the War Department relented and dramatically increased class sizes, the pendulum swinging to the extreme opposite direction in class loading. As a result,

Instead of 10, class sizes averaged 19 cadets during the first nine months, 46 during the next twelve, and 75-80 during the following months. Therefore the size of entering classes increased sharply and continuously from the beginning to a point in 1944.[46]

But due to the initial small class sizes and higher than projected attrition rates, the 99th Pursuit Squadron still did not reach its full pilot strength until July 1942, exactly one year after Class 42-C had started training.[47] As one newspaper editorial noted,

In the first airplane fashioned of wood and wax by his ingenious father, Daedalus, young Icarus sought to flee from Crete to Greece, but he soared too near the sun, the wax wings melted and he hurtled to earth and to his death.

Today we have many black Icaruses trained to fly in cunningly fashioned machines, the best airplanes in the world, but they are kept on the ground because the sun of racial segregation is so hot that it immobilizes their planes.

The 99th Pursuit Squadron, composed entirely of Negroes (and the only Air Corps unit in which black aviators may serve) was set up at Tuskegee, Alabama in July, 1941, over a year ago, with capacity for training only 33 aviators at a time while the Army was crying for hundreds of thousands of aviators...

If this snail's pace were general throughout the U.S. Air Corps, the war would soon be lost and we would have to sue the Axis powers for peace. While the War Department has been stalling along with its segregated Tuskegee set-up trying to turn out one all-Negro pursuit squadron, thousands of American, Dutch, British, Canadian and Chinese pilots have been trained at air fields all over the United States, are displaying their wings and participating in bombing and combat in actual warfare.

Black Icarus requires two years for training, it seems, while white Icarus is ready for the front in a year or less because his wings are not warped by segregation growing out of official adherence to the hated race and blood theory which the Nazis flaunt.[48]

Additional African-American Pursuit Squadrons

With the increased class sizes, Tuskegee now had too many aviation cadets in the pipeline to feed a single squadron. In December 1941 the War Department announced that a second all-black unit, the 100th Pursuit Squadron, would be formed at Tuskegee.[49]

The 100th Pursuit Squadron was officially activated on May 26, 1942 and it was envisioned as a sister squadron to the 99th Pursuit Squadron, which explains the consecutive numbers.[50] As with the 99th Pursuit Squadron, all associated enlisted training for the 100th Pursuit Squadron was conducted at Chanute Field. Unlike the 99th Pursuit Squadron, however, enlisted training was not completed in advance of pilot training, which caused excessive delays in the 100th Pursuit Squadron coming to full strength. As a result, the 99th Pursuit Squadron deployed overseas as a solo unit before the 100th Pursuit Squadron was fully constituted and certified combat ready.

Class 42-C Enters Advanced Training

Upon completion of Basic training on January 11, 1942, Class 42-C moved on to Advanced training, transitioning into the North American AT-6 *Texan*. During advanced training, the Tuskegee Airmen also traveled to other nearby U.S. Army Air Forces fields for specialized training. Even on military bases, the three horsemen of discrimination, prejudice, and intolerance were always close at hand. Davis recalled,

Not even the fact that we were about to go off and fight for our country saved us from the abuses of racism. In advanced training, we flew air gunner and bombing missions at Dale Mabry Field in Tallahassee, Florida. We had not been expecting much in the way of hospitality at Dale Mabry, but it sent a chill through us to learn we were to stay in a building that had been used as a guardhouse for black prisoners.[51]

Class 42-C Graduates

Class 42-C's Advanced training was completed in early March 1942, less than 33 weeks after starting Preflight. Only five members of the original class remained, eight class members having been attrited, yielding a 39% graduating rate, much lower than the 56% graduation rate for white aviation cadets. A wise decision was made to use as many African-American graduates of the Civilian Pilot Training Program Secondary flight course at the Tuskegee Institute as possible, to close the gap between white and black aviation cadets graduation rates.[52] In fact, 11 of the first 24 pilots assigned to the original 99th Pursuit squadron were successful graduates of the Civilian Pilot Training Program.

Commissioned as second lieutenants in the U. S. Army Air Forces, this group was the first class of Negro cadets.

The Negro as a Military Airman

by FRANK LAMBERT

Preconceived notions about Negro flyers have been proved false by the U.S. Army training program. A thorough analysis of the subject is presented here.

The Army now has a small number of Negro pilots; more are being trained. The author, actively engaged in flight instruction for a number of years and more recently associated with Negro flight training, here presents a studied analysis of a much-discussed program.—Ed.

RECENTLY the Army graduated its first class of Negro military aviators. This class was small, but significant. It was the first group of Negro military aviators ever to be trained as such, anywhere in the world. These Army pilots are the first products of a complete program of training for Negro pilots in Army aviation. A little more than one year ago, this entire program was merely a problem in the minds of a few Air Forces officers. Between that time and the present much planning and a great deal of effort has been expended. After the decision to train Negro military aviators had been made, the first important action was the selection of a site. Several were considered, but Tuskegee, Ala., was soon picked as the logical location for the first Negro school. The job of planning and building a basic and advanced flying school was begun immediately and the actual work was started in the spring of 1941.

Before basic and advanced training could begin, however, it was necessary to provide primary training for Negro students. In line with the policy of the War Department, every provision for training of Negroes was required to be identical with the provisions for the training of other students. Since all Army pilots now receive their primary training in civil contract schools, a plan was worked out whereby Negro cadets would receive their training in the same manner. Tuskegee Institute, through its department of mechanical industries, had gained experience in the training of pilots in the CPTP. The Institute assumed the contract for training Negro students according to the program, schedules and standards which had already proved so successful in the training of all Air Forces flyers.

Assisted by Army advice and supervision, the Institute secured a suitable tract of ground a few miles north of Tuskegee, and construction was begun on a primary flying field. The flying field, hangar and other installations were built in their entirety by a Negro contractor and almost entirely by Negro skilled and unskilled labor. Despite an exceptionally rainy summer, the field was partially completed in time to begin flying training in August, 1941.

Cadets were housed and fed on the campus of Tuskegee Institute, and these

Written by Frank Lambert, a white flight instructor at Tuskegee, a five page article appeared in the July 1942 issue of *Flying* magazine detailing the training of black flight students at Tuskegee.

I GOT WINGS

A Negro Army flier—one of the first Negroes ever commissioned in Uncle Sam's Air Force—tells how "my wild, fantastic, impossible dream" came true. This stirring story of devotion and determination brings one more proof that Americans, regardless of color and creed, stand united today against the common enemy

The author . . . "a Jap or a German is all the same to me"

"OKAY, that's it!"

That motor sure sounds swell as it roars like one thousand thunderstorms. I swing the whip onto the concrete runway for the take-off. Faster, faster. Hangars flash past. At first it's as bumpy as riding in a jalopy with one flat tire. Then, the never-failing miracle, the bumps smooth off. We're in the air. Out of this world. Free.

Upstairs, at 2,000 feet, I look around. Below me, the Tuskegee Army Flying School, where nearly 50 colored officers and over 1,000 colored enlisted men are working like industrious ants to make a success of the first Army aviation post for Negroes.

Around me, stretching away to the horizon, the red clay of Alabama, dotted with the corn and cotton fields where the Negroes are working. The same fields where their ancestors worked—as slaves. A little knot of people in one field look up at me. A couple of them wave. I feel a catch in my throat.

My people. . . .

I'm a Negro, too; one of the pioneer class at Tuskegee. There were 13 of us to begin with, but 8 got washed out. That left 5, and we all got our wings together. Those bright, silver wings that had never been awarded to any colored men before. Captain Ben Davis, Jr., a West Point graduate and son of Brigadier General Davis, the only Negro to become a general in American history; Lem Custis, who used to be a cop in

Hartford, Conn. George Roberts, who worked with the CAA in West Virginia. Mac Ross, ex-inspector in a Dayton, Ohio, steel mill. And myself.

A voice crackles in my earphones: "*Lieutenant De Bow, proceed to . . .*"

As I carry out the assignment, I remember the civilian who stopped me on the street in Montgomery the other day. "You one of those new colored fliers over at Tuskegee?" he asked.

"Yes, sir," I replied proudly.

"Tell me one thing," he said. "What do you boys want to fly for, anyhow?"

If my skin hadn't been black, I don't suppose he'd have asked me. But I've been thinking it over ever since, and I think I've cleared it up in my own mind.

First of all, I'm flying for Uncle Sam. We're in a war for the future, and I want no part of the Fascist future. Our democracy isn't perfect, but it's the only system that opens the way to perfection. Maybe tomorrow, maybe months from tomorrow, I might be shipped off for combat duty. East or west, I don't care which. To help protect this way of life, a Jap or a German is all the same to me.

I'm flying for Dad and Mom, too. Dad's a porter in a white barbershop in Indianapolis, Ind. He makes $30 a week, and Mom used to earn $20 more as a maid in a department store. When I got my commission I began sending her half my pay on condition she quit working. It took some persuading, but finally she agreed. Both of them gave up comforts

and vacations to see me through school. I can't let them down.

Finally, I'm flying for every one of the 12,000,000 Negroes in the United States. I want to prove that we can take a tough job and handle it just as well as a white man. God didn't fit me to be a great educator like Booker T. Washington, or a great scientist like George Washington Carver. But maybe I can fly so that nobody can ever again say, "Oh, Negroes are all right as janitors and handymen, but they can't learn to fly, or fight, or be good officers."

I think all of us at Tuskegee feel that way. We've got a double duty—to our country and to our race. That goes not only for the fliers, but for the ground crews, and doctors, and executive officers, and radio specialists, and supply men. Everybody. We've all got a job to do—and we're going to see it through.

I guess that's why there isn't much fooling in our outfit. Take the time Mac Ross got in trouble, a few weeks after we got our wings. He and I were flying tight formation at 6,000 feet. Wing tips 6 inches apart. Suddenly I noticed smoke whisping out of his engine. Half a second later Mac noticed it too. He signaled me, "Loosen up the formation." I moved away and radioed the field. That smoke was a black cloud now.

"Jump, you fool; jump," I breathed. But Mac stuck with his ship. 5,000 feet. 4,000 feet. He was fighting to get back to the field, to bring the ship in. "You'll

kill yourself," I thought. Finally, at 3,000 feet, he jumped. About time. I dived alongside him, and radioed the field where he landed. They picked him up 20 minutes later. He was trudging along a dirt road, the silk over his shoulder and a scratch on his hand, not from the jump, but from climbing over a barbed-wire fence.

But Mac was worried sick that night. "Maybe I did something wrong," he kept saying. "Maybe I could have brought her in."

I tried to cheer him up. "Listen, pal," I said. "Do you realize you're the first colored member of the caterpillar club?" But all the time I knew what he was thinking: "*I've wrecked a ship worth thousands of dollars. Maybe they'll start saying that Negroes can't fly.*"

But the official report put him away out in the clear: "100 per cent *matériel* failure."

That meant it wasn't his fault at all. He'd done everything possible, and jumped when he should. There's no advantage in losing a pilot as well as a plane. We went to Montgomery to celebrate, Mac and Roberts and Custis and I.

The radio again: "*Lieutenant De Bow, come in for landing . . .*"

Probably to pick up a student for instruction. The class after us graduated 3 colored lieutenants, but since then the number of aviation cadets has jumped, and the plan now is to graduate a sizable class every month. They'll be assigned to Pursuit Squadrons, ready for action any time, any place.

The student turns out to be a serious-faced boy from the deep South. A farm kid who's never been north of the Mason-Dixon. We (Continued on page 104)

by Lieut. **CHARLES H. DE BOW**
U. S. ARMY AIR FORCE
AS TOLD TO WILLIAM A. H. BIRNIE

In the August, 1942 issue of *American* magazine, 2nd Lt. Charles DeBow related how his "wild, fantastic, impossible dream" of becoming a U.S. Army Air Forces rated pilot came true.

On March 7, 1942, Class 42-C officially graduated, all members receiving their silver wings designating them as U.S. Army Air Forces aviators, the first African-Americans in history to achieve this distinction. Aviation cadets also received their commissions as 2nd Lt's.

The guest speaker at Class 42-C's graduation was Maj. Gen. George E. Stratemeyer, the U.S. Army Air Forces Chief of Staff, who said,

> I am sure that everyone present, as well as the vast unseen audience of well-wishers, senses that this graduation is a historic moment, filled with portent of great good. Our country is engaged in a hard fight for its security and freedom.
>
> Here today is opened up a new source to wage that fight. It is my hope and my confident expectation that by your skill, courage, and devotion to duty you will fully justify that confidence and trust reposed in you, and that your service records will constitute bright pages in the annals of our country.
>
> You will furnish the nuclei of the 99th and 100th Pursuit Squadrons. Future graduates of this school will look upon you as 'Old Pilots.' They will be influenced profoundly by the example which you set. Therefore, it will be of the highest importance that your service be of a character worthy of emulation by younger officers.[53]

Class 42-C's graduation was widely covered in black newspapers and many articles appeared in major national magazines, heralding to white America the unprecedented success of these black aviators in military flight training.

One article entitled *The Negro as a Military Airman* was

The two-letter fuselage code of "TU" identifies this North American AT-6 *Texan* as being assigned to Tuskegee Army Air Field. Headquarters, Southeast Army Air Forces Training Center, assigned unique identification codes to all training air fields under its jurisdiction.

published in *Flying* magazine and was written by Frank Lambert, a white flight instructor at Tuskegee, with the byline "Preconceived notions about Negro flyers have been proved false by the U.S. Army training program."[54,55] Providing a flight instructor's perspective on the training of black aviators, he noted,

> An airplane does not react to the color or appearance of the individual pilot, either favorably or unfavorably. This fact is quite obvious, but a surprising number of otherwise well informed people show a tendency to ignore it when they think of Negro aviators.[56]

Another article entitled *I Got Wings* was presented from a flight student's perspective and written by newly minted 2nd Lt. Charles DeBow, a member of Class 42-C. Published in *American Magazine,* he described the reconsideration of his answer when he was stopped by a white civilian on the streets of Montgomery, Alabama and asked why he wanted to fly,

> If my skin hadn't been black, I don't suppose he'd have ever asked me. But I've been thinking it over ever since, and I think I cleared it up in my mind.

> First of all, I'm flying for Uncle Sam. We're in a war for the future, and I want no part of the Fascist future. Our democracy isn't perfect, but it's the only system that opens the way to perfection. Maybe tomorrow, maybe months from tomorrow, I might be shipped off for combat duty. East or west, I don't care which. To help protect this way of life, a Jap or a

German is all the same to me.

> I'm flying for Mom and Dad, too. Dad's a porter in a white barbershop in Indianapolis, Ind. He makes $30 a week, and Mom used to earn $20 more as a maid in a department store. When I got my commission I began sending her half my pay on condition she quit working. It took some persuading, but finally she agreed. Both of them gave up comforts and vacations to see me through school. I can't let them down.

> Finally, I'm flying for every one of the 12,000,000 Negroes in the United States. I want to prove that we can take a tough job and handle it just as well as a white man. God didn't fit me to be a great educator like Booker T. Washington, or a great scientist like George Washington Carver. But maybe I can fly so that nobody can ever again say, 'Oh, Negroes are all right as janitors and handymen, but they can't learn to fly, or fight, or be good officers.' I think all of us at Tuskegee feel that way. We've got a double duty, to our country and to our race.[57]

Transition Training

After graduation, the newly winged pilots of Class 42-C continued training in advanced maneuvers in the AT-6 *Texan* and received intensive tactical Transition training in several hand-me-down P-40 *Warhawk's*. Davis recalled,

Several war-weary P-40 were delivered to TAAF, each a slightly different model, but every one of them leaking oil. Most and perhaps all of them had fought the undeclared war in China with the Flying Tigers, and they still had dirty, mottled green camouflage paint on their oily fuselages.

The overall appearance and condition of these P-40s were not exactly encouraging for the pilots who flew them. But after carefully reading the technical orders and pilot guides that came with the airplanes, fly them we did. The long nose and low seat of the P-40 prevented the pilot from seeing objects directly in front of him when he was taxiing. Thus, he had to "ess" the aircraft to the right and left to avoid the unforgivable sin of a taxi accident. Takeoff required a strong right leg because of the engine's torque.

At first I was disappointed with the P-40 because I expected the airspeed indicator to show much higher numbers than it did. But after a few flights I began to feel at home in it and even began to like its maneuverability. From the war stories I had heard from P-40 combat pilots, the airplane had three important virtues: turn, turn, and turn. It was vitally important that I and all the other pilots like the P-40; it was the airplane we were going to war in.

Rated pilots were permitted to take an airplane on weekend cross-country flights as long as we stayed within 300 miles of the TAAF flagpole. I took full advantage of this opportunity to increase my flying hours and improve my proficiency, sometimes flying solo and sometimes carrying nonrated military passengers in the backseat (ah, ha: 2-seaters!). Some of these cross-country flights took me to Savannah, Nashville, and New Orleans.

Most historians agree that it was highly unlikely that the Tuskegee Airmen were flying former Flying Tigers P-40's but everyone concedes that the aircraft was dangerously worn-out. One line chief recalled their condition,

In a few cases, we had to hold hoses on those old Allisons due to overheating while warming up. It was a shame to think that our boys were expected to fly those things. It was all my men could do to keep them airworthy. We lived in continual fear that someone wouldn't return due to a failure beyond our control. When they returned from a flight, it appeared quite frequently as though they'd flown through an oil storm.[58]

Captain Davis Promoted

In mid-May 1942, Captain Davis was promoted to major and

An aviation cadet provides his guest a tour of a PT-17 Kaydet. It was not always work for the aviation cadets as Tuskegee hosted balls and dances for the flight students and families attended graduation ceremonies.

to tease him his wife named their new puppy Colonel. But a few days later the U.S. Army announced that all members of Davis' West Point class were immediately promoted to lieutenant colonel to fill the need for more wartime, senior officers. So the puppy was demoted back to Major, as Davis himself explained: "because we could not have two colonels around the house."[59]

First African-American Commanding Officer of a Fighter Squadron

On May 15, 1942 the U.S. Army Air Forces redesignated all pursuit squadrons as fighter squadrons.[60] In rapid succession, new classes of graduating African-American pilots followed Class 42-C into the 99th Fighter Squadron, which had been under the command of three separate white officers.

That changed on June 1, 1942 when 1st Lt. George S. Roberts, a graduate of Class 42-C, assumed command of the 99th Fighter Squadron, the first African-American to command a squadron in the history of the U.S. military.[61] Davis' unexpected leap to lieutenant colonel had "caused some problems in the TAAF white-black hierarchy" resulting in his temporary assignment to a new billet created specifically for him entitled "executive of troops."[62]

A few months later new orders were received and on August 22, 1942, Davis relieved Roberts as commanding officer of the 99th Fighter Squadron.[63] Davis's assumption of command was extremely gratifying to Tuskegee's President Dr. Patterson and Director Washington,

There is nothing more delightful than flying in an open-cockpit airplane on a sunny day, unless you have a flight instructor in the rear seat critiquing your every maneuver.

Certainly particularly so to Dr. Patterson who made the special request in the very beginning that he be transferred from Fort Riley to undergo flight training with the first class of cadets with a view to becoming the commander of the 99th Pursuit Squadron. This was in keeping with our rationale, earlier mentioned, and gave assurance that the first squadron would go into combat under a Negro commander.

I am not sure that too many people knew of how Colonel Davis (now a general) got into the Air Corps picture at Tuskegee. Tuskegee thought highly of him. He was a professor of military science and tactics, as was his father some time before him.[64]

Davis was not the only African-American in the running to become commanding officer of the 99th Fighter Squadron. Many supporters, not without justification, believed that the air combat-experienced John C. Robinson, who fought in the Ethiopian-Italian war, was also a strong candidate, an opinion published in a newspaper article.[65] According to one story, Robinson, who commanded the Imperial Ethiopian Air Force with the rank of colonel, was offered the rank of 2nd Lt. in the U.S. Army Air Forces but he declined, stating "Second lieutenants are a dime a dozen."[66] Although Robinson corresponded directly with Washington about the position, Patterson and Washington preferred Davis and Robinson was considered only for a staff instructor position.[67] Therefore, it was Lt. Col. Davis who prepared the 99th Fighter Squadron for pre-combat certification and eventual deployment into a combat zone.

Meanwhile, classes continued to convene at the Tuskegee Institute, and of these follow-on classes, the one we are most interested in is Class 43-B, which counted among its members a young man from Pensacola, Florida named James R. Polkinghorne Jr. ▪

Chapter Eight
James R. Polkinghorne Jr.'s Flight Training

Polkinghorne's Hometown, Pensacola, Florida

Pensacola was first established by Spanish explorer Don Tristan de Luna who arrived on August 14, 1559 to attempt the first European colony in the United States. Devastated by a hurricane that sank most of his supply ships and decimated by harsh living conditions, this colony lasted for only two years before it was abandoned. The Spanish returned to Pensacola on November 21, 1568 when Don Andes de Arriola established a permanent settlement on the present grounds of Naval Air Station Pensacola. Control of this desirable deep water port city on the Gulf of Mexico shifted back and forth several times between Spain, France and Great Britain. On July 17, 1821 permanent possession of Pensacola transferred to the United States as Spain ceded Florida according to the terms of the Adams-Onis Treaty.

In October 1825 the United States Navy established the Pensacola Navy Yard seven miles southwest of the city of Pensacola to combat pirates in the Gulf of Mexico and the Caribbean Sea. Over the years the fortunes of the Pensacola Navy Yard ebbed and flowed with strategic requirements, politics, wars and expeditions, yellow fever epidemics, and the availability of warship maintenance, repair, and construction funding. On October 20, 1911 the Pensacola Navy Yard was officially closed but not entirely abandoned as caretakers were left behind to monitor the property.

On January 3, 1914 the U.S. Navy announced that the entire Naval Aeronautics Corps, 32-men and 7-airplanes strong, was to be permanently transferred to Pensacola to establish the first Naval Aeronautical Station (later renamed Naval Air Station) in the United States. World War II transformed the base and its associated airfields into the most extensive aviation training complex in the world. At its peak during 1943-1944 more than 1,000 U.S. Navy, U.S. Marine Corps, and U.S. Coast Guard pilots graduated each month, none of whom were African-Americans.

Approximately 50 miles east of Naval Air Station Pensacola is located Eglin Field (later renamed Eglin Air Force Base). Activated on June 14, 1935 the site was used for bombing and gunnery training for U.S. Army Air Forces pilots. This base also underwent tremendous growth and expansion during World War II.

Pensacola was a prosperous international seaport during

1934 Pensacola city directory advertisement for James R. Polkinghorne Jr. father's business. PH.G. is an abbreviation for a graduate degree in pharmacy, which is no longer offered in the United States.

Photograph of Dr James R. Polkinghorne Sr. as a young man. A highly respected businessman, he was the first African-American to seek public office in Pensacola.

The Polkinghorne children, from the left, Neomi, Maggie, James, Lillian and Vera.

the 19th century and with its exposure to a "variety of mores, religions and ideas, it could better counteract the typical pressures in a southern community of this time toward conformity and intolerance."[1] As a result, the position of "middle class blacks during the period from the late 1890s to 1910 was one of moderate commercial and residential integration and comity."[2] At the beginning of the 20th century, this social acceptance of African-Americans changed dramatically with the increased migration of Southern whites to Pensacola who encouraged segregationist attitudes. The first Jim Crow laws soon appeared in Pensacola and African-Americans increasingly became more disadvantaged

to the point where they became "Pensacola's most restricted and publicly ghettoized group."[3]

Polkinghorne's Family

Polkinghorne's father, Dr. James Reed Polkinghorne Sr., was born in Natchez, Mississippi, and graduated in May 1912 from the School of Pharmacy at Flint Medical College, a segregated school in New Orleans, Louisiana.[4] He then moved to Pensacola to manage the Pensacola Drug Store for a Dr. H. G. Williams, a prominent black physician originally from Jamaica.[5,6,7]

In May 1914 Polkinghorne became the proprietor of his own drug store when he opened the Palace Pharmacy at 509-518 W. Belmont Street after purchasing a stock of drugs and a 1914 model 'Walrus Iceless' soda foundation in Montgomery, Alabama.[8] In 1916 Polkinghorne entered in a partnership with M.C. Beverette, M.D. and they renamed the drugstore to The Belmont Pharmacy.[9]

It is not known how they met but in the fall of 1914 in Pensacola Polkinghorne married Maggie Ridley, who was born in Evergreen, Alabama. Their first child, Miriam Cornelia, was born the next year on July 1, 1915. Census data recorded James and Maggie's race as mulatto, as at that time census takers used the term "black" to categorize full-blooded African-Americans and "mulatto" to categorize a person of mixed white and black ancestry.[10] In 1930 these census instructions were changed and all persons of mixed white and black ancestry were classified as "Negro," which was used to categorize Polkinghorne family members in all subsequent censuses.

Over the years Polkinghorne delved into several enterprises, including serving as a notary public and as a bail bondsman as well as representing several companies, including the Afro-American Insurance Company, E. A. Welters Tooth Powder Company, and the Rest-Well Medicine Company. Dr. Polkinghorne also assumed a leadership role in the Belmont-Devilliers Business District and served as an active member of several prominent civil associations.

The 1920 census recorded the family as living in their own home at 527 West Belmont Street and on June 16, 1921 James Reed, their second child and only son, was born. Four additional daughters, Vera Louise, Neomi Marilyn, Lillian Elaine, and Maggie Beatrice, followed to complete their family.

By the 1930 census, the family had moved to 523 North Reus Street, which remains the family home to this day. During the Great Depression Polkinghorne was forced to close his drugstore and he decided to add on to his house and operated his pharmacy business from there.[11]

In 1950 Polkinghorne ran successfully in the Democratic primary for Precinct 55 Committeeman, the newspaper noting that "as far as is known Polkinghorne is the first Negro to seek public office at an election in Pensacola."[12] In 1951 he ran for City Council as a Democratic candidate and announced that "This is an

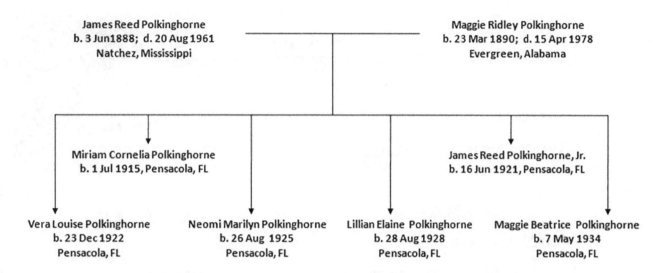

The family tree of James R. Polkinghorne Jr. He was the second of six children born to James and Maggie Polkinghorne and he had five sisters.

age of integration and should be a government of the people, for the people and by the people."[13] He later dropped out of the race, stating that "he did not want to disturb the racial harmony in the city."[14]

James Reed Polkinghorne Jr.

As he grew up in Pensacola young Polkinghorne was no stranger to segregation. He attended segregated schools and graduated from Pensacola's Booker T. Washington High School in 1938. He worked as a bellboy at the famous San Carlos Hotel located in downtown Pensacola. This 157-room hotel was built in 1910, and during Polkinghorne's youth, it was a haven for military aviators from nearby Naval Air Station (NAS) Pensacola. The hotel was managed by Lee Conner Hagler, who also served as mayor of Pensacola and for whom Pensacola's civilian airport is named.

His sister Maggie recalled that her brother,

> Would bring ice cream for her when he returned home from working at the San Carlos Hotel in downtown Pensacola. He'd bring ice cream and he'd wake me up and feed me ice cream....I can remember the ice cream hurting my head, but I wouldn't say anything because I didn't want him to stop giving it to me...oh, he was a good brother.[15]

After high school graduation, Polkinghorne attended Florida Agricultural and Mechanical College, now known as Florida A&M University, in Tallahassee, Florida, which at that time was also a segregated school. He enrolled in the Division of Liberal Arts and Sciences, which was designed to "lay a foundation for training in some special field which the student will receive in his junior and

BEGIN TRAINING
James R. Polkinghorne, 523 North Reus, and Ben Brown, West Zaragossa street, both Negroes, yesterday entrained for Maxwell field, Ala., to begin their flight training for commissions in the Army Air force. Both men are graduates of the Florida A and M colleeg at Tallahassee.

This puzzling article appeared in the June 30, 1941 of The *Pensacola News-Journal*. Polkinghorne had not yet registered for the draft and he had only completed his junior year at Florida A&M. He was most likely heading to Maxwell Army Air Field for his initial screening.

senior years."[16]

School records are not available for this era so it is unknown whether he majored in the Bachelor of Arts program to study the social sciences or whether he majored in the Bachelor of Science program to study biology or chemistry and perhaps follow in his father's footsteps as a pharmacist.[17] Perhaps the former as his sister Maggie indicated that her brother wanted to study law.[18]

Polkinghorne Enlists and Begins Flight Training

It is not known how Polkinghorne learned of the U.S. Army Air Force's training program at the Tuskegee Institute or whether he had ever flown in his life before reporting to Tuskegee. On June 30, 1941, shortly after Polkinghorne's 20th birthday, a puzzling article appeared in The *Pensacola News-Journal* stating that

HEADQUARTERS
66TH AAF FLYING TRAINING DETACHMENT
TUSKEGEE INSTITUTE, ALABAMA

August 7, 1942
(Date)

ROSTER OF STUDENTS

Class No. 43-B

Started Training   August 6, 1942
(Date)

STUDENTS	SERIAL NUMBER

Aviation Cadets

*	1	Andrews, Robert Warren	13050130
*	2	Cleaver, Leroy Jr.	38048919
	3	Davis, Russell Edward	14103346
*	4	Dickson, William Henry	-34064589
*	5	Donms, Walter Mo	14095441
	6	Govan, Claude Benjamin	12078762
*	7	Griffin, William Eugene	-14091210
	8	Harris, James Houston	18105370
	9	Jeffries, Jesse Willard	14091211
(-) *	10	Jones, William Alfred	13080192
*	11	Mills, Arthur Lawrence	38047318
*	12	Polkinghorne, James Reed	14024023
*	13	Prowell, John Henry Jr.	34167039
	14	Richardson, Milton Hiram	34271313
	15	Richburg, Lawson Thomas	14091212
(-) *	16	Robinson, James Howard	14099413
	17	Smith, Herschel John	14095359
*	18	Stapler, John Talmadge	14091213
*	19	Walker, William Harold	36021054
*	20	Spencer, Roy Maxwell	13076700

*   Denotes remaining members of Class.
(-) Indicates previous CPT Training.

For the Commanding Officer:

HOWARD T. FRAZIER,
2nd Lt., Air Corps,
Adjutant.

Official roster of Polkinghorne's Class 43-B classmates. Of these 20 flight students, only seven would earn their wings.

Formal portrait of James R. Polkinghorne Jr. at the age of about 21 wearing his flight gear as an U.S. Army Air Forces aviation cadet at Tuskegee Army Air Field.

James R. Polkinghorne Jr's World War II draft registration card

Master training schedule for Polkinghorne's Tuskegee Class 43-B. A note at the bottom indicates that all students in his class were to attend the Civilian Pilot Training Program Elementary course at Tuskegee.

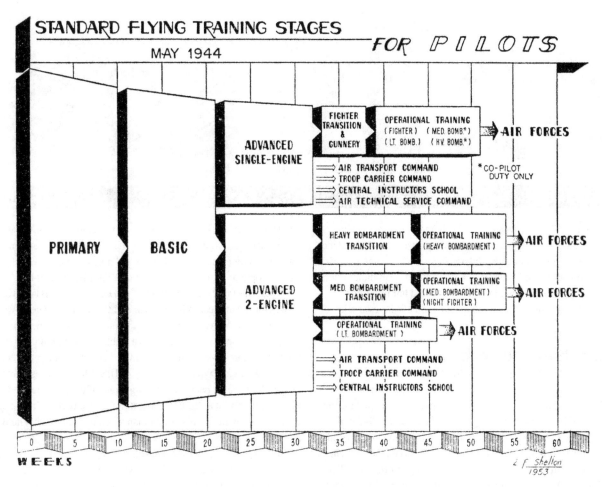

This U.S. Army Air Forces flowchart diagrams the pilot flight training progression in effect when aviation cadet James R. Polkinghorne Jr reported to Tuskegee. The track includes both fighter pilot and bomber pilot training, which started in 1943.

Polkinghorne and another Pensacola man named Ben Brown had "entrained for Maxwell Field, Ala., to begin their flight training."[19]

Service records indicate that Polkinghorne did not register for the draft until February 16, 1942 and that he did not officially enlist into the U.S. Army Air Forces until May 31, 1942. He and Brown may very well have reported to Maxwell Army Air Field for a screening flight physical, the first step in the U.S. Army Air Forces application process, described as one Tuskegee Airman as being typified by,

> Tenseness and anticipation. When the cadet reports for his physical examination, he undergoes his first step toward becoming a pilot. Upon successfully completing the physical examination, he meets a board of qualified Army Air Force officers, and if everything is well, he relaxes for a short while waiting for his appointment. Days pass waiting for that one letter to come through. Finally the day arrives, the Cadet immediately departs from his hometown to a basic training center for classification. He Cadets, and is assigned to a pre-flight school.[20]

It does not appear that Polkinghorne participated in the Civilian Pilot Training Program, despite a directive that ordered all flight students entering training at Tuskegee Army Air Field after December 1941 to complete the Elementary flight course in an attempt to reduce attrition in military flight training.[21] This is confirmed by an annotation on Polkinghorne's official class starting roster at the 66th AAF Flying Training Detachment which indicated that he did not have previous Civilian Pilot Training Program training.[22] While Polkinghorne was ultimately successful in earning his U.S. Army Air Forces wings, it appears that Brown started flight training in Tuskegee Class 42-D but did not complete flight training.

When Polkinghorne was notified of his acceptance, he left his studies at the end of his junior year at Florida A&M University and enlisted as a private in the U.S. Army Air Forces Eglin Field,

CLASS SE-43-B

Walter M. Downs   Claude B. Govan   William E. Griffin   James R. Polkinghorne   John H. Prowell   Roy M. Spencer   William H. Walker

Polkinghorne's classmates in single engine (SE) Class 43-B.

located about 50 miles distant from his home in Pensacola and about 150 miles from his university. He was listed as 5'10" inches tall and weighing 138 pounds. Interestingly, he indicated that his occupation was "actor," although he was definitely an undergraduate student at the time and his little sister could not imagine why he wrote that down, as she has no recollection of him ever taking the stage.[23]

Polkinghorne Reports to Tuskegee Army Air Field

When aviation cadet James R. Polkinghorne Jr. stepped off the train at the Chehaw railroad station in the summer of 1942 and made his way to the Tuskegee Army Air Field, it must have been an exhilarating moment for this young man. Three local airfields were active with the Tuskegee Institute running multiple Civilian Pilot Training Program courses at Kennedy Field and Moton Field

and U.S. Army Air Forces military flight operations in full swing at the Tuskegee Army Air Field. On the ground, multiple formations of aviation cadets marched passed him while overhead flew a cornucopia of Piper J-3 *Cubs,* Waco YPT-14s, Fairchild PT-19 *Cornells,* Boeing PT-13 and PT-17 *Stearmans,* Vultee BT-13 *Valiants,* North American AT-6 *Texans,* and Curtiss P-40 *Warhawks.*

As a native of Pensacola, Polkinghorne was accustomed to these aerial displays, so in their own right, they would not have been that impressive to this young man. But these aircraft were not manned by the white U.S. Navy or U.S. Marine Corps pilots of his youth. Instead, nearly every single one of the airplanes had a black student pilot at the controls. It must have been a singularly inspiring moment for this young man when he realized that he was about to learn how to fly among them.

Polkinghorne reported to Tuskegee Army Air Field and began Preflight training in July 1942. He was assigned to Class 43-B along with 20 other class members.[24] His was the 11th class to

First Solo!

Obviously staged for the photographer preparing a booklet on flight training at the Tuskegee Army Air Field, it is doubtful that Polkinghorne received such a friendly sendoff on his first solo flight. More likely, he was sent off alone for the first time at an isolated outlying field under the wary gaze of only his flight instructor.

convene at the Tuskegee Army Air Field, and on August 6, 1942 Class 43-B transferred to Primary flight training.

By the completion of Advanced training, only seven members of his class remained, a 65% attrition rate. Members of Polkinghorne's graduating class included Roy M. Spencer, Claude B. Govan, John R. Prowel, William H. Walker, William E. Griffin, and Walter M. Downs.

On February 16, 1943 in front of family and friends, the aviation cadets of Class 43-B were proudly commissioned as 2nd Lt.'s in the U.S. Army and received their silver wings to reflect their designations as rated U.S. Army Air Forces pilots. In Polkinghorne's case, his mother and father attended his graduation while his sisters remained at home.[25]

Emeldia Zaragoza and Neomi Polkinghorne

Not only men served alongside the 2,000 flight students that passed through U.S. Army Air Forces training at the Tuskegee complex.[26] There was also a large number of women hired as civil service employees and employed as mechanics, riveters, welders, dispatchers, clerks, parachute riggers, and medical personnel.[27,28,29] In total, more than 14,000 ground personnel supported the Tuskegee Airmen at home and overseas. All of these personnel, both male and female, black and white, military and civilian, are known as Documented Original Tuskegee Airmen (DOTA), and they are afforded all the same respect and honor as that given to the airmen.[30]

Two extraordinary women who worked at Tuskegee had close ties to 2nd Lt. Polkinghorne. The first was his own sister, Neomi, who was only 17 years old when she left Pensacola to work at the Tuskegee Army Air Field at the same time James was going through flight training. Her youngest sister Maggie explained why her parents allowed such a young girl to leave home on her own,

> My mother and father definitely emphasized the importance of education and the need for a college degree. My sister Neomi, though, was the only one of us who did NOT want to go to college. And I think that was one of the reasons why they let her go to Tuskegee to work. She was kind of headstrong and she told them that she just did not want to go to college.

While Neomi's parents knew that her brother James could keep somewhat of an eye on her, they took greater solace in the fact that Neomi had convinced her closest friend, Emeldia Zaragoza, to apply, pass the civil service entrance tests and accompany her to Tuskegee.[31]

Emeldia, who was only 18 years old herself and had never been away from home, lived with her parents, Willie and Theresa, and one brother and four sisters at 118 S. De Villers Street in Pen-

Neomi Polkinghorne served at Tuskegee Army Air Field alongside her brother James, making them a rare sister/brother Documented Original Tuskegee Airmen (DOTA) combination.

Emeldia Zaragoza, a Documented Original Tuskegee Airman in her own right, wears the silver wings presented to her by 1st Lt. James R. Polkinghorne Jr.

Formal photograph of Polkinghorne's graduating Class 43-B. Polkinghorne is second from the left.

sacola. Both her parents were native Pensacolians and her father's occupation was a shrimper and fisherman.

In a beautiful letter on file with the Tuskegee Airmen National Historic Site, Emeldia's daughter Angie Colasanti related how her mother came to serve at Tuskegee Army Air Field alongside Neomi,

> Born June 16, 1923 in Pensacola, Florida my Mother, Emeldia Zaragoza, was the second eldest of six children. Like in most small communities at that time, just about everyone knew each other. And it was there Emeldia met and fell in love with James Polkinghorne, the only son of the local pharmacist.
>
> When James went to Tuskegee to become an airman, Emeldia, against her parents' wishes, decided to go with him. She, along with James' sister Neomi, took and passed the civil service exams for civilian work at the Tuskegee Airbase. Being the best of friends, Emeldia and Neomi were also roommates during their stay in Tuskegee.
>
> James Polkinghorne was assigned to a... fighter squadron in

Italy. Five months into his assignment, he was shot down somewhere over Italy and his remains were never found. Left with only the silver wings James had given her and a broken heart, my Mom couldn't face going home to Pensacola. Instead, she went to Pennsylvania with a girlfriend she met at Tuskegee.[32]

It is not known in which specialties the two young women were trained and utilized, but Emeldia later completed a 122-hour specialized course in aircraft fabrics, including shop training topics on blueprint reading, mechanical drawing, seam construction, aircraft covering and code markings.[33] Neomi and Emeldia shared a room in a house within walking distance of the base owned by a widowed, elderly black woman who "looked after them like their own mothers."[34] The two young girls felt safe and comfortable, and there were strict house rules, including no boys permitted in the rooms.

As a graduation present, Polkinghorne presented Emeldia with a miniature, duplicate set of his silver wings, which she kept for her entire life and was donated in her memory to the Tuskegee Airmen National Historic Site by her daughter Angie.

Tuskegee Army Air Field Overcrowded

Now rated aviators, Polkinghorne's Class 43-B was ready for Advanced training in the North American AT-6 *Texan*, squadron assignments and combat training in operational fighters. For the first time, this specialized training occurred at an airfield far from Tuskegee.

The reason was that Tuskegee Army Air Field was loaded well beyond capacity with personnel and aircraft. The War Department's initial intention was to train only a small cadre of black pilots to staff a single squadron, hoping that this small effort would suffice to silence any criticism. But much to the U.S. Army Air Forces dismay, input to the pilot training pipeline continued unabated and the production of winged African-American pilots was succeeding beyond anyone's expectations. By mid-1942, with the U.S. Army Air Forces leadership unwilling to deploy the 99th Fighter Squadron into overseas combat, almost 220 officers, 3,000 enlisted personnel and a staggering number of aircraft were packed into Tuskegee Army Air Field.[35] As one Tuskegee Airman recalled,

EAGER AND READY TO DO THEIR JOB

Eager and ready to take their places in line with other American airmen fighting on many fronts against the enemy, these Tuskegee hawkmen look over the types of ships they will fly. Left to right, Second Lieutenants Roy Spencer of 1526 South Adams street, Tallahassee, Florida; Claude B. Cowan of 142 Somerset street, Newark, N. J.; James R. Polkinghorne of 523 North Deus street, Pensacola, Florida; John H. Prowell Jr., Box 12, Lewisburg, Alabama; William H. Walker of 328 North Illinois avenue, Carbondale, Illinois; William E. Griffin of 811 17th street, Birmingham, Ala., and Walter H. Downs, Box 5, McComb, Mississippi.

Informal photograph of Polkinghorne's graduating Class 43-B that appeared in the papers. From the left, Roy Spencer, Claude Govan, James Polkinghorne, John Prowell, William Walker, William Griffin, and Walter Downs

> The War Department didn't know what to do with the black pilots it had trained. The Tuskegee plan hadn't been expected to succeed nearly so well; no real consideration had been given beyond their training. It was decided to move the men to 'another location,' so they would think some action was being taken. But where would the army send them?"[36]

Another issue that compounded the overcrowding at the Tuskegee Army Airfield was the status of attrited flight students. At other U.S. Army Air Forces training sites when white aviation cadets were unsuccessful in pilot training, they were transferred to different bases and assignments. Due to the U.S. Army's segregationist policies, however, attrited black aviation cadets at Tuskegee Army Air Force had no such options. One pilot remembered,

> There were a lot of good pilots who didn't make it. Some cadets were not suited to fighter planes. White cadets could go to the Air Transport Command or to B-17 bombers. We couldn't. In fact, there was only one place for a black wash-

out to go, he became a buck private at Tuskegee. It was the ultimate humiliation.[37]

The eventual solution to the overcrowding was to form three additional all-black squadrons, the 100th, 301st, and 302nd Fighter Squadrons and place them under the segregated operational control of the newly formed 332nd Fighter Group. The organizational structure of the all-black 332nd Fighter Group now mirrored the organizational structure of standard all-white fighter groups, which were also assigned three fighter squadrons.

This left the 99th Fighter Squadron, which had its full complement of trained pilots and ground support personnel unlike all the other squadrons in the new 332nd Fighter Group, as a lone wolf.

332nd Fighter Group Transferred to Selfridge Army Air Field

As a stop-gap measure to relieve the overcrowding at Tuskegee Army Air Field, the 332nd Fighter Group and its assigned squadrons were ordered to Selfridge Army Air Field, located about

One of Emeldia Zaragoza's training certificates reflecting her training in aircraft fabrics. Polkinghorne's sister, Neomi, also served at Tuskegee, making a rare combination of brother-sister Documented Original Tuskegee Airmen (DOTA).

30 miles northeast of Detroit, Michigan. After having survived Alabama's fiery sunshine and blanketing humidity under "circumstances which might have exasperated Job," one can only imagine how these now warm-blooded Southern-trained aviators managed to cope with such bitter-cold Northern conditions that aircraft engine oil congealed under icy field conditions.[38]

On March 26, 1943, the 332nd Fighter Group, under the command of a white officer, Lt. Col. Sam W. Westbrook, Jr., along with the ground echelon of its three assigned fighter squadrons, departed by train from the Tuskegee Army Air Field for Selfridge Army Air Field.[39] The first echelon of the squadrons' airplanes followed on March 28, 1943 but not before buzzing Tuskegee Army Air Field during their farewell departure to the delight of everyone present. The 99th Fighter Squadron remained behind at Tuskegee Army Air Field as it awaited its own separate orders to deploy overseas independently from the 332nd Fighter Group.

This relocation marked a historical milestone as these were the first African-American squadrons to desegregate a U.S. Army Air Forces airfield, albeit only temporarily as the 332nd Fighter Group anticipated being shipped overseas rather quickly once all pre-deployment training was completed and they were certified operationally ready for combat,[40]

The men of the 332nd were overjoyed to leave the segregated and dehumanizing South for the promised land of the North. The men were shocked and disappointed to find that segregation extended beyond the geographical boundaries of the South. Their new base, Selfridge, located near Detroit, was also racially segregated.[41]

Conditions at Selfridge Army Air Field were exacerbated when race riots broke out in nearby Detroit. The black airmen were confined to base, surrounded by white sentries placed by commanders fearful that they might aid the rioters.[42]

In April 1943 a snapshot of the personnel strengths of the 332nd Fighter Group showed:[43]

- Headquarters, 332nd Fighter Group under the command of Lt. Col. Samuel W. Westbrook, Jr., a white officer, consisted of 15 officers and 33 enlisted men
- 100th Fighter Squadron under the command of 1st Lt. Mac Ross, a black officer, had 34 officers and 268 enlisted men

- 301st Fighter Squadron under the command of 1st Lt. Charles H. DeBow, a black officer, had 13 officers and 250 enlisted men
- 302nd Fighter Squadron under the command of 2nd Lt. William T. Mattison, a black officer, had 6 officers and 291 enlisted men

Oscoda Army Air Field

Despite the "warm breezes of spring driving old man winter from hibernation in northern Michigan," living conditions for the 332nd Fighter Group took a further downturn on April 12, 1943 when the first elements the squadrons departed Selfridge Army Air Field aboard a 100-vehicle convoy for primitive training facilities at Oscoda Army Air Field.[44]

Located about 200 miles north of Selfridge Army Air Field in Iosco County, Michigan, Oscoda Army Air Field was used for aerial gunnery and dive bombing training on local ranges and other training sites situated in nearby frozen Canada.[45]

Shortly after their arrival in Iosco County, 332nd Fighter Group personnel learned,

That the War Department had rejected a request by the Board of Supervisors of Iosco County demanding that a contingent of the 332nd F Gp personnel stationed at Oscoda, Michigan be moved elsewhere because Negroes at the Base would create social and racial problems. Meantime, Governor Harry Relley, Senator Homer Ferguson, and Arthur Vandenburg, vigorously denounced the Board of Supervisors, stating that under no circumstances would such a move be supported.

Investigations of this incident reveals the Board of Supervisors of Iosco were not the originators of such a resolution. It still remains a mystery to be solved as to the origin of the Iosco County Resolution, however, the training program was not interrupted and things proceeded according to plan.[46]

Yet not every experience at Oscoda Army Air Field was terrible,

On 15 May 1943, three Greyhound Busses, loaded with one hundred and five (105) hostesses and chaperones journeyed to Oscoda to entertain the enlisted personnel. This array of feminine talent was headed by Mrs. Ardenah Stephens, Director of the John R. U.S.O. Club and members of the Y.W.C.A. respectfully. The hospitality of Mayor Lloyd D. McCraig and civilians of the Oscoda community will long be remembered.[47]

L, SUNDAY., APRIL 4, 1943

Polkinghorne Is First Local Negro To Get His Wings

From hopping bells at the San Carlos hotel to piloting planes for Uncle Sam is the record made by James R. Polkinghorne, Jr., 523 North Reus street, who has just received his wings in the Army Air corps.

Lieutenant Polkinghorne, who is home now visiting his parents, was graduated from the Tuskegee Army Flying school at Tuskegee, Ala., March 6, and has been assigned to Selfridge field, Mich.

He is the first Pensacola Negro youth, and the only one so far, to gain his wings at Tuskegee.

Lieutenant Polkinghorne, whose father has operated a drug store here for 30 years and who as a notary public has married hundreds of couples, was graduated from Washington High school and was in his junior year at Florida A. & M. college when he went into the Army's flying school.

Pensacola News Journal April 4, 1943 article celebrating 2nd Lt. James R. Polkinghorne Jr. earning of his U.S. Army Air Forces wings.

P-40 *Warhawks* on the line at Oscoda Army Air Field in May 1943.

Polkinghorne Assigned to 301st Fighter Squadron at Selfridge Army Air Field

As a newly winged aviator and after some well-deserved leave at home with his family, it was to Selfridge Army Air Field that Polkinghorne reported to on April 14, 1943 for combat training in the Curtiss P-40 *Warhawk*.

Polkinghorne was assigned to the 301st Fighter Squadron

Emblem of Polkinghorne's 301st Fighter Squadron, a caricatured cat piloting a .50 caliber machine gun with a wing tank under each wing.

whose emblem was officially described as being,

> On a light turquoise blue disc, edged black, a caricatured cat wearing a red cape, brown aviator's helmet and white goggles, piloting a gray .50 caliber aerial machine gun with red and white tail, winged yellow-orange, with an auxiliary gray wing tank under each wing, all in flight toward dexter, in front of a large, white cloud formation.[48]

Polkinghorne's 301st Fighter squadron repositioned to Oscoda Army Air Field on May 3, 1943, where he was taught the intricacies of air-to-air and air-to-ground combat.[49]

> Over the sandy pine shores of Lake Huron, pilots of the 332nd F Gp polished up their flight and gunnery tactics for that inevitable test of their skills and courage, which will eventually lead them to pursuit and battle in the skies of Europe and Asia.[50]

301st Fighter Squadron's First Casualty

On May 9, 1943 Polkinghorne's 301st Fighter Squadron suffered its first casualty when 2nd Lt. Wilmeth W. Sidat-Singh, a gifted Syracuse University athlete, was killed while on a training mission over Lake Huron. Although he was seen to bail out of his P-40F before it crashed into the water, his body was not recovered for several weeks. When his sunken aircraft was finally located by divers, he was found with his parachute snagged on the outside of his airplane.[51,52]

This was not the first time Polkinghorne had encountered death while in military flight training. Many aviation cadets were killed at Tuskegee Army Air Field, some well-known to Polkinghorne but others not. But the loss of a squadron-mate, someone with whom one flies, trains, and lives with in close quarters every single day, is a different matter.

This wonderful 36-page booklet documented aviation cadet life and U.S. Army Air Forces flight training at the Tuskegee Institute and the Tuskegee Army Air Field.

Accident report photographs documenting Polkinghorne's left landing gear which collapsed upon landing at Oscoda Army Air Field on May 6, 1943, causing him to swerve off the runway.

Polkinghorne's Three Curtiss P-40 *Warhawk* Training Accidents

U.S. Army Air Army Forces records indicate that Polkinghorne was involved in three separate Curtiss P-40 *Warhawks* accidents at Selfridge Army Air Field and Oscoda Army Air Field. He was never seriously injured or professionally disqualified for these mishaps, and in each instance, he was quickly returned to flying status.

The first accident occurred on May 6, 1943 after landing at Oscoda Army Air Field in a P-40F *Warhawk*. The official report of the aircraft accident stated,

> Lt. Polkinghorne was seen flying around with his left wheel not fully retracted. On his approach for a landing the gear appeared to be normal. He made a normal 3 point landing and as he continued his roll his left gear collapsed, throwing the plane off the runway onto the land. On examination of the plane after it was raised, it was found that the retracting strut had been broken and that there was a solid movement on the hand pump regardless of where the left wheel was. Material failure was the cause of the accident. [53]

The accident record showed that Polkinghorne had 13.7 total pilot hours in the P-40 *Warhawk* and 243.3 total pilot hours since he had started flight training on August 6, 1942, 39 weeks prior.

Col. Selway Relieves Lt. Col. Westbrook as 332nd Fighter Group Commander

On May 16, 1943, Col. Robert R. Selway, Jr., a white officer, relieved Lt. Col. Westbrook as commander of the 332nd Fighter Group. Instituting the motto of "Get to your damn guns," Selway established a rigorous training schedule, and by the fall the squadrons were flying 2,000 flight hours a week.[54,55] One eloquent squadron historian recorded his impressions of the group's progression,

> Amid heavy humidity and high temperature, intense training usurps, the traditional glamour once boastfully treasured by the nymphs, a design of what might have been a difficult task, molds into a painting which warrants the envy of the artist. Bitter determination, courage and ability oils the wheel as we advance cautiously, but definitely toward the goal. Under the guidance of the new command, emphasis was placed on individual training so as to prepare each Officer and EM for efficient and timely execution of specialized duty within the organization.[56]

Polkinghorne's Second Accident

Polkinghorne's second accident occurred slightly more than two weeks later on May 25, 1943 when he attempted to land at Selfridge Army Air Field in a P-40L *Warhawk* after a cross-country flight from Oscoda Army Air Field. In his official statement, Polkinghorne stated,

> I took off from Oscoda on a scheduled flight to Selfridge Field at 1220. Upon arriving at Selfridge I found that there was a 90-degree crosswind and came in on the best available runway to land. I landed and the plane rolled toward the end of the runway. I attempted to keep it from going into the mud but applied brake too firmly. The plane nosed up and damaged the prop and airscoop. Time of Accident 1325.[57]

The accident investigation board was a little more detailed and less kind in their description of Polkinghorne's actions,

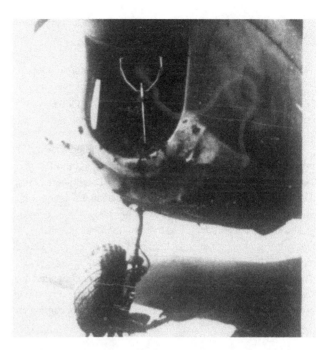

Fighting high crosswinds, Polkinghorne landed long and ran off the runway on May 25, 1943 at Selfridge Army Air Field. His P-40 *Warhawk* nosed over in soft dirt and these accident report photographs document a bent prop and a damaged air scoop.

On May 25, 1943 at 1329 EWT, 2nd Lt. James R. Polkinghorne in P-40L-20CU No. 42-11113 made a high, fast approach and landed on the last third of the East-West runway. As the plane ran off the end of the runway the pilot was braking heavily and the plane nosed up when the wheels hit the soft dirt. At the time of the accident a 60-degree crosswind prevailed and the tower was unable to contact the plane by radio, however the red light was given the pilot when it was evident that he was overshooting.

The Accident Classification Committee met at Selfridge Field, May 30, 1943. It is the opinion of this Committee that the pilot used very poor judgment in not going around again when he was obviously overshooting.[58]

Col. William B. Wright, Commanding Officer of Selfridge Army Air Field, concurred with the committee's findings. But other than a damaged ego, it appears that 2nd Lt. Polkinghorne suffered no other action against him and he was returned to a flying status The accident record showed that Polkinghorne now had 47.7 pilot hours in the P-40 *Warhawk* and 288.7 total flight hours.

Polkinghorne's Third Accident

Polkinghorne's third training accident occurred on June 29, 1943 while he was conducting a two-airplane formation takeoff from Oscoda Army Air Field in a P-40E *Warhawk* with 2nd Lt.

William J. Faulkner as flight lead in a P-40F *Warhawk*. In his statement, Polkinghorne said,

This is to certify that I James R. Polkinghorne, was taking off on a routine training flight from O.A.A.F., Oscoda, Michigan in extended formation at about 1445 EWT on the right side of my formation leader, while rolling down the runway the left wing of the plane dropped due to a strong gust of wind picking up the right wing. The plane began to swerve to the left and I attempted to pick the left wing up by giving right rudder and aileron, I then applied full throttle. The ship continued to swerve into the other plane I succeeded in getting the plane off the ground crossing in front of the other plane while doing so. The plane stalled and went into the ground on the left wing and motor, the plane was demolished. The wind at the time was a gusty crosswind from the right.[59]

The accident investigation committee's comments were,

This pilot was taking off in formation on the upwind side with his element leader. He started overtaking him and the cross wind drafted him toward the leader. Rather than cut his throttle, he used full throttle and attempted to pull off the ground. He pulled off the ground, slid across his leader over the top, and stalled on his left wing. The lead plane kicked his plane to the right but his wing failed to miss the tail section of the wing man's plane. The leader hit the tail section and caused him to ground loop.

The responsibility for this accident is attributed to pilot error, 100%, judgment in that he failed to maintain air position on his leader. Recommendations are that all pilots take off individually in strong winds or in cross winds. [60]

Both pilots were uninjured although Polkinghorne's P-40 *Warhawk* cartwheeled and 2nd Lt. William J. Faulkner's P-40 *Warhawk* ground looped into a cloud of dust. Polkinghorne must have been held in high regard because once again no action was taken against him and he returned to flying status.

The accident record indicated that Polkinghorne now had nearly 300 total flight hours, including 91.8 flight hours in several versions of the P-40 *Warhawk*.

While the first two accident P-40 *Warhawks* were repaired and eventually returned to service, it appears that the third aircraft was written off. Polkinghorne was dangerously close to becoming an "enemy ace."

99th Fighter Squadron Combat Deployment Withheld

Meanwhile, the 99th Fighter Squadron, at full strength and combat-ready, still awaited deployment orders at Tuskegee Army Air Field. The 99th Fighter Squadron was assigned operationally to the 3rd Air Force Headquarters, which was responsible for training combat replacement units and was located at MacDill Field in Tampa, Florida. Inspectors from the 3rd Air Force pronounced the 99th Fighter Squadron ready for deployment in September 1942. [61]

Upon completion of this final pre-deployment certification, the next logical step should have been an overseas combat assignment. Yet despite having successfully completed all required training in air-to-air and air-to-ground combat operations, U.S. Army Air Forces leadership refused to deploy the 99th Fighter Squadron, paralyzed by indecision due to two troublesome issues.

First and foremost was implicit racism by theater commanders who refused to accept an African-American squadron into their area of operations. The second more administrative dilemma was that a U.S. Army Air Force Fighter Group was customarily comprised of three squadrons. Integrating a fourth African-American squadron into the command structure not only violated segregation policies but was also too unconventional for leadership tastes.

So while other white fighter squadrons flew off to war, the 99th Fighter Squadron trained,

And trained. And trained. They trained for a year and went through three training cycles "until we were bored," said Jamison. "We had several hundred hours, which would have been unusual for white pilots before going into

combat." [62]

The squadron languished at Tuskegee Army Air Field, "overtrained and restless, if not disillusioned." [63] Finally, Tuskegee Institute's President Dr. Patterson decided to take matters into his own hands and bypass local U.S. Army Air Forces officials. He flew to Washington, DC,

> He had reached a point where it seemed he needed to contact President Roosevelt. He wasn't available immediately, and Dr. Patterson got to see Mrs. Roosevelt. After talking to her, I believe he felt the message would reach the President. At least he came back to Tuskegee satisfied with accomplishments in Washington. [64]

Decision Made

It worked. Combined with political pressure from the black press and other influential, sympathetic civil rights activists, in the spring of 1943, the U.S. Army Air Forces finally decided to deploy the 99th Fighter Squadron to fight in North Africa. To minimize racial troubles and operate within the bounds of U.S. Army Air Forces mandated segregation, the 99th Fighter Squadron deployed as a separate squadron within the command structure of the North African Theater of Operations, U.S. Army (NATOUSA).

Although operationally attached to the 33rd Fighter Group under the command of Col. William W. Momyer, a white officer, the 99th Fighter Squadron, in reality, maintained an independent identity and was often billeted away from white squadrons. In fact, organizational tables for major combat operations during this period either omit the squadron entirely or identify it as "99th Fighter Squadron (Detached)". [65]

Nonetheless, the 99th Fighter Squadron was eager to be tested in the red-hot forge of combat. They were perhaps the most combat-ready squadron ever deployed during World War II, and their actions were followed closely by Polkinghorne and his fellow squadronmates of the 332nd Fighter Group, who hoped to follow right behind them. ∎

Chapter Nine
99th Fighter Squadron Goes To War

Tactical Situation Ashore: The African Campaign

In conjunction with Germany's blitzkrieg across Europe, Hitler's Axis partner Benito Mussolini, prime minister of Italy, invaded British-controlled Egypt in September 1940. Mussolini sought to expand his country's territorial holdings by gaining control of the Suez Canal and commanding access to Middle East oil. Initially, the assault was successful, but an Allied counteroffensive destroyed the Italian 10th Army, and in February 1941 the Germans dispatched the Afrika Korps commanded by Lt. Gen. Erwin Rommel to North Africa to reinforce the faltering Italians. Rommel won a series of startling victories until the Battle of El Alamein in October 1942 when he was decisively defeated by British Lt. Gen Bernard L. Montgomery, who sent the Axis forces into a chaotic 1,400 miles retreat across Libya to Tunisia.

Seeking to trap Rommel in a pincer movement, in November 1942 the Allies opened up a second front against Rommel by landing forces at Algeria, Oran, and Morocco in Northwest Africa. The Twelfth Air Force was formed to provide air support for these ground forces who advanced eastward to link up with Montgomery's forces moving westward. Eventually, the Axis forces were surrounded, and after months of bitter fighting, combat in North Africa ended with a complete Axis surrender on May 13, 1943.

99th Fighter Squadron Sails to North Africa

On April 2, 1943, more than a month before the Axis surrender in North Africa, the 99th Fighter Squadron boarded a train in Chehaw, Alabama and departed Tuskegee Army Air Field for Camp Shanks, New York in preparation for overseas movement They left their weary P-40 *Warhawks* behind in anticipation of being assigned newer aircraft once overseas. On April 16, 1943, the squadron boarded the former luxury liner SS *Mariposa* now converted to troopship use for the nearly 10-day trans-Atlantic convoy journey to North Africa.

Once ashore the 99th Fighter Squadron's pilots became the first African-American aviators to fly in air combat since Eugene J.

In April, 1943, the 99th Fighter Squadron rode the troopship SS *Mariposa*, a converted luxury ocean liner, from New York to Casablanca, Morocco for their first combat assignment.

Bullard fought for the French in 1917, John C. Robinson for the Ethiopians in 1935, and James Peck for the Spanish Republicans in 1937. The 99th Fighter Squadron remained in nearly continuous combat operations for the next two years before peace was declared in Europe and they returned home. Lt. Col Davis, their Commanding Officer, noted,

> The squadron was small and tightly knit, and it is inevitable for such closeness to grow among people who go to war together. We were that much closer because we were racially isolated, lonely blacks in a sea of hostile whites.[1]

Lt. Col Davis was assigned as troop commander aboard the SS *Mariposa*, the senior officer of all embarked military personnel, only 15 percent of whom were African-Americans. Davis noted,

> Contrasted with the anonymity and facelessness of the segregated treatment we had endured at TAAF...as we left the shores of the United States on the morning of 15 April, we felt as if we were separating ourselves, at least for the moment, from the evils of racial discrimination. Perhaps in combat overseas, we would have more freedom and respect than we had experienced at home.[2]

25 of the 26 original pilots of the 99th Fighter Squadron who deployed to North Africa in April, 1943 under the command of Lt. Col. Benjamin O. Davis Jr.

By the time the 99th Fighter Squadron docked at Casablanca, Morocco on April 24, 1943 the war in North Africa was nearly over. After a short period in a bivouac area, the squadron moved 150 miles east across French Morocco to Oued N'ja, a former Luftwaffe base near the town of Fez, to prepare themselves for combat.

They were soon equipped with brand-new Curtiss P-40L *War-hawks,* an updated version of the worn-out P-40's they had flown in the United States. Davis recalled,

> While no AAF unit had gone into combat better trained or better equipped than the 99th Fighter Squadron, we lacked actual combat experience. So as we approached our first missions, my own inexperience and that of my flight commanders was a major source of concern. On the other hand, we had averaged about 250 hours per man in a P-40 (quite a lot for pilot who had not yet flown their first missions), and we possessed an unusually strong sense of purpose and solidarity.[3]

Since no one in the 99th Fighter Squadron had actual combat experience, they relied on the nearby 27th Fighter Group based at Ras el Ma for guidance,

> A strong bond exists among those who fly regardless of race,

and we got along well with the men of the 27th. Col Philip Cochran, a famous veteran of the winter air battles following the North African landings and the real-life prototype of Flip Corkin in 'Terry and the Pirates,' the comic strip by Milt Caniff, flew several training missions with the 99th. We all caught his remarkable fighting spirit and learned a great deal from him about the fine points of aerial combat. Maj. Robert Fackler and Maj. Ralph Keyes, both combat experienced pilots, also advised us during this phase of our preparation and alleviated our vague anxieties about the job we were about to undertake.[4]

On May 30, 1943, after nearly a month of training at Oued N'ja, the 99th Fighter Squadron traveled a thousand miles east across Algeria to Fardjouna, Tunisia. This airfield was located on the Cape Bon peninsula, surrounded by the Gulf of Tunis and within striking distance of Sicily.

They were assigned to the 33rd Fighter Group commanded by Col. William W. Momyer, who later almost singlehandedly caused the removal of the 99th Fighter Squadron from combat and nearly prevented Polkinghorne and his squadronmates in the 332nd Fighter Group from deploying to a combat zone at all.

The 33rd Fighter Group already had three squadrons assigned, so the 99th Fighter Squadron was identified as "detached" and operated independently of the three other squadrons, although it

Launching from a dirt airfield in Fardjouna, Tunisia, the 99th Fighter Squadron's first combat missions were raids and bomber escort missions against the islands of Pantelleria, Lampedusa and Sicily.

received its operational orders from the 33rd Fighter Group.[5]

Tactical Situation Ashore: Pantelleria and Lampedusa

With the surrender of Axis forces in North Africa on May 13, 1943 Allied leadership next turned toward preparations for an invasion of Sicily followed by landings on the Italian mainland. But two small islands under Italian control posed a potential threat to any Allied operations in the Mediterranean Sea.

These heavily fortified islands lying off the coast between Tunisia and Sicily were named Pantelleria and Lampedusa. Refusing to surrender despite Allied offers, beginning on May 31, 1943, these islands were relentlessly attacked, providing the 99th Fighter Squadron with their first actual combat experience.

99th Fighter Squadron's First Combat Mission

On June 2, 1943, Lt. Col Davis assigned Lt. William Campbell and Lt. Charles Hall to fly the 99th Fighter Squadron's first combat mission, a strafing and bombing raid against the island of Pantelleria. This was the first air combat mission ever flown by African-Americans on behalf of the U.S. military, earlier black aviators having taking wing in defense of foreign countries.

From this point on, the 99th Fighter Squadron averaged about two missions a day, including bomber escort missions. They had their first encounter with German fighters on June 9, 1943 when four German Me-109s attacked a bomber formation escorted by the 99th Fighter Squadron and Lt. Willie Ashley damaged one aircraft.[6]

The campaign against Pantelleria and Lampedusa was short-lived. On June 11, 1943, only 12 days after the air campaign began, Pantelleria surrendered with Lampedusa yielding the next day. The path was now cleared for an Allied invasion of Sicily, and on July 2, 1943, the Twelfth Air Force began eight days of concentrated air attacks against targets on the island of Sicily.[7]

More importantly, the 99th Fighter Squadron had performed well under fire and none other than Henry L. Stimson, the Secretary of War, reported in a press release that the squadron had "weathered its first aerial combat test very credibly."[8]

Sidebar: Bell P-39 *Airacobra*

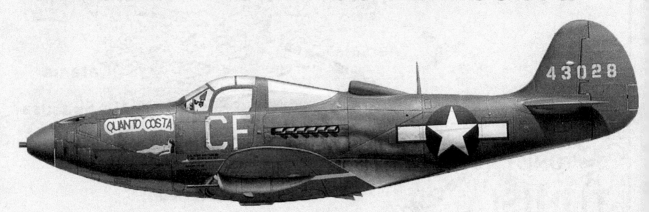

On his final mission Polkinghorne flew P-39Q-20 serial number 44-3077 equipped with an Allison V-1710-85 engine and armed with a M4 37mm cannon and four Browning M2 .50 caliber guns. Per his Missing Air Crew Report (MACR), he was not armed with a bomb, although the aircraft was capable of carrying one. This P-39Q was flown by 1st. Lt. Samuel Curtiss of the 100th Fighter Squadron from Capodichino, Italy in May 1944.

The Bell P-39 *Airacobra* was the second of two combat fighters flown by 1st Lt. James R. Polkinghorne Jr and the airplane he flew on his final mission.

The origin of the P-39 is traced to a 1937 design submitted by the Bell Aircraft Corporation to meet U.S. Army Air Corps specifications for a new fighter with a "tactical mission of interception and attack of hostile aircraft at high altitude."[1] On October 7, 1937 the U.S. Army Air Corps ordered a single prototype with the assigned military experimental designation of XP-39.[2]

The XP-39 took to the air for the first time on April 6, 1938 and was designed as a single-seat, single-engine, low-wing fighter of all-metal construction, except for fabric-covered but metal framed flight control surfaces, including electrically operated flaps. An innovative design for its time, it was one of the first fighters to use a tricycle landing gear configuration, the retractable gear raised and lowered by an electric motor.[3] On a previous design, the XFM-1, Lawrence D. Bell, founder and

president of Bell Aircraft Corporation, had named the aircraft the *Airacobra*, a combination of airplane and barracuda.[4] For the P-39 the named was slightly modified to *Airacobra*, a combination of the words airplane and cobra.

As originally designed, the P-39 *Airacobra* was powered by a turbo-supercharged, electrically-started, 12-cylinder 1,150 horsepower Allison V-1710-17 liquid-cooled inline engine, the supercharging system used to deliver compressed combustion air for high altitude combat operations. For balance purposes, the engine was located behind the pilot, which raised concerns about the possibility of the pilot being crushed in an accident. A ten-foot driveshaft extension used to transmit power to a gearbox behind the three-bladed propeller. This long shaft assembly, designed to accommodate deflections of up to two inches, emitted a loud whirring sound beneath the pilot's legs, which although harmless, often proved unsettling to new P-39 *Airacobra* pilots.[5]

Flight testing was a success and on October

12, 1939 the U.S. Army Air Corps placed the first of many production orders and also made the momentous decision to delete the turbo-supercharger from production aircraft.[6,7] The intent was to use the P-39 *Airacobra* primarily in a low-altitude, close air support role instead of a high-altitude fighter interceptor. As a result, the P-39 *Airacobra* lacked the engine performance necessary to dogfight against newer German and Japanese fighters that were capable of flying and fighting at higher altitudes than the non-turbo-supercharged P-39 could reach.[8] Thus, the P-39 *Airacobra* was unfairly criticized by U.S. and Allied pilots for being unable to perform a mission for which they were assigned, but the aircraft was not capable of executing. More than 20 variants of the Bell P-39 *Airacobra* were eventually built, P-39Q being the last and most produced variant.[9]

The design of the P-39 *Airacobra* was dictated more by the placement of its Oldsmobile-built T-9 cannon than aerodynamic considerations. For greater firing accuracy, the cannon, which fired a 37-millimeter shell, was located on the fuselage's center line and shot through the opened center of the propeller spinner. Two Browning M2 .50 caliber machine guns were nose-mounted on the fuselage and synchronized to shoot through the propeller arc. Two additional .30 caliber machines guns were also mounted in the wings, but depending on the purchase order, some variants flew with 20mm cannons or with the .30 caliber machine guns removed and replaced by two .50 caliber machine guns mounted in streamlined under-wing pods.[10]

A fuselage centerline rack provided for the carrying of a single bomb weighing up to 500 pounds, although there were reports of some squadrons successfully carrying a 1,000-pound bomb in combat.[11] An external 175-gallon fuel drop tank could also be taken in place of a bomb to supplement the fuel carried in the six self-sealing wing tanks, their capacity varying from 86 gallons to 120 gallons depending on the variant.

Harmonization of the three guns was complicated by the fact that all three weapons had different ranges and trajectories, making

The P-39 *Airacobra's* cockpit was designed for a 5-ft 8-inch pilot. Polkinghorne stood nearly 5-ft 11-inches tall.

Excellent close-up of the P-39 *Airacobra's* automobile-style cockpit door. This particular P-39 was flown by the Tuskegee Airmen at Selfridge Army Air Field.

Staff Sgt. James McGee working on a P-39 *Airacobra* in Italy. Always the unsung heroes of any squadron, mechanics labored under extreme field conditions to keep their fighters combat-ready.

aiming difficult.[12,13] As compared to the high-speed, very flat trajectory of the .50 caliber bullets, the 37mm cannon shells, which lacked a high-velocity cartridge, had a slow, very curving trajectory that required extensive training before the pilot became effective. The cockpit was presumably fume-tight, but pilots reported that "when you flipped on all three gun switches and fired your entire arsenal, there was a great roaring noise, braaaaap, and the cockpit filled with smoke so your eyes ran."[14]

Two automobile-styled doors with roll-up windows and emergency door jettison handles were located on either side of the fuselage to permit easy access to the non-pressurized cockpit, which was designed to accommodate a pilot who was five feet eight inches tall and weighed 200 pounds with a parachute.[15] The windows could be rolled down in flight for extra air in warm climates, and the pilot was well-protected in the cockpit, which featured armored bulkheads, armored plating, bullet-proof glass, a sturdy roll-over structure directly behind the seat, and excellent visibility in all directions.

Demand was so great for the P-39 *Airacobra* that Bell Aircraft that at the height of production more than 50,000 employees were producing 20 P-39 *Airacobra's* a day.[16] But its time was limited. The P-39 *Airacobra* did not have the high-altitude performance necessary to defend deep strike U.S. bombers like the Boeing B-17 *Flying fortress* and Consolidated B-24 *Liberator* against attacks from better performing German Luftwaffe fighters. On

July 25, 1944 all production of the Bell P-39 *Airacobra* ceased with a grand total of 9,558 aircraft produced.

In the final analysis, the Bell P-39 *Airacobra*, also known as "The Iron Dog" by its detractors, excelled in its designed role as a ground-attack fighter with its tremendous firepower, and even in air-to-air combat below 10,000 feet. But for the lack of a turbo-supercharger, it may have also excelled in its dual role as a high-altitude interceptor and avoided the scorn and criticism it suffered during its active service.

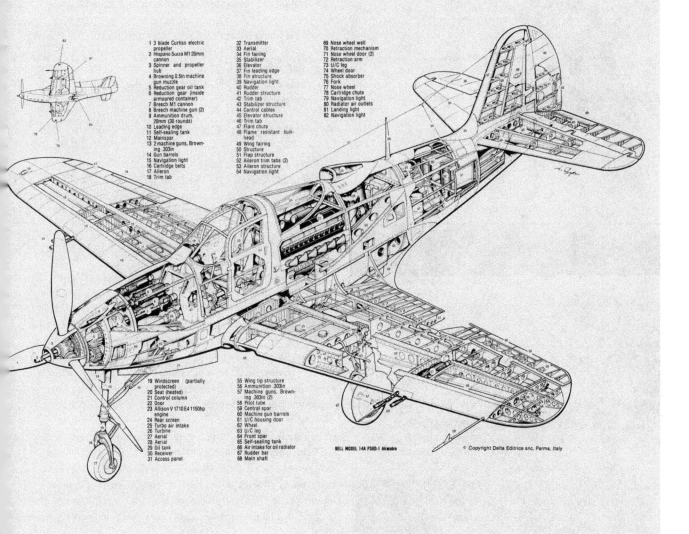

1 3 blade Curtiss electric propeller
2 Hispano Suiza M1 20mm cannon
3 Spinner and propeller hub
4 Browning 0.5in machine gun muzzle
5 Reduction gear oil tank
6 Reduction gear (inside armoured container)
7 Breech M1 cannon
8 Breech machine gun (2)
9 Ammunition drum, 20mm (30 rounds)
10 Leading edge
11 Self-sealing tank
12 Mainspar
13 2 machine guns, Browning .303in
14 Gun barrels
15 Navigation light
16 Cartridge belts
17 Aileron
18 Trim tab

19 Windscreen (partially protected)
20 Seat (heated)
21 Control column
22 Door
23 Allison V 1710 E4 1150hp engine
24 Rear screen
25 Turbo air intake
26 Turbine
27 Aerial
28 Aerial
29 Oil tank
30 Receiver
31 Access panel

32 Transmitter
33 Aerial
34 Fin fairing
35 Stabilizer
36 Elevator
37 Fin leading edge
38 Fin structure
39 Navigation light
40 Rudder
41 Rudder structure
42 Trim tab
43 Stabilizer structure
44 Control cables
45 Elevator structure
46 Trim tab
47 Flare chute
48 Flame resistant bulkhead
49 Wing fairing
50 Structure
51 Flap structure
52 Aileron trim tabs (2)
53 Aileron structure
54 Navigation light

55 Wing tip structure
56 Ammunition .303in
57 Machine guns, Browning .303in (2)
58 Pilot tube
59 Central spar
60 Machine gun barrels
61 U/C housing door
62 Wheel
63 U/C leg
64 Front spar
65 Self-sealing tank
66 Air intake for oil radiator
67 Rudder bar
68 Main shaft

69 Nose wheel well
70 Retraction mechanism
71 Nose wheel door (2)
72 Retraction arm
73 U/C leg
74 Wheel door
75 Shock absorber
76 Fork
77 Nose wheel
78 Cartridge chute
79 Navigation light
80 Radiator air outlets
81 Landing light
82 Navigation light

BELL MODEL 14A P39D-1 Airacobra

© Copyright Delta Editrice snc, Parma, Italy

First 99th Squadron Air Victory

On June 29, 1943 the 99th Fighter Squadron was assigned to the 324th Fighter Group commanded by Col. William K. McNown and began flying bomber escort missions between Fardjouna, Tunisia and the Axis-occupied island of Sicily.

On July 2, 1943, the first aerial victory by a Tuskegee Airman occurred when 1st Lt. Charles B. Hall shot down a Focke-Wolfe 190 while escorting B-25 bombers on a raid into Castelvetrano in southwest Sicily. Hall noted,

"GOOD HUNTING, SON, – YOU'RE ON YOUR OWN NOW !!! "

Editorial cartoon depicting the 99th Fighter Squadron's first combat missions against Axis forces on the islands of Pantelleria.

Notwithstanding the air combat achievements of Bullard, Robinson, and Peck before him, 1st Lt. Charles B. Hall arguably became the first black fighter pilot in American history to shoot down an enemy airplane.

It was my eighth mission and the first time I had seen the enemy close enough to shoot at him. I saw two Focke-Wulfs {sic} following the bombers just after the bombs were dropped. I headed for the space between the fighters and bombers and managed to turn inside the Jerries. I fired a long burst and saw my tracers penetrate the second aircraft. He was turning to the left, but suddenly fell off and headed straight into the ground. I followed him down and saw him crash. He raised a big cloud of dust.[9]

Hall was personally awarded the Distinguished Flying Cross for his actions by Gen. Dwight D. Eisenhower, then assigned as Supreme Commander Allied Expeditionary Force of the North African Theater of Operations. But he received a much sweeter reward from one of his own squadronmates. While in Morocco, 2nd Lt. Louis Purnell had found a bottle of Coke and deposited it in the squadron safe to celebrate the squadron's first aerial victory,

Lou [Purnell] retrieved the Coke from the safe and from a town fifteen miles away got a block of equally precious ice. In the shade of a grove of olive trees the Coke, perhaps the only one in the Mediterranean Theater, 'came to a well-deserved end.'[10]

First Wartime Casualties

The joy of Hall's victory was tempered by the sorrow of the unexplained losses of 1st Lt. Sherman White Jr. and 2nd Lt. James L. McCullin, who disappeared during that same mission and were presumed shot down. Their bodies were never recovered.

Sicilian Campaign

The Allied invasion of Sicily began on the night of July 9, 1943 with landings by airborne forces followed by an amphibious assault on the early morning of July 10, 1943. Code-named Operation Husky, Allied plans called for an assault on Sicily by two armies, the Western Task Force commanded by Lt. Gen. George S. Patton with his Seventh Army and the Eastern Task Force led by Gen. Bernard L. Montgomery and his Eighth Army. Allied air forces flew fighter sweeps to prevent the Luftwaffe from harassing ground forces and conducted tactical bombing and strafing missions.

In a study of contrasts between land and sea flight operations, the 99th Fighter Squadron's airfield at Fardjouna was "so dusty that sometimes we had to take off 12 P-40s abreast, each plane maintaining its heading and position by reference to the plane on its right."[11] The pilots were "uncomfortably conscious of the distance that had to be flown across the water from North Africa to Sicily."[12]

As invasion forces moved inland, Allied squadrons quickly

Hall was personally congratulated by Gen. Dwight D. Eisenhower and awarded the Distinguished Flying Cross for his actions.

repositioned to captured Axis airfields to provide close air support to advancing troops. On July 19, 1943 the 99th Fighter Squadron was reassigned back to the 33rd Fighter Group commanded by Col. William W. Momyer. On the same day, the 99th Fighter Squadron left North Africa permanently when it shifted to Licata air base on the south coast of Sicily.

The Sicilian invasion proceeded swiftly. On August 17, 1943, less than six weeks after the beginning of the assault, Axis forces surrendered, but not before successfully evacuating an enormous amount of troops and equipment to Italy. With Sicily successfully captured, the next target for the Allies was the Italian mainland.

Lt. Col. Davis Returns to the United States

Quite unexpectedly, Lt. Col Davis received orders to return to the United States. His assignment was to assume command of the 332nd Fighter Group, comprised of the 100th Fighter Squadron, 301st Fighter Squadron, and 302nd Fighter Squadron and prepare them for overseas combat operations. Davis recalled,

> Except for its white commander, Col. Robert R. Selway, Jr., and his white training personnel, the 332nd was an all-black fighter group. Having commanded a squadron in combat, it was logical for me to command the 332nd if it had been specified that the unit was to have a black commander. These orders, however, took me completely by surprise. Colonel Selway was probably expecting to accompany the unit overseas, so he may have been equally surprised when he learned that I had been chosen as the group's new commander.[13]

Lt. Col. Davis turned over command of the 99th Fighter Squadron to his operations officer, Maj. George Roberts, on September 2, 1943. Roberts had previously served as the very first commander of the 99th Fighter Squadron while the unit was still at Tuskegee Army Air Field.

Davis had been in continuous combat for nearly three months, and he left Sicily confident that the successes of the 99th Fighter Squadron under his command had paved the way for the squadrons of the 332nd Fighter Group to enter combat. In fact, only a few weeks before his departure, Davis had flown to Tunisia to meet with Secretary of War Henry L. Stimson, who showered praise on the performance of the 99th Fighter Squadron at a press conference.[14] But evil forces were afoot determined to remove the 99th Fighter Squadron from combat and put an end to the 332nd Fighter Group.

Col. Momyer's Memorandum and Times Magazine Article

Shortly after Lt. Col. Davis' departure, Col. William W. Momyer, 33rd Fighter Group commander, wrote a memorandum to his immediate superior, Maj. Gen. Edwin J. House, XII Air Support Command, questioning the combat efficiency of the 99th Fighter Squadron.

On September 16, 1943, Maj. Gen. House forwarded his own memorandum on the subject to his superior, Maj. Gen. John K.

Better than a General's handshake, 1st Lt. Charles Hall celebrates the first aerial victory by a Tuskegee Airman with the "Famous Coke."

Cannon, Deputy Commander, Northwest Tactical Air Force, using Momyer's information and stating,

> Based on the performance of the 99th Fighter Squadron to date, it is my opinion that they are not of the fighting caliber of any squadron in this Group. They have failed to display the aggressiveness and desire for combat that are necessary to a first-class fighting organization. It may be expected that we will get less work and less operational time out of the 99th Fighter Squadron than any squadron in this Group.

> ...on many discussions held with officers of all professions, including medical, the consensus of opinion seems to be that the negro type has not the proper reflexes to make a first-class, fighter pilot. Also, on rapid moves that must be a part of this Command, housing and messing difficulties arise because the time has not yet arrived when white and colored soldiers will mess at the same table and sleep in the same barracks. No details in this connection have been brought out because it is desired that administrative features not be a part of this report.

> ...I believe it would be much better to assign the 99th to the Northwest African Coastal Air Force, equip it with P-39's and make the present P-40's available to this Command as replacements for the active operations still to come in this theater.

Maj. George S. Roberts earned his private pilot license in the Civilian Pilot Training Program, graduated with Davis in the first class at Tuskegee Army Air Field, twice served as Commanding Officer of the 99th Fighter Squadron, and later commanded the 332nd Fighter Group.

> ...It is recommended that if and when a colored group is formed in the United States, it be retained for either the eastern or western defense zone and a white fighter group be released for movement overseas.[15]

House's memorandum was forwarded through the chain of command to Lt. Gen. Carl A. Spaatz, Twelfth Air Force Commander in theater. On September 19, 1943 Spaatz endorsed the report and forwarded it to Gen. H. H. Arnold, Commanding General, U.S. Army Air Forces, who was located in Washington.[16] Arnold recommended to Gen. George C. Marshall, Jr., Chief of the Army, that the 99th Fighter Squadron be removed from tactical operations, that the 332nd Fighter Group be sent to a noncombatant area, and that plans for the formation of an all-black bombardment group be shelved.[17]

Lt. Col. Davis first found out about the criticism of his 99th Fighter Squadron's performance only after he arrived back in the United States in early September 1943. Davis was justifiably furious, suspecting that the real motive behind the memorandum was not a fair evaluation of the 99th Fighter Squadron's combat efficiency but rather a blatant attempt to remove African-American aviators from combat operations. Neither Col. Momyer or Maj. Gen. House had expressed any concerns to Lt. Col. Davis while he was in theater.[18]

Davis controlled his emotions and accompanied by his father Brig. Gen. Benjamin O. Davis Sr., held a press conference with twenty newspaper editors on September 16, 1943 in a War Department conference room in the Pentagon.[19,20] He defended the combat record of the "Black Eagles" of the 99th Fighter Squadrons and noted that they had flown "more than 800 sorties over enemy territory and had demonstrated the ability of the Negro pilot to live up to the highest standards of the Army Air Forces."[21,22]

Time Magazine Article

On September 20, 1943, shortly after Davis' press conference and only four days after Maj. Gen. House had forwarded his memorandum, *Time* magazine published an article titled *Experiment Proved?* stating in part,

> Unofficial reports from the Mediterranean theater have suggested that the top air command was not altogether satisfied with the 99th's performance; there was said to be a plan some weeks ago to attach it to the Coastal Air Command, in which it would be assigned to routine convoy cover. In any case, the question of the 99th is only a single facet of one of the Army's biggest headaches: how to train and use Negro troops. No theater command wants them in considerable numbers; the high command has trouble finding combat jobs for them.[23]

TRAINING

Experiment Proved?

To Washington last week came tall, lath-straight Lieut. Colonel Benjamin O. Davis Jr., until recently commander of the 99th Fighter Squadron, the Air Forces' first all-Negro fighter outfit. At a press conference West Pointer Davis, who led the 99th in Tunisia and Sicily, said that in his opinion Negro pilots had made the grade, and training them should no longer be regarded as an experiment.

In one of their first encounters, Colonel Davis said, the 99th had two planes shot down, but got one German fighter definitely, two probables and three damaged. On every bomber escort mission his men met superior enemy forces and managed to break a little better than even. His conference finished, Colonel Davis, son of the Army's only Negro general officer, Brigadier General Benjamin O. Davis Sr., departed. His new command: the 332nd Fighter Group, to be formed of three Negro squadrons.

So little operational data on the 99th had reached Washington that it was impossible to form a conclusive opinion

TIME, SEPTEMBER 20, 1943

Anonymous sources intent on discrediting the combat performance of the 99th Fighter Squadron provided classified information for this 20 September 1943 *Time* magazine article.

This article not only discredited the performance of the 99th Fighter Squadron but also indicated that someone had leaked classified information to the press.[24]   One newspaper editor provided his thoughts on the article,

Of course the top command is not satisfied with the 99th's performance. It would not be satisfied if the 99th had shot every Axis plane out of the skies. Indeed, it would less satisfied because it would be in more of a dilemma. It was never planned to use Negroes as military aviators or in mechanized combat services, and if it had not been for the tremendous propaganda carried on by this newspaper, the other Negro newspapers, the NAACP, the Urban League and practically every institution and organization in Negro life,

there would be no such units today.[25]

Equally incensed, Davis's wife, Agatha Scott Davis, wrote a letter to the editor of *Time* magazine, which was published on October 18, 1943,

Are you justified in saying that the record of the 99th Fighter Squadron is only fair? My husband tells me that his judgment, based on comparison with the work done by six veteran P-40 squadrons in the same area on the same types of missions over the same period of time, is that the record of the 99th Fighter Squadron is at least worthy of favorable comment.

My indictment is that by publishing an article based on "unofficial reports" you have created unfavorable public opinion about an organization to which all Negroes point with pride. You should realize that these few printed words in TIME—words which may be creating a false impression—have struck at one of the strongest pillars upholding Negroes' morale in their effort to contribute to the winning of the war.[26]

On October 16, 1943 Davis was ordered to appear before the War Department's Committee on Negro Troop Policies. Unofficially known as the McCloy Committee in deference to its head, Assistant Secretary of State John J. McCloy, the McCloy committee was created in 1942 to "formulate racial policies for the segregated armed forces and to issue information on race relations to white officers commanding black troops."[27] The committee, which included Lt. Col. Davis' father, Brig. Gen. Benjamin O. Davis Sr. of the U.S. Army's Office of the Inspector General, had studied House's memorandum and wanted to hear Lt. Col. Davis' opinion.[28]

Davis powerfully refuted every point in Maj. Gen. House's memorandum, and noted,

During the actions against Pantelleria and Sicily, the 99th had performed as well as any new fighter squadron, black or white, could be expected to perform in an unfamiliar environment. I painted a vivid picture of the growth of our combat team from inexperienced fliers to seasoned veterans, giving the example of the bomber escort mission I had led on 2 July and describing how we had stayed right with our bombers and absorbed the attacks of the enemy planes.

The squadron's training had been entirely adequate, but our lack of combat experience had inevitably led to some mistakes in the first missions. This would have been true of any squadron handicapped by a lack of experienced pilots. I told the committee that if there had been any lack of aggres-

One of the most iconic war bonds posters of World War II, then 2nd 1st. Lt. Robert W. Diez was credited by the Treasury Department as being the model for this 1943 portrait. In January 1944, while serving as a fighter pilot with the 99th Fighter Squadron, Diez shot down two German planes in two days over the Anzio beachhead.

sive spirit in the 99th at first, we had soon made up for it as our pilots gained confidence and began to work successfully as a team.[29]

Indeed, at the same time that Davis was appearing before the McCloy Committee, the 99th Fighter Squadron had detached from Col. Momyer's 33rd Fighter Group and reported to the 79th Fighter Group under the command of Col. Earl E. Bates, Jr. Now based on the Italian mainland, the squadron was averaging 36 to 40 close air support missions a day in support of the Allied advance up the peninsula, for which the squadron would later be awarded a Distinguished Unit Citation.[30]

U.S. Army Air Forces Study Officially Clears the 99th Fighter Squadron

Davis' passionate defense of the 99th Fighter Squadron and his insistence that it had performed as well as or better than the other P-40 squadron stationed in theater achieved its desired effect. General Marshall, aware of the power of the black press and the political fallout of any action taken by the U.S. Army Air Forces, directed no action be taken until a study was conducted comparing the operations of the 99th Fighter Squadron with other comparable P-40 squadrons in the Mediterranean Theater of Operations (MTO).[31]

This study was completed on March 30, 1944 and the 99th Fighter Squadron was vindicated. The first sentence of the report stated,

> An examination of the record of the 99th Fighter Squadron reveals no significant general differences between this squadron and the balance of the P-40 squadrons in the Mediterranean Theatre Operations.[32]

The racially motivated memorandums of Col. Momyer and Gen. House, which nearly ruined the reputation of the 99th Fighter Squadron and almost ended any future opportunities for African-American military aviators to serve in combat, were quashed. Forever a positive person, Davis said,

> The report had a secondary effect. It sent us to the Fifteenth Air Force, and took us out of the nasty, dirty close air support business, and put us into sort of glamour business, escorting bombers[33]

That would come later. At present Lt. Col. Davis needed to focus his leadership skills and recent air combat experiences on preparing an untested fighter group and its three new fighter squadrons for war. ∎

Chapter Ten
1st Lt. James R. Polkinghorne Jr. Goes to War

Mechanics from the 332nd Fighter Group perform engine maintenance on a P-40 *Warhawk* at Selfridge Army Air Field in 1943.

332nd Fighter Group Returns to Selfridge Army Air Field

While the 99th Fighter Squadron was fighting over the islands of Pantelleria, Lampedusa and Sicily the 332nd Fighter Group and its three squadrons continued their pre-deployment training at Oscoda Army Air Field, Michigan. Yet a tremendous influx of officer and personnel into Oscoda soon overwhelmed that facility's ability to accommodate everyone.

So in July, 1943 the 332nd Fighter Group began to process of gradually moving squadrons back to Selfridge Army Air Field, although individual pilots and squadron detachments continued to shuffle back and forth between Selfridge Army Air Field and Oscoda Army Air Field for various gunnery and bombing training qualifications. The 100th Fighter Squadron and the 301st Fighter Squadron returned to Selfridge Army Air Field, leaving behind only the 302nd Fighter Squadron which was in the process of being fully manned.[1]

But the unceasing flow of new pilots from Tuskegee Army Air Field and enlisted men from various technical schools continued non-stop into Selfridge Army Air Field. Soon there were so many surplus officers and enlisted men aboard the station that a fourth squadron, the 332nd Provisional Squadron, was established by necessity to account for and supervise these men until they could be reassigned to the 332nd Fighter Group's three fighter squadrons or the 99th Fighter Squadron serving overseas.[2] The U.S. Army

332nd Fighter Group mechanics at Selfridge AAF have removed the Allison engine from this P-39 *Airacobra*, providing an excellent illustration of its placement behind the pilot.

Air Force's segregationist policies and delays in transferring the 332nd Fighter Group overseas had created a personnel bottleneck at one of only three airfields in the country available to station black airmen.

A critical pre-deployment milestone was achieved on July 23, 1943 when the 332nd Fighter Group and its three squadrons were relieved from assignment to the Third Air Force, which was responsible for initial training, and transferred to the First Air Force, which was responsible for operational training in preparation for overseas combat deployments.[3]

The 332nd Fighter Group was slowly being molded into a fighting team,

> Under the clear blue Michigan skies, the personnel of the 332nd FGp toiled on with fiendish desire to accomplish the task before them. To have followed the metamorphism of the unit during this period, one could not help but observe the growing pride that was gradually being instilled in every individual. It was heartening to see this intangible and sel-dom discussed subject, squadron pride, develop among men from all walks of life with all sorts of pre-formed ideas and from every state in the union.[4]

332nd Fighter Group historians continued to wax eloquent in their daily reports about the training grind, one observing in the fall of 1943,

> The wind changed from a still to a semi-brisk pace, evening began to shorten her pleasant and much-enjoyed stay and night slowly pulled her curtain of darkness at an earlier hour.

The leaves began to fall lazily to the ground and the grass changed its color from a rich to a pale green.

To the average American youth it was "back to school" with just enough time left to lay aside his baseball equipment, hang up his tennis rackets, store away his fish pole, change from summer sport to fall and winter sport clothes and help usher in the current season of the great American sport Football.

But to the 332nd Fighter Gp it was "Step-up" time in order to meet the demands of a bigger and more important pro-gram. New pilots pour in from Tuskegee, more planes were brought in and the mechanics worked long strenuous hours in order to meet the demands of maintenance, and to the pilots it was Fly - Fly - Fly.

If you happened to be near the operations office, you could not but overhear a conversation such as this: 'Lt have you checked the bulletin board? Lt you will have class today. Lt you are behind in your link time, you need more cockpit time, you are expected to attend a movie for pilots today and to-night Lt you are scheduled for night classes. Just a minute Lt, to-morrow you will fly. Fly - Fly - Fly. [5]

Introduction to the Bell P-39 *Airacobra*

It was at Selfridge Army Airfield and Oscoda Army Air Field in the fall of 1943 that the squadrons were first introduced to the Bell P-39 *Airacobra*. Training in the P-39 *Airacobra* came as a

The differences are apparent between the P-40 *Warhawk* (left) and the P-39 *Airacobra*. The 99th Fighter Squadron flew the P-40 *Warhawk* in their first combat missions in Africa while the 100th, 301st and 302nd Fighter Squadrons flew the P-39 *Airacobra* upon their arrival in Italy.

surprise to the 332nd Fighter Group pilots and turned out to be a shadowing of missions to be assigned once they were overseas.

The first Tuskegee Airman to fly a P-39 was, surprisingly, an aviation cadet, Ed Gleed, back in Tuskegee,

> We had just finished the fourth week (of advanced training) when I got called out of class. A lieutenant said, 'Cadet Gleed, you're supposed to read up on the P-400.' 'P-400! I never heard of it!' It turned out to be the P-39 *Airacobra*. He said, 'They're going to bring three here, and you've been elected to fly one.' 'What?' 'Yeah, they're going to have a cadet and an instructor fly them.'[6,7]

Training was nothing more than a cockpit familiarization brief, and although he admitted to being terribly frightened, Gleed managed to get the P-39 *Airacobra* airborne and even have some fun with some mild aerobatics. The approach to landing was a different story,

> It wasn't until the third pass, after I'd settled my nerves, that I realized I was stalling that thing, holding the nose too high. This time I came round and made a smooth landing of it. Next the white instructor went up. He held the nose way back when he landed, dragged his tail and damaged it. The guys said, 'No way you're going to wash out after this.' But I damn near washed me out.[8]

Gleed went on to graduate first in his class at Tuskegee Army Air Field, and at Selfridge Army Air Field he was amply rewarded for his single flight in a P-39,

At first we were flying P-40s, then they decided to give us P-39s. I'm the only guy who had flown one, so one day in June 1943 I found myself being told I was now the squadron commander of the 302nd as a second lieutenant.[9]

To ease the transition, the Bell Aircraft Corporation formed an "*Airacobra* College" at Selfridge Army Air Field, staffed by civilian specialists who provided around-the-clock training to pilots and ground crews.[10] The aircraft was greeted with excitement, and an analysis of assigned airplane serial numbers indicates they were relatively new, perhaps even fresh off the production line, P-39Q-10-BE's.

Combat training by its very nature is inherently dangerous, and P-40 *Warhawk* and P-39 *Airacobra* accidents were all too common at Selfridge Army Air Field and Oscoda Army Air Field with several pilots killed and others permanently removed from flying duties due to unsatisfactory performance.

One possibly fatal accident, however, was avoided by quick thinking on the part of the young pilot,

> 2nd Lt Spurgeon N. Ellington, 100th F Sq received top honors for his daring exploit, while flying his P-39 *Airacobra,* he became lost from his formation and descended through an overcast to find a well-traveled four-lane highway below. He had used his reserve tank and since he couldn't get his bearing he decided to make a forced landing. Circling several times to find a break in the traffic, Lt Ellington made a perfect landing on the highway and taxied the *Airacobra* up to a filling station.[11]

Members of the 100th Fighter Squadron toured Bell Aircraft Corporation's P-39 *Airacobra* production plant in Buffalo, New York.

Davis Assumes Command of the 332nd Fighter Group

Lt. Col Davis reported to the at Selfridge Army Air Field on October 4, 1943 and on October 7, 1943 assumed command of the 332nd Fighter Group, becoming the first African-American to command a fighter group in the history of the U.S. Army aviation.[12]

Davis was surprised to find the squadrons equipped with Bell P-39 *Airacobras*, rather than the P-40 *Warhawks* he had flown in combat with the 99th Fighter Squadron. He described the P-39 *Airacobra* as a,

> Beautiful, small-looking fighter-bomber with a tight, crowded cockpit, especially tight when it was flown by a six-footer. My head rubbed against the canopy, and I had to keep my back bowed. Although the Russians had used the P-39 successfully on the eastern front and it was doing well in the war in the Pacific, it could not fly as high as the FW-190s and Me-109s we were likely to encounter in Europe...

> I actually would have preferred another airplane, but because the P-39 had already been chosen for the unit, I

declared it to be the best airplane we could possibly have and belittled all criticism of it, such as its rumored tendency to tumble. This rumor arose from the fact that the engine sat behind the pilot in the center of the aircraft, and its nose was not as heavily weighted as those of most other planes.

> After my first flights in the P-39, I flew up to our gunnery camp at Oscoda, where I flew the strafing, dive-bombing, and skip-bombing maneuvers I supposed would be our bread and butter in Europe. [13]

Davis' task was to prepare the 332nd Fighter Group for combat. He was concerned,

> It was a fighter group in name only. Most of its pilots were recent flying school graduates, and they had not flown together enough to identify themselves as members of a team. The enlisted men in the three squadrons, which had gradually grown to authorized strength at Oscoda, hardly knew each other. Gradually the new arrivals from technical schools were absorbed into the squadrons, and the pilots began to fly together as well-organized teams. [14]

332nd Fighter Group's
Deployment Warning Order

On October 19, 1943 the 332nd Fighter Group finally received orders to begin preparations for movement to a port of embarkation in anticipation of orders to a combat zone.[15]

Officers and Enlisted Men were constantly seen on the firing range blazing away at the distant targets. There was a grimace now as they went about their duties because the time for actual combat was close at hand. Men could be seen huddled in small groups discussing the possibility of their squadron seeing action over New Britain, the Burma Road, the rugged mountains of Italy or across the Straits of Dover.[16]

The final phases of bombing and gunnery training were completed for each squadron and on November 5, 1943, despite snow and freezing temperature, Polkinghorne's 301st Fighter Squadron was ordered to Oscoda Army Air Field for ten days to complete their final phase of bombing and gunnery training. Once complete, the Bomb and Gunnery and Detachment at Oscoda Army Air Field was officially closed.[17]

All military organizations have their rumor mills and grapevines, deemed "Scuttlebutt " in the U.S. Navy and "Spratmo" in the U.S. Army Air Forces.

Rumors! Rumors! Rumors! Leave it to the G.I. of the 332nd Fighter Group. They have a system of gathering information that is unparalleled with any in the states. If critical analysis were rendered there is little doubt that it would far outshadow the system that once gave aid to General Channault {sic} and his flying tigers. The G.I. of the Group have a terrific communique system called "Spratmo" which can be considered as a very reliable agency. The source from which their information is gathered will no doubt never be known but there is yet to be a case that "Spratmo" predicted that was wrong.[18]

The 332nd Fighter Group's training in the United States was nearly complete, and the men's interest turned to speculation into which combat zone they might be ordered,

Morale was exceptionally high because every man, Sq Comdr and Private, pilot and mechanic knew with his heart; theirs' was a good outfit, well trained and capable of meeting and defeating the enemy overseas, in Asia, Europe, or the South Pacific.

As the moment for fame drew close, Spratmoe [sic] concerning their destination gained momentum. In the morning

"Airacobra College" Started At Selfridge Field; Base Using Bell Aircraft Plant Facilities

SELFRIDGE FIELD, Mich.— An "Airacobra college" now is in operation at Selfridge Field, as the Army Air Forces capitalize on teaching facilities of the Bell Aircraft Corporation.

Nearly a score of Airacobra specialists have arrived from the Bell plant in Niagara Falls, N. Y., to give a thorough schooling in P-39 Airacobras to pilots and ground crews of the 332nd Fighter Group. This is the all-Negro Fighter Group, already oriented to P-40's and P-47's. Its personnel now become the first members of their race to handle the Army's P-39 pursuit ship.

Twelve civilian instructors, the director of Bell's field training section, and two of Bell's service representatives arrived last week to assist Army teachers in the program arranged by Col. Robert R. Selway, jr. in cooperation with Arthur Fornoff and Kenneth Frey of the Bell Service Department. Also concurring in the arrangements was Col. A. R. DeBolt of the First Fighter Command, Mitchel Field, N. Y.

mock-ups or actual working units of such structures as the landing gear, the machine guns, the instruments and other electrical units. Built on wheels, the mock-ups are rolled out in front of a class and put into operation. Students then see just what happens when a switch is turned on in the cockpit. Classrooms have sprung up in nearly every available place. A combination hangar - gymnasium, lined with bleacher seats, was made into several classrooms. Each Bell Corporation instructor stands on the basketball court with his particular mock-up directly in front of each group.

Overseas Instructors Teach

Other classes are conducted in corners of various hangars and on the concrete apron where P-39's are prepared for flight. Here, mechanics surround instructors or actually work on Airacobras, putting to practical use knowledge gained in classes. Pilots are given special lectures about flight characteristics and operation of the P-39. They are told how the plane

In October 1943 Bell Aircraft Corporation provided specialized mechanic and pilot training on the P-39 *Airacobra* at Selfridge Army Air Field.

it was New Guinea, at noon Salerno and by bedtime they were going to the Burma Road.

Actually nobody knew where they were going, but there was a singularity of purpose; wherever they landed their best would go towards making the world safe for democracy. [19]

The men were granted leave during Thanksgiving as they would be shipped overseas before the Christmas holidays.

Old Man Winter was beginning to make himself evident with occasional snow flurries and cold gusts of penetrating winds; Officers and EM were taking long awaited leaves and furloughs to pay a last visit to their loves ones and homage to their friends. Men looked forward to Thanksgiving with hopeful hearts not for the cherished turkey but prayerfully that this would be the last Thanksgiving of a horrible war.[20]

P-39 *Airacobra's* on the line at Selfridge Army Air Field in 1943.

Polkinghorne most likely traveled home to Pensacola during this period, given how close he was to his family. Sadly, this would be the last time that his mother, father, and five sisters would see him alive.

Polkinghorne Promoted to 1st Lieutenant

On November 27, 1943 Polkinghorne was promoted to 1st Lt., a little over nine months since he had been commissioned a 2nd Lt. at Tuskegee Army Air Field.[21]

As a 1st Lt. his yearly base pay increased to $2,000, which was increased by 50% for serving as a rated pilot. He also received a subsistence allowance of $21 a month as a bachelor and a monthly rental allowance of $60. Therefore, his total yearly salary of $3,972 was equivalent to about $56,241 in 2017 inflation-adjusted dollars. Also, his base pay was further increased by 10% while serving in a foreign country, equivalent to an additional $4,248 per year in 2017 dollars.

Polkinghorne often shared his well-earned wealth with his family,

> Kindness and generosity was a trait that Polkinghorne displayed throughout his short life. He was a prolific letter writer, writing mostly to his parents and sisters. His letters usually conveyed warm feelings for his family and concern that his parents were receiving the money and packages he routinely sent home.[22]

332nd Fighter Group Sets Sail

In early December 1943 the 332nd Fighter Group and its three assigned squadrons successfully completed their final pre-deployment operational training requirements and inspections by higher headquarters. All flying was secured, and the squadrons packed up their organizational equipment and materials for shipment overseas. Their exhausted P-40 *Warhawks* and P-30 *Aircobras* were left behind, hopefully, to be replaced by newer front-line fighters like the P-47 *Thunderbolt*.

Movement orders were received, and the destination of the 332nd Fighter Group was now confirmed: Italy. Personnel were to move by rail from Selfridge Army Air Field to arrive at Camp Patrick Henry, Virginia, on Christmas Eve, December 24, 1943. [23]

Before departing, separate farewell parties were held for all of the officers, enlisted men, family and friends assigned to the 332nd Fighter Group. One wonders if Emeldia Zaragoza and Neomi Polkinghorne traveled to Michigan to say one last goodbye to James,

> On the night of 20 December 1943, the Officers of the Group bid farewell to the citizens of Detroit, wives and sweethearts and their happy playground, 'The Vally' [sic] by celebrating their last farewell Party at the beautiful Labor Temple. This too, was the last night of freedom before departure of the 332nd Fighter Group for overseas duty. This Party will be well remembered by all who attended on the evening of the 20th, Sweethearts and wives looking their best in their most alluring semi-formal outfits and a glance around the ballroom revealed a spectrum of colors. Amid gaiety and laughter, the eye caught couples with a gloomy and remorseful look, revealing the finality of the affair and the parting of an amiable friendship.[24]

In sub-zero temperatures and with the Selfridge Army Air Field band "providing lively tunes to keep everyone in good spirit," the 332nd Fighter Group headquarters staff and the 100th Fighter Squadron boarded the first of two trains departing Selfridge Army Air Field bound for Camp Patrick Henry, their staging area before proceeding to Hampton Roads, Virginia, their port of embarkation for overseas transport to Italy.[25] Lt. Col. Davis was troop commander of this train, and they departed at 1945 on the evening of December 23, 1943, arriving at Camp Patrick Henry as scheduled at 1145 on December 24, 1943.

A second train commanded by Capt. Charles H. DeBow carrying Polkinghorne's 301st Fighter Squadron and the 302nd Fighter Squadron arrived at Camp Patrick Henry on December 25, 1943, "a pretty gloomy Christmas for most of the men."[26] Capt. DeBow trained alongside Lt. Col. Davis in Class 42-C, the first graduating class at Tuskegee Army Air Field, and served under his command overseas, one of many former 99th Fighter Squadron pilots rotated back to the United States who were willing to return to combat with the 332nd Fighter Group.[27]

For operations security (OPSEC) reasons, the men were restricted to Camp Patrick Henry, a 1,700-acre complex situated in a forest in Newport News, Virginia. The men received orientation training, including lectures on mail censorship policies, and practiced abandon ship drills. Telephone calls were permitted although the wait times at the telephone exchange booths were two to six hours with no head of line privileges granted to officers.[28]

On January 1, 1944 a New Year dawned and the 332nd Fighter Group historian captured the mood of the men,

> Deep within the heart of each individual there was one thought, first and foremost which was so vividly expressed on their faces that even a child could readily understand. It was an aching anticipation of what awaited them in the near future. Will they as a combat group be given an opportunity to prove their capabilities? Or will their efforts be stymied by mal [sic] assignments to secondary roles. Whatever the task may be, no matter how difficult, there is but one paramount objective which is an inherent quality imbued in the minds of the 332nd F Gp - 'Do that which is most difficult now, the impossible will take a little time.'[29]

On January 3, 1944 the men were ordered to be prepared to march before dawn with full field packs from the Camp Patrick Henry staging area to a nearby train depot. An officer recorded the move,

> It may be a meteorological phenomena or just coincidence but with each move that I have witnessed for the 332nd, there has always been a forerunner, rain, rain, and more rain. At approximately 0445, 3 January 1944, the 332nd Fighter Group at the Rendezvous Point amid an intermittent sprinkle of raindrops which in a very short while developed into an incessant downpour of rain which lasted until, well to be exact all day.
>
> After two and one half (2 1/2) hours of standing with full field pack, duffle bag and all its accessories, the Group finally moved off soaked from head to foot with not a dry

Rank	Insignia	Yearly Pay	Rent Allowance (Mo.) with dependents	single
General	✯✯✯✯✯	$8,000	$120	$105
Lt. General	✯✯✯	8,000	120	105
Maj. General	✯✯	8,000	120	105
Brig. General	✯	6,000	120	105
Colonel		4,000	120	105
Lt. Colonel	(Silver)	3,500	120	105
Major	(Gold)	3,000	105	90
Captain		2,400	90	75
1st Lieutenant	(Silver)	2,000	75	60
2nd Lieutenant	(Gold)	1,800	60	45
Warrant Officer (chief)	(Brown)	2,100	75	60
Warrant Officer (j.g.)	(Brown)	1,800	60	45
Flight Officer	(Blue)	1,800	60	45

54 OFFICIAL AAF GUIDE

In the above, all officers with dependents receive $42 per month (30 day period) subsistence allowance; single officers, $21. (Exception: Lt. Col. and Maj., married, receive $63.)

FLYING PAY—Flying officers and enlisted men receive an increase of 50% of their base pay when by orders of competent authority they are required to participate regularly and frequently in aerial flights and when as a result of orders they do participate in such flights. Non-flying officers receive flying pay at the rate of $60 per month when they participate in regular and frequent aerial flights ordered by competent authority.

Official pay chart for U.S. Army Air Forces officers in effect when Polkinghorne was promoted to 1st Lt. in 1943. His annual salary in 2018 inflation-adjusted dollars was about $56,241, which is surprisingly equivalent to the pay today of an active duty officer of that same rank.

stitch of clothing anywhere. A brief ride on the "Chattanooga Train" ended with the Group at docks of Hampton Roads, Va. An arousing welcome was accorded the men by the Port Band playing the Air Corps song and other hot tunes. In a short while all personnel was aboard the ferry boat "Mohawk" on their way to those dear old 'Liberty Ships' lying across the bay.[30]

Polkinghorne's 301st Fighter Squadron was assigned to the Liberty ship SS *Clark Mills*, an EC2-S-C1 class transport built in Mobile, Alabama in 1942 with a cruising speed of about 11 knots.[31] On January 3, 1944, the convoy departed Hampton Roads for Italy,

The first days out, the sea was fairly rough, and most of our

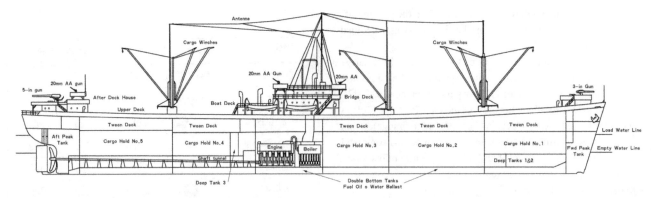

Line drawing of a typical mass-produced U.S. Liberty ship used to transport personnel and war materials overseas. More than 2,700 were built during World War II with an average construction time of 42 days.

men were confined to their bunks because of certain green pallor about their gills. After those first few days, though, the sea calmed down, and we were able to enjoy fairly decent weather for the remainder of our voyage.

When we were about seventy (70) miles off the African coast we got our first and only 'sub' scare. Destroyer Escort vessels began dodging in and out of the convoy dropping depth charges, indiscriminately, or, at least, it seemed so to us. We never did see any evidence of a sub, but anyway it did show us how fast our men could move in an emergency.[32]

Sgt. Stewart Gandy, an armorer with the 302nd Fighter Squadron, recalled his time aboard ship in a diary, giving the reader an idea of the conditions Polkinghorne endured during a winter trans-Atlantic crossing,

January 3, 1944
We boarded a small ship for a short trip to the one we were going over in. Saw it at last. On deck we went down the hole (that's right) and they said take a bed. (Bed my ass) Bunks stacked five high. I grab the top one and fell out my first night aboard ship. "Hard Living" Roger and out.

January 4, 1944
Most of the day was spent in Port. Sure had a rough night. Those bunks don't come with any mattresses. Well all day we did nothing but put our stuff away, find the chow line and talked about where we were going. About 2 o'clock the tugs hooked on and we moved out into open water and heard our engines for the first time. We took one last look at the US, threw a kiss and went below.

January 5, 1944
Here we go. The old ship she reeled, the old ship she rocked

and the fish began to eat at regular intervals from guys on the rails who were seasick. I am not sick yet but that sure is hard living. The sea sure is rough.

January 6 to 19, 1944
The sea is still rough and guys are vomiting everywhere. Set the bed on the floor but I'm still holding my own. I was first in the chow line, first to bed and first on deck when we had a drill. We got our position in the convoy and doing

Allied forces invaded the Italian mainland on September 3, 1943 with Lt. Gen Mark Clark's Fifth Army driving up the eastern side of the Italian peninsula and Gen. Bernard Montgomery's Eighth Army moving up the western side. Field Marshal Albert Kesselring commanded all German forces in Italy.

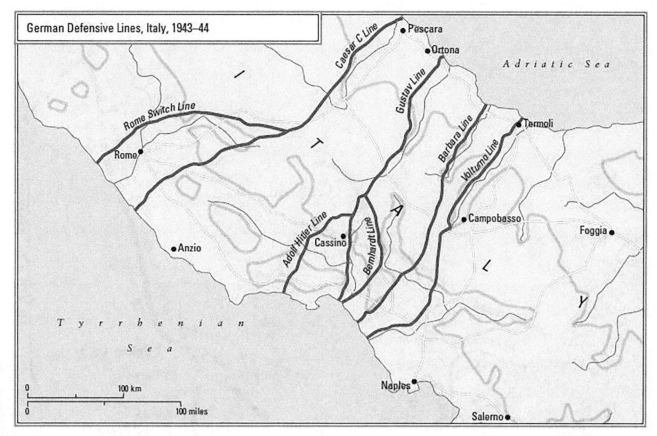

German Field Marshal Kesselring's strategy to defend the Italian peninsula was to fall back into a series of fortified defensive lines that spanned the entire width of Italy. The most formidable was the Gustav Line anchored in the mountainous terrain behind the town of Cassino.

okay. Talk about time on your hands. I have never wanted something to do more in all my life. All day I walk the deck and look. What do I see more ships, sky and water....my kingdom for the sight of land.[33]

Tactical Situation Ashore: Italian Mainland Campaign

Stepping off from their victories in North Africa and Sicily, the Allies invaded the Italian mainland on September 3, 1943, driving northward to Rome on two fronts, one on each side of the Apennine Mountains.

On the western side of Italy's coastline along the Tyrrhenian Sea, Lt. Gen. Mark Clark's Fifth Army landed at Salerno and was tracking up the old Appian Way while on the eastern side Gen. Bernard Montgomery's British Eighth Army landed at Calabria and Taranto and was slowly moving up the Adriatic Cost.

Meanwhile, Benito Mussolini had been ousted from power and replaced by Gen. Pietro Badoglioa, who secretly negotiated an armistice with the Allies that was signed on September 3, 1943 and announced on September 8, 1943. Thus, during on mainland Italy, the Germans, not the Italians, were the enemy fought by Allied forces.

Rather than demoralize the Germans, the Italian surrender served to stiffen their resolve to defend Italy and reinforcements were rushed in to halt the Allied advance and protect Rome. Luftwaffe aviator Field Marshal Albert Kesselring was placed in sole command of German forces in Italy and his strategy to defend the Italian peninsula was to slow the Allied attack by falling back into a series of fortified defensive lines.

The most formidable reinforced position was named the Gustav Line, and it spanned the width of Italy at its narrowest point, running from the Tyrrhenian coast, over the Apennines Mountains, and to the Adriatic Coast.

One of the key strong points in the western half of the Gustav Line was the town of Cassino, located about 60 miles north of Naples and 90 miles south of Rome. Surrounded by mountainous terrain, its steep peaks provided the German defenders clear

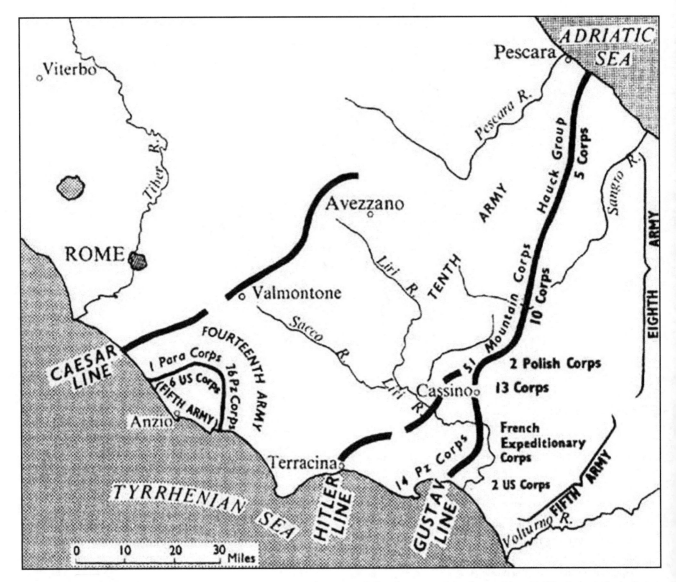

The Anzio beachhead was approximately 40 miles southeast of Rome and 60 miles west of the Gustav Line. Polkinghorne's final mission was in the vicinity of the town of Terracina near the Hitler Line.

observations of Allied troop movements while thousands of well-defiladed artillery pieces, tanks, antiaircraft guns, turreted machine-gun emplacements, pillboxes, bunkers, anti-tank ditches, minefields, and barbwire emplacements made the area nearly impregnable. Allied forces alone suffered more than 125,000 battle casualties between September 1943 and June 1944 before successfully breaking through these fortifications and heading towards Rome.[34] German losses during the battle and subsequent retreat were much more massive and deemed incalculable by Fifth Army Commander Lt. Gen. Clark, who suggested that they could only be measured by the nearly 16,000 prisoners-of-war captured.[35]

Naples was captured on October 1, 1943 but it was not until December 1943 that the Allied assault forces reached the Gustav

Line, where fierce resistance by the Germans, rugged terrain, and adverse weather conditions combined to stall the Allied ground campaign.

During the bitter winter months, the Italian campaign deteriorated into a stalemate in which the two separate Allied armies, the American Fifth Army on the west coast and the British Eighth Army on the east coast, were unable to penetrate the well-entrenched German lines.

Movements of the 99th Fighter Squadron

Meanwhile, the 99th Fighter Squadron, operating independently of the 332nd Fighter Group, continued to leapfrog across Italy, relocating to freshly captured or newly constructed airfields as necessary to provide air cover and close air support for advancing Allied ground troops.

The squadron had been operating on the Italian mainland since transferring from Sicily in October 1943. Attached to the 79th Fighter Group and flying from airfields on the Adriatic Coast, the squadron supported the British Eighth Army advance on the eastern coast of Italy and developed close ties with the group. On January 16, 1944 the 99th Fighter Squadron moved to Capodichino airfield three miles northeast of Naples to support the Anzio landing and beachhead.

Anzio

In an attempt to break the deadlock and outflank the Germans, a surprise amphibious landing by Fifth Army forces was made on January 22, 1944 at Anzio, about 60 miles behind the Gustav Line. Although initially delayed in their reaction, the Luftwaffe subsequently exploded violently against the Anzio beachhead with fighters and bombers.

The 99th Fighter Squadron had been flying in combat operations since June 1943 with only one confirmed air victory to show for their efforts.[36] That total changed dramatically while providing overhead protection to the Anzio landing force. Flying from Capodichino airfield near Naples, the 99th Fighter Squadron distinguished itself by shooting down 13 German FW-190's over the Anzio beachhead in a two-day period between January 27 and January 28, 1944.

Described in one newspaper article as the "black pearl of the Allied air forces in Italy," these air victories instantly silenced any critics of the squadron's combat efficiency and drew high praise from Gen. Arnold.[37][38] In stark contrast to their critical article *Experiment Proved?* published five months earlier, *Time* magazine published a new article titled *Sweet Victories* that heralded the 99th Fighter Squadron's achievements defending Anzio,

> On the operations-tent bulletin board at a U.S. advanced fighter base in Italy good news was pinned up last week: an official commendation by Army Air Forces' Chief "Hap" Arnold. Reason for the commendation: the squadron had shot down eight German aircraft in one day, four in another. Score for three days' missions had totaled twelve kills, two probable's, four damaged.
>
> Any outfit would have been proud of the record. These victories stamped the final seal of combat excellence on one of the most controversial outfits in the Army, the all-Negro 99th Fighter Squadron.
>
> Its pilots had survived disappointments, discouragements

BAGS NO. 14

Credit for the 14th Nazi plane destroyed over Italy by the 99th Fighter Squadron went to 2nd Lt. Elwood T. Driver, of Trenton, N. J. Lieutenant Driver shot down the German plane over the Anzio beachhead below Rome on February 4.

The 99th Fighter Squadron's performance over the Anzio beachhead drew high praise from none other than Gen. Arnold. The 332nd Fighter Group was still aboard ship making their way to Italy when they received word of the squadron's victories.

Polkinghorne and his squadronmates endured a nearly15-hour journey from their arrival port of Taranto to Montecorvino, their assigned airfield near the town of Salerno. They traveled in open trucks, unprotected against driving rain, sleet, and snow.

and months of routine operations in which they did not even sight an enemy. They had finally got their big chance flying cover for the Allies' Nettuno beachhead, and they knew what to do with it...The Air Corps regards its experiment as proven.[39]

While the Anzio landing may have initially taken the Germans by surprise, the Allied landing force was unable to break out of the beachhead and remained surrounded by the Germans throughout the remaining winter.

332nd Fighter Group and Polkinghorne Arrive in Italy

In late January 1944, the convoy carrying the 332nd Fighter Group steamed through the Straits of Gibraltar,

> For security purposes no one was allowed upon deck but from the portholes of the ships' crew, one could see the Rocks' lion couchant silhouette against a star, with its' flanks sprinkled with pin points of light, a memorable sight which will find its' way into the memory of many.[40]

The convoy dispersed and the four ships of the 332nd Fighter Group arrived in Italy at different times between January 29 and February 3, 1944, disembarking at the ports of Bari, Naples, and Taranto.

Polkinghorne's ship arrived at the port of Taranto, one of the pilots noting,

> It was a terrible sight because of the bombings...rusting ships were overturned in the harbor. Most of the Italian structures were built out of stone and masonry, and they had

been bombed by the Americans first and then, of course, when the Allies took it, the Germans bombed the port too. As the ships pulled up on the dock, we saw these people, these human beings in ragged clothes, with babies. They were going around begging and looking into garbage cans for food. It was a very disturbing sight.[41]

The SS *Clark Mills,* whose namesake was a famous American sculptor, had safely delivered her precious cargo; a few months later she would be lost off of Bizerte, Tunisia after an aerial torpedo attack.

After 26 days at sea, the 44 officers and 258 enlisted men of Polkinghorne's 301st Fighter Squadron walked ashore on January 29, 1944. Sgt. Gandy recalled,

> Happy is a day in the sunshine. Dropped anchor last night, in port. 'How about that mess.' Up on deck we could see land, and it is beautiful from here. We packed in nothing flat. Wondering if I can walk on land again after so long on a rolling deck. At about 10 o'clock we set foot on land in Taranto, Italy. Sure felt good but not for long before bad news. We marched four miles with full pack to camp and dropped dead. I made it and don't ask me how, and found awaiting tents and rocky ground.[42]

Italian winter weather was not kind to the men, who slept on the ground in pup tents,

> Attempts were made to stabilize tents that almost folded to the sweeping wind and rain that visited during the night... complete changes from rain to snow developed on the hour. Since we were without over-shoes, it was impossible to keep feet dry.[43]

332nd Fighter Group Assigned to Montecorvino Airfield

The 332nd Fighter Group and its three squadrons were assigned to the Twelfth Air Force's 62nd Fighter Wing, under the command of Col. Robert S. Israel Jr. The squadrons were ordered to Montecorvino airfield near the city of Salerno, located about 90 miles south of the Gustav Line.

Montecorvino was a former Luftwaffe base that had been captured and heavily damaged during the Salerno invasion. The facility, once considered "one of the best airfields along the whole lower stretch of the Italian west coast," was cluttered with burned-out German tanks and about 40 wrecked German airplanes. [44,45] To the delight of no one, Montecorvino was also trapped in a cold Italian winter. Constant rain, wind, snow, fog, and low clouds limited visibility and hampered flight operations throughout the 332nd Fighter Group's stay there.

On February 7, 1944 Polkinghorne's 301st Fighter Squadron departed the Taranto staging area at 0730 by motor convoy for their new home, about 170 miles away. They arrived at Montecorvino at 2200 in the evening, pup-tents providing the men their first night's lodging until larger tents could be issued. [46]

Sgt. Gandy recalled the journey that the personnel of the 332nd Fighter Group, including Polkinghorne, made,

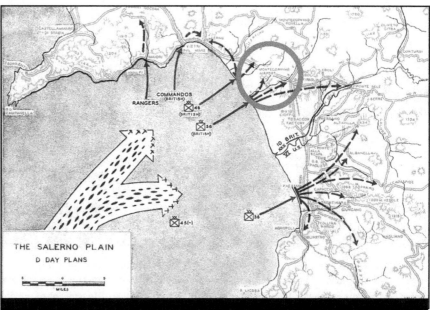

Montecorvino air base on the western coast of Italy was a former Luftwaffe field captured during the Salerno landings in September 1943.

> February 6, 1944
> Another one of my most unforgettable days. We packed our blankets, we loaded it on a truck...then we began the ride to end all rides. Paul Revere had a cliché. Our trucks didn't have tops on them and it started to snow about 30 minutes out. It got cold and we climbed. Never knew a man could climb so and get so cold. We climbed all day through rain, sleet, snow and a little sunshine, but it was beautiful country. After going as high as the air would permit we started down. Jack, we came down for a while. Finally reached our destination [Montecorvino] near Salerno. To top off a hectic day we had to pitch pup tents and eat cold C rations. Stole hay to sleep on.

> February 7th to 14th, 1944
> So after getting our pup tents up, we were told we would have to move. So we moved about a half-mile and pitched tents again...on the eighth we were given eight-man tents. It had been raining all night and mud was everywhere. So we pitched tents in the rain and mud...there was as much mud and water inside as out. The first night we slept on some boards we stole. The next night we didn't even have them. I slept with my feet in mud and water, my head on a duffel bag and my ass in my helmet. 'Hard Living' Stopped raining at last and we made beds out of trees and lie like men not pigs. Our guys are going to start flying.

> February 21 and 24th, 1944
> Today the 21st we move somewhat nearer to the airfield... same old story, muddy Italy. King mud as I called him.

Living conditions slowly improved as the men improved their facilities, eventually moving to permanent buildings that were enhanced when generators were procured to provide lighting. Davis recalled,

> When we first arrived in Italy we had lived in tents and were constantly fighting the mud, but by now we had set up headquarters in a not-too-unattractive building on the Montecorvino airfield. We had our own mess, a good enlisted men's club, and a good officers' club. I was personally comfortable. I had an electric light and a stove made out of a five-gallon gasoline can with a hole cut in it for draft and four or five bricks piled inside. Another can dripped gasoline from a petcock for fuel. I could put a basin of water on my stove and have a hot bath, and naturally the world looked a lot better when I was warm and clean. [47]

Rare ground-eye view of the field conditions at Montecorvino air base in Italy, showing several 332nd Fighter Group's P-39 *Airacobra's*, tents, and plenty of mud. Polkinghorne flew all his missions from this airfield.

Slowly, other amenities arrived, including mail service; religious services, an American Red Cross unit with coffee, doughnuts, and candy; a post exchange; fresh food from nearby villages; a movie theater; sporting equipment and events; a piano and ping pong tables; and even ice cream. Additionally, personnel received passes to visit Naples, and it is assumed to other nearby villages, cities or historical sites near their airfield.

At Montecorvino the 332nd Fighter Group replaced the 81st Fighter Group, which had been transferred to India. In a harbinger of what was to come, the 81st Fighter Group's three squadrons had been flying P-39 *Airacobras* on convoy escorts, harbor protection, fighter scrambles against unknown or enemy aircraft, and coastal patrols.

332nd Fighter Group Assigned Bell P-39 *Airacobra's*

Before coming ashore, Spratmo hinted that the 332nd Fighter Group's squadrons would be equipped with the Republic P-47 *Thunderbolt* or perhaps even the newer North American P-51 *Mustang.* Instead, to the disappointment of everyone, the aircraft they were assigned was the all too familiar Bell P-39 *Airacobra.*

How these aircraft were obtained could not be determined but based on an analysis of 332nd Fighter Group P-39 *Airacobra* accident aircraft serial numbers during this period, it appears that the squadrons were assigned a mix of older P-39 *Airacobra's* and brand-new P-39Q-20-BE models. It is possible that most, if not all of the older aircraft were left behind by the 81st Fighter Group. Records indicate that the 332nd Fighter Group received 75 brand-new P-39Qs in February 1944, one of the last U.S. Army Air Force units to receive the P-39 *Airacobra* as all fighter squadrons were slowly being re-equipped with the more capable Republic P-47 *Thunderbolts* or North American P-51 *Mustangs.*[48]

To replace the older airplanes and to offset attrition, the 301st Fighter Squadron alone received ten brand-new P-39Q models

on March 13, 1944.[49] On March 22, 1944 nine pilots boarded a B-25 and were flown to Sidi Amor, Tunisia to ferry back nine P-39 *Airacobras* of unknown model type to Montecorvino.[50]

When the 332nd Fighter Group did eventually transition to Republic P-47 *Thunderbolts* it is assumed that their P-39 *Airacobras* were declared surplus and transferred to Fifteenth Air Force storage at the Capodichino airfield. In turn, these airplanes were released to the Italian Co-Belligerent Air Force at the Campo Vesuvio airstrip.[51] The Italian Co-Belligerent Air Force was comprised of Italian squadrons aligned with the Allies after the armistice had been signed.

332nd Fighter Group Assigned Coastal Patrol Duties

In what many squadron members considered to be an intentional insult, instead of being assigned close air support missions in support of the assault on the Gustav line, the 332nd Fighter Group was assigned coastal patrol duties in the Cape Palermo, Gulf of Policastro, and Ponza Island area, mainly the Tyrrhenian Sea shoreline adjacent to the major port city of Naples and points south.

Coastal patrol was an unglamorous support role tasked with providing air security for Allied convoys. These men were fighter pilots; glory was to be gained through air-to-air combat, not by serving as a nursemaid. What made matters worse was visits by pilots of the 99th Fighter Squadron, including their Commanding Officer Maj. George Roberts, who regaled the 332nd Fighter Group with tales of their own adventures of aerial combat over North Africa, Sicily, and the Italian mainland.

Lt. Col. Davis was convinced that this assignment was a direct result of Col. Momyer's derogative memorandum that questioned the combat efficiency of the 99th Fighter Squadron (the report *Operations of the 99th Fighter Squadron Compared with Other P40 Squadrons in MTO* that exonerated the 99th Fighter Squadron

Oblique view of Montecorvino air base taken by an American reconnaissance airplane on June 13, 1944, showing the runway facing into mountain ranges. In the foreground is the shore of the Gulf of Salerno.

Slightly closer and higher view of Montecorvino air base taken by a US reconnaissance airplane on April 23, 1944.

332nd Fighter Group maintenance personnel repairing a P-39 *Airacobra* in the open at Montecorvino air base.

was not officially released until late March 1944).[52]

Davis was furious that his men had been assigned to these mundane duties.

> To assign the group to a noncombat role at a critical
> juncture in the war seemed a betrayal of everything we
> had been working for, and an intentional insult to me
> and my men. I expressed my feelings to no one, how-
> ever. I had to show to all concerned an
> attitude that what we were doing was vitally important
> to the theater mission, whether I believed it or not.[53]

Boring Missions and Bad Airplane

Despite Davis' brave face, his pilots didn't believe in their mission or their airplane. Various narratives abound on their views,

Pilot Charles McGee: We began operations on February 14, 1944, patrolling Naples Harbor to the Isle of Capri, and we also did coastal patrol. My first patrol was on February 28. We moved up to Capodichino on March 4, and did the rest of our tactical patrolling from there. The P-39Q was too slow and essentially a low-altitude aircraft, we flew at 10,000 to 15,000 feet, and by the time we reached even that altitude to intercept intruders, they were usually back in Germany. It was frustrating.[54]

Pilot Clarence Lester: A fighter pilot flying coastal patrol was like a brain surgeon being a physician at a Boy Scout camp: it was just about the most boring mission you could perform. And the P-39s were dogs if I ever saw one, rickety old things, just lousy airplanes. It had the engine behind the pilot and a shaft with the cannon ran between your legs and shot out through the propeller spinner. It was good-looking, it had doors on it like an automobile, but it had very funny flying characteristics because the center of gravity was off because of the engine placement. It was lousy for air-to-air combat but pretty good for ground support because of its heavy shielding underneath. I didn't mind the airplane too much, because I could fly it. But there were a lot of pilots who were scared to death of it.[55]

Pilot Woodrow Crockett: [The P-39] was a little faster than the P-40, but it couldn't turn. You could change your heading, but you couldn't change your direction, it just mushed. And I didn't like running interference for a big engine behind me. If you were tall you had to put the seat down all the way to the bottom. I'm five-foot-eleven, almost the limit, so I had to press my head down to get inside the door. There is no P-39 Pilots' Association today, apparently no one thought very much of it.[56]

Pilot Harry Sheppard: We got the P-39s back from Russia and England, some of the old Lend-Lease planes we had sent them. They very gleefully give them back to us when we got to Italy. I never did trust it. It had very poor aerodynamic characteristics in combat situations; it didn't like sudden changes in altitude or direction. In a real tight turn where you're pulling streamers off your wing, it had a nasty habit of snapping into a spin, which was quite exhilarating.[57]

Pilot Warren Sparks: The *Airacobra* had no range, bad stall characteristics, would flat spin and snap out of high G situations. However, it was not as bad as depicted by the guys back home...the P-39 fit in very well to our air-to-air ground combat role. The cannon would really raise havoc with the barges and ships we attacked. The four .50s and the 37mm would devastate everything that happened to get in the way. It served me well and brought me home consistently."[58]

Flying During the Italian Winter

Additionally, flying the P-39 *Airacobra* during a cold Italian winter was not a pleasurable experience as one pilot remembered,

Under winter conditions the P-39 was a breezy airplane, there being no engine in the front to heat the air that filtered into the cockpit. The situation was not aided by the fact that the aircraft heaters had been disabled; they operated from the fuel system and were rumored to thin the mixture and damage the engine. Numerous ingenious methods were employed to solve the problem. Everything that could be taped over, was taped over, including the left-hand door. (The P-39 was almost unique in being a 'right-hand' type, with hand holds on the starboard side.) {One officer} "acquired" unused canvas summer tent caps and covered the gun ports in the cowl by placing the canvas under the cover plate and trimming the excess; these could be shot though if necessary. Many pilots stuffed newspaper into the legs of their flying suits for insulation.[59]

Polkinghorne's 301st Fighter Squadron Suffers First Pilot Loss

Despite the dull monotony of their assignment, the pilots of the 332nd Fighter Group dutifully manned their P-39 *Airacobras* and provided air cover for Allied convoys and harbor patrols over the Gulf of Naples.[60] There was some benefit to these flights as this was the first time most of the pilots in the 332nd Fighter Group had been airborne in over two months as flight operations had been secured in early December to prepare for overseas movement.

Polkinghorne's 301st Fighter Squadron flew their first combat patrol, a convoy protection flight, on February 15, 1944. Regardless of their dull and routine nature, there were always inherent dangers embedded in these overwater missions, flown all too often in poor weather conditions. On February 23, 1944 Polkinghorne's 301st Fighter Squadron lost their first pilot overseas,

Four of our pilots were up on a Training Mission around

Avellino when the weather closed in on them. One of them, Lt. U.S. Taylor, was forced to bail out in the sea. Luckily, he was picked up by a motor launch, after staying in the water for a little less than an hour, and taken to a hospital where he was treated for shock and exposure.

Another, Lt Langston, had quite a bit of difficulty with his plane, going into spin after spin. Finally he decided to jump but just when he was about to leave the plane, he spotted the coast line through the soup, righted his plane, and landed at Pompeii, sans door.

The third man, Lt Wiggins, managed to get back to the base without a mishap.

The fourth man, Lt Harry Daniels, was lost soon after they got into bad weather, and no trace of either he or his plane has been found since. Lt Daniels was a very likable fellow, and the entire Squadron grieved his loss.[61]

Less than two weeks later, Polkinghorne's 301st Fighter Squadron lost a second pilot when Lt. Wayne V. Liggins crashed during a training mission and was killed. The squadron logbook noted that, "his death, along with the many accidents that had been occurring within the squadron, hit both the men and the Officers pretty hard."[62]

Several other 332nd Fighter Group pilots were also killed in the following months not due to enemy action, but because of engine failures and in-flight fires in their P-39 *Airacobras*.

100th and 302nd Fighter Squadrons Depart Montecorvino

The 332nd Fighter Group's stay at Montecorvino was not very long. Following the "cardinal principle that if optimum tactical results are to be obtained air bases must be as close as possible to the battle lines," the group was ordered to conduct a phased transfer 60 miles northwest to Capodichino airfield near Naples, where the 99th Fighter Squadron was presently located. [63]

The 100th Fighter Squadron departed first, leaving Montecorvino on February 21, 1944 for Capodichino. A few days later a twin-engine, two-pilot, three-passenger UC-78 *Bobcat* (nicknamed *"Cessina"* by the pilots) was assigned to the 332nd Fighter Group so personnel could fly between Montecorvino and Capodichino to coordinate logistics.

The 302nd Fighter Squadron departed on March 6, 1944 leaving behind at Montecorvino only the 332nd Fighter Group headquarters staff and Polkinghorne's 301st Fighter Squadron, who were still awaiting their official transfer orders. Of interest, during March 1944 Polkinghorne's 301st Fighter Squadron flew 130 combat sorties.

The first German combat aircraft that pilots of the 332nd Fighter Group came into contact with was the Junkers Ju-88, a twin-engined, multirole aircraft used primarily in a reconnaissance role during the Italian campaign. The Ju-88's better performance let it easily outrun pursuing P-39 *Airacobra*'s.

Polkinghorne's P-39 *Airacobra* Accident

On March 7, 1944 Polkinghorne was involved in a P-39 *Airacobra* accident. According to his official statement,

> I certify that while on a scheduled patrol mission on March 7, 1944 in P-39M AC#42-4572, the motor cut out on takeoff. I dropped the belly tank and after switching tanks was making preparations to make a forced landing when the motor caught again. The motor continued to cough intermittently, I checked the instrument reading and they checked normal. I continued on the mission.
>
> While carrying out the mission the engine began to cough again, I called the controller and notified him that my fuel was getting low and was told to return to the field. When I got on my downwind leg the motor began to cough rapidly and motor quit on crosswind leg. I made a normal landing and rolled as far down the runway; as far as possible.
>
> I attempted to start the motor up to taxi off runway and smelled smoke; I glanced at engine and flame was shooting out. I left plane after Fire Fighting Equipment arrived; I returned to plane and checked switches.[64]

The accident investigation committee, ever looking to place blame, did so and split the difference equally between man and machine. They faulted Polkinghorne on his attempt to restart the engine and clear the runway after his emergency landing, which any combat pilot would have done out of consideration for other airplanes seeking to land,

> It is the decision of the Aircraft Accident Committee that the accident was caused by 50% pilot error.

Questioning the line chief revealed that the pilot over primed the hot engine on starting; the fire started in the exhaust stacks and then on through to the carburetor. In view of the fact that there was an outstanding malfunctioning of the fuel system or carburetor this constitutes the other 50% of the cause. If the entire fuel system had functioned properly the accident would not have happened. An inspection of the engine after the fire could not reveal the cause of the intermittent coughing and finally the cutting out of the engine.[65]

The accident report documented that Polkinghorne had 143 hours of P-39 *Airacobra* flight time and 616.8 total flight hours. What it did not record was the courage of a young aviator who continued on his assigned mission despite a suspect engine.

Operation STRANGLE

Allied intelligence estimated that seven German divisions were surrounding the Anzio beachhead and nine German divisions holding the Gustav Line.[66] With Allied ground forces unable to penetrate the Gustav line and the Anzio landing forces pinned down, Allied leadership turned to the use of air power to hinder the Germans' ability to supply and reinforce their troops.[67]

Therefore, on March 19, 1944 Operation STRANGLE was initiated to continuously and simultaneously attack trains, motor transports, marshaling yards, bridges, tunnels, and even open roads with the hope of breaking the current stalemate and leaving the Germans weakened and incapable of stopping a major Allied ground offensive in the spring.

With terrible winter weather and poor flying conditions enveloping the deadlocked battle fronts at Anzio and the Gustav Line, Allied tactical air units were released from close air support missions and directed to focus solely on the complete destruction of German lines of communication in Central and Northern Italy.[68]

Luftwaffe Ineffective on Italian Mainland

To the frustration of hungry Allied fighter pilots and the relief of friendly ground forces, the Luftwaffe was generally not a factor during Operation STRANGLE, or during the entire Italian campaign for that matter, with the one exception of the concentrated attacks against the Anzio beachhead. As a result, many Allied fighter pilots never sighted an enemy airplane while on patrol.

Two factors enabled the Allies to achieve near air supremacy during the Italian mainland campaign.[69] The first was that the Luftwaffe had withdrawn most of its fighters and bombers from the Mediterranean area of operations for service elsewhere.[70] The second factor was that the Allies had conducted an aggressive series of counter-air bomber attacks against Luftwaffe airfields. Strikes not only destroyed aircraft on the ground but more importantly, severely damaged landing fields and facilities to the extent that many were unusable.[71]

As a result, what few Luftwaffe fighters that remained in the theater were repositioned to airfields in Northern Italy and southern France. The Luftwaffe, however, did employ long-range Ju-88 bombers with some success, which provided the 332nd Fighter Group with its first enemy contact.[72]

332nd Fighter Group's First Ground Encounter with German Aircraft

Polkinghorne and the 332nd Fighter Group's first encounter with German aircraft occurred while most of the men were sleeping. On March 15th, 1944 at 2:00 a.m. the Luftwaffe attacked Montecorvino airfield. As one wit noted,

Enemy aircraft flew over our area. Anti-aircraft guns blasted the peaceful stillness of the night for about fifteen minutes. They told us about it the next morning. We were asleep. Either the Squadron was very brave or very tired.

In the afternoon of the same day, the Squadron had its first scramble. Lts Wiggins and Gomer attempted to intercept a Reconnaissance Plane that was seen flying around over our heads. Interception was not made.[73]

332nd Fighter Group's First Airborne Encounter with German Aircraft

During their time at Montecorvino airfield, none of the pilots of the 332nd Fighter Group claimed air-to-air kills. However, pilots from the 302nd Fighter Squadron on two separate sorties did damage two German Ju-88's conducting reconnaissance.

The exact dates vary depending on the source consulted, but the 332nd Fighter Group's history states that the first encounter occurred on March 17, 1944 when 2nd Lt. Larry D. Wilkins from the 302nd Fighter Squadron and his wingman 2nd Lt. Weldon K. Groves sighted a Ju-88 "near Ponza Island, off Gaeta Point in the Tyrrhenian Sea." Wing records indicate Wilkins,

Chased it as far as the Anzio beachhead, getting several bursts into the ship before his guns jammed. Just as low fuel forced him to return to base, he saw metal parts fly from the enemy plane, which then went out of control and fell several hundred feet before the German pilot recovered and climbed out of sight into the sea mist. Because an airplane must be seen to crash or disintegrate, or its pilot bail out for a victory to be credited, Lieutenant Wilkins missed that distinction, but it was doubtful that the Ju-88 got home safely.[74,75]

The second encounter occurred on March 28, 1944 when,

Lt. Roy Spencer spotted a Ju-88 off Ponza, due west of the Volturno River line. Spencer called Lt. William Melton to join in the chase, spraying it with machine-gun bullets until his guns jammed. Melton closed in and expended all his ammunition, observing smoke from the right engine of the target airplane. They followed the Ju-88 for some 60 miles and saw him lose speed, but they were unable to fire and complete the kill.[76,77]

Melton himself recalled that "those *Airacobras* just didn't have enough to close in, and at that altitude, he just walked away from us."[78] His recalled what it was like pitting the P-39 *Airacobra* against the Ju-88,

I was the first guy in the Group to encounter the enemy, a severely damaged Junker 88 bomber, while on patrol at the mouth of Naples harbor. They used to come over at a very low altitude and take pictures; they'd be low enough to throw wakes in the water with their props. They were always there a certain time of day, and we used to sit out there and wait for them. I thought I'd get one, but that old 37-mm gun jammed on me. The P-39 was a notoriously underpowered airplane, especially at sea level, so the Junker got away.

Going over as we did, we didn't have combat returnees to lead us, and I learned more in the first three or four hours in combat than in all the prior months. One white pilot recommended hanging our dog tags over our gunsights to tell our position with reference to the ground in case our instruments got shot out, whether we were skidding, whether our wings were level. That became a ceremony. My crew chief would take my tags off and hang them over the gunsight.[79]

Mount Vesuvius Erupts

In surely what must have been a shock for Polkinghorne and his squadronmates, between March 18 and March 28, 1944, Mount Vesuvius erupted, shooting flames and billowing smoke high into the sky, while throwing fiery rocks, and splashing a stream of red-hot lava down the mountainside towards Naples.

Volcanic cinders and ash were spread for miles around, including Montecorvino airfield, located a little over 30 miles away. Flying was suspended for several days after a four-inch layer of volcanic ash blanketed the airfield and airplanes. A squadron officer logged,

> Now the Squadron has seen it all. Today it is raining volcanic ash. Vesuvius is erupting and doing a truly noble job of it. The Squadron is awaiting orders to "put that volcano out."[80]

Lt. Col. Davis recalled that "The fine texture of the ash particles made them particularly dangerous. Many of our men wore gas masks; others wore eye masks."[81]

One of Polkinghorne's squadronmates, 2nd Lt. Joseph P. Gomer, remembered taking off from Montecorvino and "swinging over the coast. I could see all that red lava just flowing down. A beautiful sight."[82]

Another pilot, 1st Lt. Chris Newman of the 100th Fighter Squadron, decided to take a closer look and flew directly over Vesuvius,

> Suddenly his engine started sputtering, the sulfurous air had little oxygen, and he immediately headed out. 'If I'd gone down a little deeper, I might not have made it.'[83]

While no American lives were lost, the 340th Bomb Group stationed at nearby Pompeii airfield lost 88 North American B-25 *Mitchell* bombers due to hot ash that burned fabric flight control surfaces and ruined Plexiglas, which prompted one wag to note that it was the "only group to lose its planes to enemy rocks."[84]

Weather-wise, the men of the 332nd Fighter Group were ready for the Italian winter to end, one officer noting that "sunny Italy proves to be another Trojan horse as inclement weather prevails."[85] Another wrote,

> On March 21, 1944, the men of the Gp were immensely touched by the essence of Spring, her beauty which has a simple charm and the delicate vigor of a wild flower. With the pathetic pleading for Winter to let her assume command, Spring tried her utmost to illuminate the sky with its precise blue color, but each attempt was in vain as rain clouds and dust prevailed. With the residue of Winter unable to resist Spring with its warm forcible winds, it was necessary to

One of the some 88 North American B-25 Mitchell's lost in March 1944 during the eruption of Mount Vesuvius when volcanic ash and cinders blanketed the aircraft and burned through fabric-covered flight control surfaces.

give way to another season and let Spring assume full command. Thus we find the Group assiduously at their duties for there is yet a task to accomplish and Spring fever has no control of freedom within the organization.[86]

301st Fighter Squadron Overland Familiarization Missions

The utter boredom of flying routine convoy protection missions was broken in April 1944 when Polkinghorne's 301st Fighter Squadron flew its first familiarization flights overland in preparation for bombing and strafing missions in support of Operation STRANGLE.

The timing was no coincidence as the official report *"Operations of the 99th Fighter Squadron Compared with Other P-40 Squadrons in MTO, 3 July 1943-31 January 1944"* that exonerated the 99th Fighter Squadron's combat record had just been released a few weeks before.[87]

The 301st Fighter Squadron's Commanding Officer, Capt. Lee Rayford, an experienced 99th Fighter Squadron combat veteran, was the formation leader for all of these familiarization flights and every pilot in the squadron participated.

Bombing and strafing of entrenched German troops and supply lines were tough, down in the dirt, perilous missions. Bombing attacks were made from extremely low altitudes; the "usual tactics were to dive quite low and release the bomb with a sharp pull-out to escape the blast effects and to get away from anti-aircraft fire.[88]

Intelligence officers cautioned all the 332nd Fighter Group squadrons that pilots who had conducted attack missions against German ground units had found the anti-aircraft fire to be extremely heavy.[89]

1st Lt. James R. Polkinghorne Jr was about to experience that reality. ■

Chapter Eleven
1st Lt. James R. Polkinghorne Jr.'s Final Mission

A P-39 *Airacobra*, the same type of aircraft that Polkinghorne flew on his final combat mission, sits in the mud at Montecorvino airfield.

Italian Spring

In April 1944 the Italian winter finally broke at Polkinghorne's 301st Fighter Squadron home field at Montecorvino,

> The surrounding area of the Field has renewed itself into a garden of sweet poppies which tend to open the morning with a gladness as they break through their carpet of dew. It was noticed that time stepped up a pace and the personnel were up about their duties an hour earlier.[1]

99th Fighter Squadron Assigned to 332nd Fighter Group

On April 2, 1944 the 99th Fighter Squadron shifted to Cercola airfield, located about 4 miles from Capodichino where it was attached to the 324th Fighter Group. Three months later, in July 1944, the 99th Fighter Squadron was finally transferred to the operational control of the 332nd Fighter Group.[2] No longer set apart as the "332nd Fighter Group and the 99th Fighter Squadron," this order created the only four-fighter squadron fighter group in the European theater of operations.

In April 1944 Lt. Gen. Ira C. Eaker (far right), Mediterranean Allied Air Forces commander, met with Lt. Col. Davis (far left) and Lt. Col Beaufort Buchanan of the 62nd Fighter Wing to discuss a welcomed mission change for the 332nd Fighter Group.

This merger of the four original Tuskegee fighter squadrons was not well-received by all pilots of the 99th Fighter Squadron, who valued their association with the 79th Fighter Group, or by some pilots of the 100th, 301st, and 302nd fighter squadrons,

> Pilots of the 99th felt that the War Department was reverting to segregation policies practiced in the states. They felt that transferring them to the 332nd was based purely on race, particularly since they believed they were to become part of the 79th Fighter Group, and actually had received a few P-47's before being released from the group. Many felt that a larger segregated Negro group would mean loss of identity. Many veterans of 50 or more missions were fearful of becoming wingmen to men with no combat experience at all. On the other hand, the 332nd feared the experienced pilots of the 99th would be assigned all the responsible positions. Soon, however, all fears proved groundless, and the union was accomplished.[3]

On April 15, 1944 the 332nd Fighter Group headquarters staff departed Montecorvino and permanently transferred to Capodichino airfield, joining the 100th Fighter Squadron and the 302nd Fighter Squadron already located there.[4] This left only elements of Polkinghorne's 301st Fighter Squadron at Montecorvino as the squadron slowly repositioned to the new field.

On April 20, 1944 Lt. Gen Ira C. Eaker, Mediterranean Allied Air Forces commander, inspected the 332nd Fighter Group and dined in the Officers Mess.[5] Eaker informed the officers that all squadrons were to be reequipped with Republic P-47 *Thunderbolts* or North American P-51 *Mustangs* and moved to Ramitelli airfield on Italy's east coast to escort heavy bombers on deep strikes into Europe.

On April 25, 1944 six 332nd Fighter Group pilots were transported to Lesina, Italy on the Adriatic Sea to ferry back the group's first P-47 *Thunderbolts*, which were distributed equally among the three squadrons. A few weeks later Brig. Gen. Dean C. Strother of the 306th Fighter Wing visited to coordinate the transfer in May of the 332nd Fighter Group from the Twelfth Air Force to the Fifteenth Air Force.[6]

Tactical Situation May 1944

With the end of the cold, wet winter season and the arrival of warmer, dry spring weather, the Allies were ready to resume their full-scale ground offensive against the Gustav Line. Dubbed Operation DIADEM, the renewed Allied drive to Rome was scheduled to begin on May 11, 1944. With Operation STRANGLE hopefully having achieved its goal of interdicting Axis supply lines, the Allies hoped to face weakened German forces.

Once the Gustav Line was overrun, two strategic roads leading to Rome capable of handling Allied heavy mechanized forces such as tanks, armored personnel carriers, and self-propelled artillery, needed to be taken. The first was Route 7, the ancient Appian Way, the main road which traveled along the Italian west coast; and Route 6, a lesser road through the Liri River valley. [7]

Route 7 emerges from the mountainous terrain that faced the Allies at the Gustav Line at the coastal town of Terracina, located less than 50 miles southeast of Rome,

> The mountains come down to the sea at Terracina in a high, finger-like ridge, on the slopes of which the older part of the town is built; the road itself runs on a narrow strip less than 100 yards wide between the cliffs and the sea. Every avenue of approach to the town is dominated by the mountains.[8]

Beyond Terracina lay the flat, malaria-ridden Pontine Marshes which stretched to Anzio and had been flooded by the Germans as a defensive measure. Terracina was not located on the central Naples to Rome railway line but 23 miles away from the town of Sezze, situated on a high hill, commanded a view of the Pontine plain.

The Germans had also established a series of secondary, fallback defensive positions in the event the Gustav Line was breached. One such area was the Hitler Line that ran northeast from the town of Terracina. As a result, the surrounding mountains in this area were heavily fortified with pillboxes, bunkers and

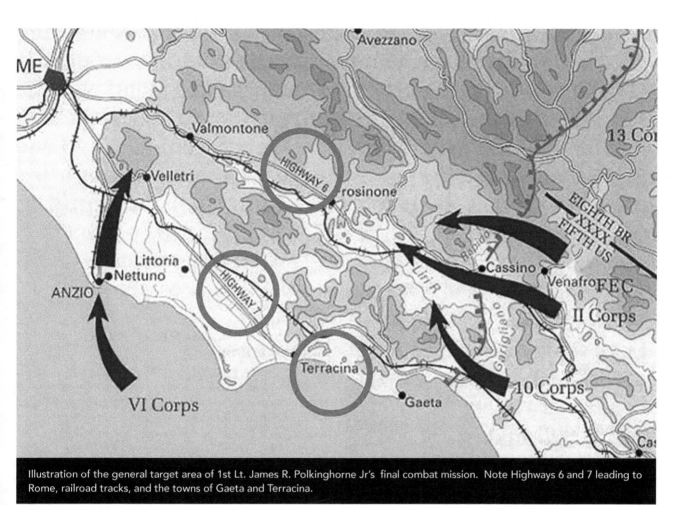

Illustration of the general target area of 1st Lt. James R. Polkinghorne Jr's final combat mission. Note Highways 6 and 7 leading to Rome, railroad tracks, and the towns of Gaeta and Terracina.

gun positions.

While Allied intelligence knew in great detail the German order of battle along the Gustav Line and the surrounded Anzio beachhead, less was understood about the composition of German forces defending the Hitler Line, Terracina, and Sezze. Intelligence was aware that one regiment of the 15th Panzer Grenadier Division was garrisoned near Terracina to oppose any attempted Allied amphibious landings there. The 26th Panzer Division was also being held in reserve near Sezze.[9,10]

It was along Route 7 in the vicinity of Terracina and Sezze, with their steep mountains and extremely rugged and isolated terrain, that Polkinghorne flew his final mission.

German Ground-Based Anti-Aircraft Defense

With the German Luftwaffe generally unable to provide air support during the Italian campaign, German ground forces relied heavily on anti-aircraft artillery to defend infantry units against Allied air attacks. As a result, the number of anti-aircraft batteries

was significantly increased by the Germans during the defense of the Italian mainland.

A wide variety of German and captured Italian light and heavy anti-aircraft weapons were used by German ground forces during the Italian campaign. The most well-known was the German 88-mm anti-aircraft flak gun, flak being an abbreviation of flug-zeugabwehrkanone, or "aircraft protection cannon."[11]

88-mm flak guns were typically grouped into anti-aircraft batteries of four guns, each capable of firing a 20-pound shell to an effective ceiling of 26,000 feet, to protect vital rear areas such as headquarters, airfields, supply depots, ammunition dumps, bridges, railroad stations, and critical road junctions.[12]

An extremely mobile weapon, it was easily towed when attached to wheeled bogies and could also be mounted on railroad flat cars for self-defense. 88-mm flak guns were also installed on Panzer tank chassis to create a motorized, self-propelled anti-aircraft artillery.

Additional technological improvements to increase the gun's lethality included larger fragmentation projectiles and incendiary shells. Even more dangerous for Allied aviators flying in the slowly burning golf balls but felt like bricks when they hit us. We were flying a gauntlet! I was right next to my flight leader and less than 100 feet off the desert. The German gunners zeroed in on him, and his P-40 instantly looked as if it had been through a shredder, as small twisted pieces of burning metal fell to the desert floor below. My flight leader disintegrated before my eyes![15]

Even a near-miss could prove deadly. 1st Lt. Luke Whethers of the 302nd Fighter Squadron was part of a flight of four P-39 *Airacobras* flying from Montecorvino when "buzzin' along at about 2,000 feet when all of a sudden, whoosh!, something smacked me in the seat of my britches and I was flying upside down."[16] Bracketed by flak, Whethers righted himself and returned safely to his base, but three of the four *Airacobras* were so riddled by flak that two landed at nearby emergency landing fields and one pilot was forced to bail out when his airplane did not respond to control inputs.

Pittsburgh Courier Reporter at Montecorvino

Ollie Harrington was a *Pittsburgh Courier* war correspondent who accompanied the 332nd Fighter Group, and separately the 99th Fighter Squadron, into combat in Italy. In May 1944 he described for his readers an early morning combat mission departing Montecorvino in support of the Allied air offensive preceding the planned assault on the Gustav Line. This would be the same profile flown by Polkinghorne on his final combat mission,

With the intent of destroying and disrupting enemy supply lines as the invasion clock rapidly nears its zero hour, the deadly *Airacobras* of the group, marking their initial appearance in this theatre, were sent on the hunt in low-level strafing sorties.

Routed out of their slumber long before dawn, the anxious squadron pilots who, up till now, have been sweating out rather colorless convoy patrols, piled into bouncing jeeps and weapon carriers, and were rushed over to the operations tent. Here the intelligence officer, First Lt. Johnny B. Quick of Brooklyn, N.Y., explained the nature of the mission, pointing out the known enemy ack-ack positions, the emergency landing fields up near the front lines and all the necessary details. Capt Bob Tresville, Columbus, Ga., calmly went over the last-minute instructions, patted a few of his eager-for-a-fight pilots on their leather-coated backs, and led them down to the line where conscientious all-colored crews were giving the P-39's final check.

The German 88-mm anti-aircraft flak gun was an extremely mobile weapon and could be used in either an anti-aircraft or anti-tank role. For Allied airmen, flak was synonymous with the nearby black burst of an exploding anti-aircraft shell.

poor weather conditions of Italy, the 88-mm flak gun could also be equipped with a gun laying radar,

Capable of furnishing present azimuth, angular height and radar range to the gun director. Usually the gun batteries used radar tracking for range and optical tracking for direction. In cases where clouds or smoke obscured the bomb formations, radar controlled or barrage firing was used although it was not considered as effective as visual sighting.[13]

Light flak weapons that were extremely effective against low-flying aircraft included heavy machine guns, towed 20-mm cannons, 20-mm flak wagons, which used a light tank body with four mounted 20-mm cannons, and 37-mm towed cannons.[14]

One pilot described what it was like to witness a direct flak hit,

German anti-aircraft 88s seemed to be everywhere, and the German gunners were expert marksmen, a brutal fact I was about to realize.....suddenly, hidden German anti-aircraft fire opened upon us from the front and sides. Thousands of anti-aircraft rounds streaked our way. They looked like white,

Ollie Harrington, a reporter for the Pittsburgh Courier, was at Montecorvino airfield for Polkinghorne's final combat mission.

A few moments later, the Cobras were roaring down the strip, one after the other, and only the blue flames from their exhaust stacks could be seen in the darkness as they banked sharply and pointed their sharp, eager noses in the direction of the front lines.[17]

Capt Tresville was the Commanding Officer of the 100th Fighter Squadron, and he was reported missing in action a month later while leading another low-level strafing mission.[18] With the target area so close and ordnance expended so quickly, these were not long missions. Harrington described the flight's return shortly after dawn,

> Slight ground mist was just disappearing under the impact of the brilliant Italian sun when the first flight came roaring in. They came roaring across the field in tight formation, peeling off beautifully as they circled and approached into the wind. Their smooth Allison motors popping as the pilots cut their throttles and settled to the ground
>
> Seconds after they had taxied their ships to line, ground crews were swarming over them. Goggled pilots, still in

parachute harness, filed into operations to make their reports. Each one was carefully questioned by the intelligence officer, and their observations recorded.[19]

Polkinghorne's Final Combat Mission

Even though more than 60 years have passed since 1st Lt. James R. Polkinghorne Jr. was listed as missing in action over Italy, one cannot help but feel a great sadness when reading his Missing Air Crew Report. Perhaps it is the thought that none of the dreams and ambitions of this poised, courageous young fighter pilot would ever be fulfilled; maybe it is the consideration that he was a beloved only son and only brother to five sisters. One can only imagine the pain and suffering that his family, relatives, and friends endured after being informed of his loss.

Examining the 301st Fighter Squadron's war diary for April 1944, it is noted that Polkinghorne's squadron flew 67 combat missions, including one strafing mission, out of an overall total of 602 flights.[20]

Polkinghorne's last letter home to his parents was written on May 3, 1944, just two days before his final combat mission, from "somewhere in Italy."[21] His sisters Vera and Maggie recalled that he wanted to confirm that his family had received the money he had sent home. He wrote, "I sent you $100 on the 30th of April; please let me know you received this, also let me know if you have received the $150 I sent on the 30th of March."[22]

For his final combat mission, Polkinghorne was scheduled to launch before dawn, so he was awakened in the middle of the night to ready himself and to be fed a hot breakfast. Along with other pilots assigned to the same mission, he attended a pre-mission briefing that included expected weather over the target area, an update on the movement of enemy forces and anti-aircraft defense systems, and a mission execution brief by his flight leader, Capt. Lee Rayford.

Once the briefing was concluded and his tactical charts updated, Polkinghorne drew his flying equipment and proceeded to the flight line to be greeted by the crew chief of his assigned P-39 *Airacobra*. After a quick walk-around, Polkinghorne boarded his airplane, already warmed up and fully armed, fueled and serviced during the night for its first mission of the day. After settling into the cockpit and completing all his checklists, he patiently awaited the prearranged signal to start his engines, taxi to the runway, takeoff, rendezvous, and proceed to the target area.

It was precisely at 05:03 a.m. on the morning of May 5, 1944 that 1st Lt. Polkinghorne launched from Montecorvino airfield. Part of a strike package comprised of twelve 301st Fighter Squadron P-39 *Airacobras,* their mission was to strafe ground targets in support of Operation STRANGLE. Within only a few days, Operational STRANGLE would end and be replaced by Operation DIADEM, the Allied 5th Army's planned advance to capture Rome.

WITH GUNS BLAZING
by Susan Rothschild

1st Lt. James R. Polkinghorne Jr., USAAF,
presses home a strafing attack
over Italy, May 1944

Standing on the wing of a P-39 *Airacobra*, a pilot reviews the maintenance condition of his airplane with his crew chief. Polkinghorne would have done something very similar on his final flight.

Polkinghorne was flying a Bell P-39Q-20 *Airacobra*, serial number 44-3077. This was the most updated version of the *Airacobra* line, and it was equipped with a modified oxygen system, a 37mm cannon, two .50 caliber machine guns in the nose, and two .50 caliber machines guns carried in pods under the wing. Polkinghorne's flight was one of 79 combat missions and 107 total sorties flown by the 301st Fighter Squadron during May 1944.[23] Polkinghorne had been ashore in Italy for 97 days.

Capt. Lee Rayford was not only the flight leader of Polkinghorne's last combat mission, but he was also the 301st Fighter Squadron's Commanding Officer. A May 1942 graduate of Tuskegee Army Air Field in Class 42-E, Rayford had already completed a combat tour with the 99th Fighter Squadron, and he had volunteered to return overseas to serve with the 301st Fighter Squadron in combat. Less than a month after this flight he was injured by flak, and in August 1944 Rayford was awarded the Distinguished Flying Cross for heroic actions in southern France. Rayford survived the war and retired as a Lt. Col.

Polkinghorne's Flight

Rayford divided the twelve P-39 *Airacobras* assigned to that morning's mission into three equal flights of four airplanes each designated, Red, White and Blue. Polkinghorne was assigned as element leader to Capt. Rayford's Red flight, flying in a finger-

four combat formation with 1st Lt. Frank D. Walker and 2nd Lt. Ulysses S. Taylor.

1st Lt. Frank D. Walker, Tuskegee Class 43-F, was born in Richmond, Kentucky and went on to fly 50 combat missions over Europe before shipping home after being injured in a P-47 accident. He died at the age of 93 in 2013.

2nd Lt. Ulysses S. Taylor, Tuskegee Class 43-D, was born in Kaufman, Texas, and also survived the war, retiring as a Lt. Col.

In the finger-four formation, the flight leader is in the No. 1 position with the least experienced pilot flying the No. 2 position on the flight leader's left, tasked with maintaining a vigilant lookout.

No. 3 position, where Polkinghorne was assigned, is the secondary flight leader, flying right wing on the flight leader, ready to assume command if the flight leader has difficulties and watching carefully for hand signals to break into an independent battle formation.

No. 4 position, flying on No. 3's right wing is the third most experienced pilot in the formation, also tasked with maintaining an alert watch for enemy aircraft.[24]

Missing Air Crew Report

During World War II the War Department required all units to complete Battle Casualty Reports, called Missing Air Crew Reports (MACR) for U.S. Army Air Forces personnel. These reports were required to be submitted within 48 hours of the time an airman was reported killed or missing.

The data contained in a pre-formatted MACR is quite detailed and includes information on the location, date, and weather conditions of the mission as well as aircraft, engine, and weapons data. Statements are also taken from any person who has knowledge of the airman's loss.

1st Lt. James R. Polkinghorne simply disappeared on his final combat mission. 1st Lt. Robert S. Scurlock, the 301st Fighter Squadron's executive, submitted the Missing Air Crew Report, which included statements from Capt. Rayford, 1st Lt. Walker, and 2nd Lt. Taylor. Capt. Rayford also included a hand-drawn sketch detailing the general area in which Polkinghorne was lost.

Capt. Rayford's Statement

Capt. Rayford wrote,

My flight was airborne at 0503 hours. Lt. James R. Polkinghorne, Jr. was flying Red 3 position with Lt. Frank D. Walker flying his wing. Lt. Ulysses S. Taylor was flying Red 2. The weather was hazy over the target with a cloud bank completely covering the target area. I instructed white flight to stay above as top cover, and red and blue flights would go beneath the cloud bank.

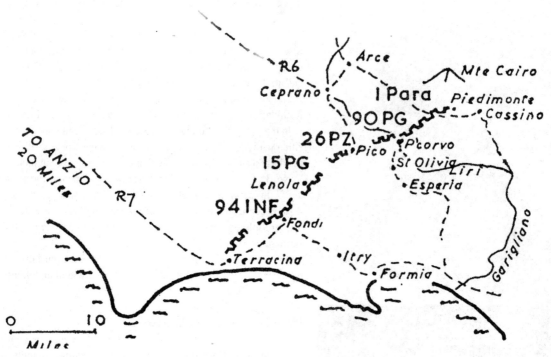

Disposition of German forces near the Hitler Line, a fall-back defensive position behind the Gustav Line, about the time of Polkinghorne's final combat mission. He most likely came into contact with elements of the XIV Panzer Corps's 94th Infantry Division, which guarded the coastal sector, or the 15th Panzer Grenadier Division, which was later rushed to the coastline to defend against any Allied amphibious landings.

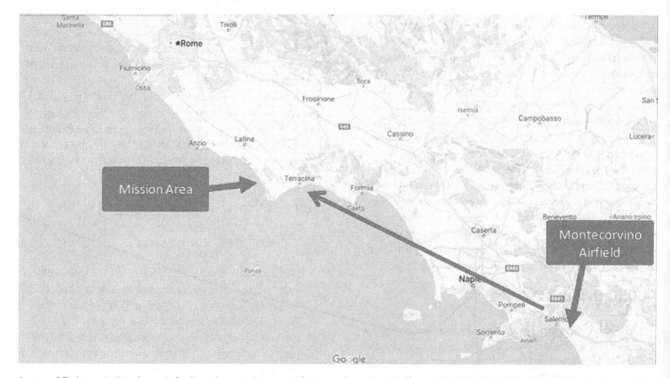

Route of flight on Polkinghorne's final combat mission, a strafing attack on German forces deployed near the town of Terracina.

1st Lt. Polkinghorne's wingmen on his final combat mission. From left, Capt Lee Rayford (Class 42-E), 2nd Lt. Ulysses Taylor (Class 43-D), Polkinghorne, and 1st Lt. Frank Walker (Class 43-F).

While losing altitude I noticed visibility become considerably worse. I decided to climb above the clouds at 1800 feet. In doing so I instructed all members to get on their instruments if necessary. I climbed to 3500 feet.

When I broke through the cloud bank I orbited and saw white flight above. Blue flight was returning to base. During this time flak bursts were seen, also tracers from automatic weapons. I lost sight of Lt. Polkinghorne over the target area at 0540 hours.

In my opinion Lt. Polkinghorne was an exceptionally good pilot, and was in good physical condition the morning of the flight.[25]

2nd Lt. Frank D. Walker's Statement

2nd Lt. Frank D. Walker's report,

We were approaching the target at or about 4,000 or 5,000 feet in places, the overcast below us was broken. We started letting down and after getting in the overcast we started back out.
Due to poor R.T., I started back out after receiving an inaudible message which I thought to be, 'Fly straight out of the overcast.' I last saw Lt. Polkinghorne as we started back out of the overcast.[26]

1st Lt. Ulysses S. Taylor's Statement

1st Lt. Ulysses S. Taylor's account,
On the 5th of May 1944, our Squadron was designated to strafe targets in the vicinity of Sezze. Captain Lee Rayford was leader of Red Flight, I was Red 2. Lt James Polkinghorne was Red 3 and Lt Frank D. Walker was Red 4.

As we approached the target area, the weather became exceedingly hazy with a cloud coverage of possibly 8.10. There was in the approximate vicinity of the target area what seemed to be an opening. Captain Rayford gave the signal to prepare for strafing I spread out, so did Lt Polkinghorne and Lt. Walker.

We found there was no opening. We ran into clouds as low as 1200 feet. Capt. Rayford, Lt. Walker and Lt. Polkinghorne was lost from my view by this time. Almost immediately Capt Rayford called on the R/T to get on instruments. I did and proceeded to fly to the top of the cloud cover.

I broke through alone with Lt. Walker following close behind. This was the last time that I saw Lt. Polkinghorne. Lt. Walker and I proceeded to our base. In listening to the R/T going on I think I heard Red call in, but, I'm not at all sure of this, as the transmission was inaudible. Lt. Walker, Capt. Rayford and I arrived at our base almost together. Lt. Polkinghorne did not return with the returning flights.[27]

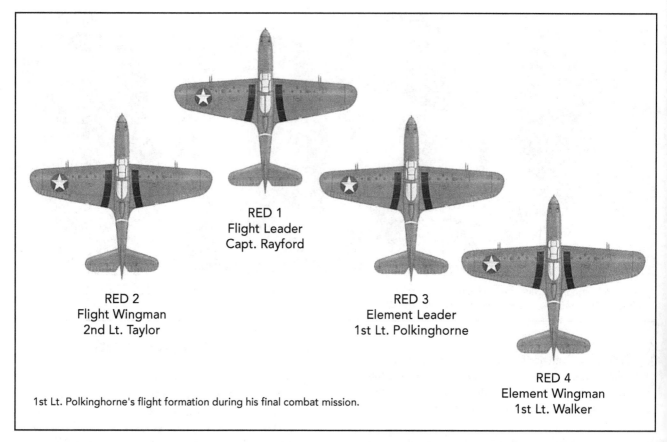

RED 1
Flight Leader
Capt. Rayford

RED 2
Flight Wingman
2nd Lt. Taylor

RED 3
Element Leader
1st Lt. Polkinghorne

RED 4
Element Wingman
1st Lt. Walker

1st Lt. Polkinghorne's flight formation during his final combat mission.

Fighter Group and Squadron War Diary Entries

The 301st Fighter Squadron's Executive Officer, 1st Lt. Robert S. Scurlock, wrote in the squadron's war diary,

> On the 5th of the Month 1st Lt James R. Polkinghorne was reported missing from a strafing mission that went over the Gaeta point area of central Italy. Lt Polkinghorne was one of the most popular officers in the squadron, liked both by the enlisted men and his fellow officers. Although he is still missing, we are all keeping faith that he is safe.[28]

The 332nd Fighter Group historian recorded,

> On the 5 May 1944, 1st Lt James R. Polkinghorne, 0-797221, Pilot, 301st Ftr Sq, was reported missing while flying on a strafing mission. Lt Polkinghorne was born in Pensacola, Fla. where he attended grammar school and graduated from Booker T. Washington High School. He attended the Florida A and M College, Tallahassee, Fla. Lt Polkinghorne was accepted as a cadet at TAAF, Tuskegee, Ala. where he received his training as a pilot. Upon completion of cadet training at Tuskegee, April 1943, he received his wings and was commissioned 2nd Lt.[29]

Speculation on Reason for Loss

1st Lt. Polkinghorne's P-39 *Airacobra* was never found or his body recovered, and the precise location of his loss covers a vast area of sea, marshland, and mountainous terrain around Terracina. While we may never know for sure what happened once Polkinghorne entered the clouds on that fateful morning, there are several possible explanations for his disappearance.

#1: Massive Explosion. As Capt. Rayford reported seeing flak bursts over the target area, Polkinghorne may have broken through the clouds and stumbled upon a battery of 88-mm flak guns or a 20-mm flak wagon protecting a high-value target. Alerted to his presence by engine noise or perhaps tracked by fire control radar, he may have suffered a direct hit and he was killed instantly, his airplane disintegrating into a shower of pieces.

#2: Uncontrollable Aircraft. Perhaps while in the clouds Polkinghorne's P-39 *Airacobra* was struck by flak or ground fire and his aircraft disabled to the point of becoming uncontrollable. He may have crashed deep into the Pontine Marshes, the Tyrrhenian Sea, or an isolated section of mountains.

#3: Damaged Aircraft. Polkinghorne's P-39 *Airacobra* may have been damaged by flak or ground fire, but it was still flyable although without an operating radio. He could have tried to nurse his broken airplane back home before experiencing a total systems failure before crashing.

#4: Disorientation. The least likely scenario for an experienced fighter pilot like Polkinghorne, who had been flying routinely in Italy's bad weather for three months, was that he might have become spatially disoriented while flying blind in the clouds, either while conducting violent maneuvers to avoid flak or turning steeply while climbing out of the clouds. He may have lost control of his aircraft and crashed into the sea, marshes or isolated mountains.

Whatever the real reason, one cannot help but wonder if 1st Lt. James R. Polkinghorne Jr.'s P-39 *Airacobra* wreckage silently waits for discovery in the depths of the Tyrrhenian Sea or in a deep crevasse in the Ausoni Mountains. ∎

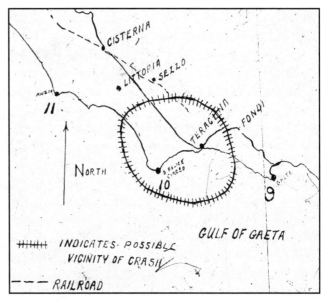

For the MACR, Capt. Rayford sketched the possible area in which 1st Lt. Polkinghorne disappeared. Note Anzio to the northwest, Gaeta to the southeast and the towns of Fondi, Terracina and Sezzo.

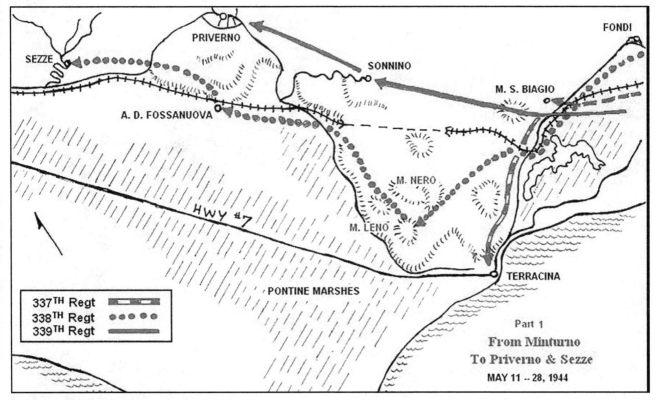

More detailed view of the general area in which 1st Lt. James R. Polkinghorne disappeared. Note the mountainous terrain and from clockwise, the towns of Sezze and Fondi connected by railroad tracks, the mountainous terrain bordering the town of Terracina, and the Pontine Marshes crossed by Highway 7 leading to Rome.

Excellent three-dimensional illustration of the mountainous terrain, marshes and sea in the general area in which 1st Lt. James R. Polkinghorne Jr. disappeared.

Chapter Twelve
Epilogue

1st Lt. James R. Polkinghorne Jr. Declared Missing

The War Department notified the Polkinghorne family that their only son had been declared missing in action in Italy by a Western Union telegram. Delivered to their home by a civilian messenger, the telegram most likely began with the heartbreaking phrase, "We regret to inform you."

Maggie Wilson, the youngest sister of James and only a small child, was home when the telegram arrived,

> I remember when the telegram came that mama didn't want to open it and somebody, maybe one of my sisters opened it, and I can just remember my mama screaming. It was a terrible time.[1]

Polkinghorne's mother never recovered from the loss of her only son and "spent years after Polkinghorne's death staring into space. All that she had to remember him, including yearbooks and letters, she kept in a cedar chest all her life."[2]

Neomi Polkinghorne, who was still working at Tuskegee Army Air Field, was so grief-stricken when she found out that her friend and roommate Emeldia Zaragoza contacted her parents and advised that they bring her home.[3] Neomi later married Ernest Nelson, also a Documented Original Tuskegee Airman, whom she met at Tuskegee.

Angie Colasanti, Emeldia's daughter, described the impact on her mother,

> Left with only the silver wings James had given her and a broken heart, my Mom couldn't face going home to Pensacola. Instead, she went to Pennsylvania with a girlfriend she met at Tuskegee. Here she met the girlfriend's brother and married him. Through this marriage my Mom had three daughters of which I am the youngest. My parents divorced when I was very young (I was around four or five years of age). My Mom didn't date nor marry again but went back to school to become a nurse...I never tired of the

1st Lt. James R. Polkinghorne Jr., U.S. Army Air Forces, missing in action over Italy in May 1944.

stories my Mom would tell me of her time at Tuskegee. She used to have a yearbook from Tuskegee and I fondly remember the hours I 'd go through it and pester her to tell the stories behind all the wonderful pictures.[4]

When her mother passed away in 2007, Angie donated the wings that Polkinghorne had given to Emeldia to the Tuskegee Airmen National Historic Site,

17 FLORIDIANS MISSING IN WAR ON 3 FRONTS

The War department Thursday released the names of 17 Floridians missing in action:

MEDITERRANEAN AREA

CRIBB, Pvt. Charles H.—mother, Mrs. Vida Cribb, Mulberry.

HUCKS, S/Sgt. James W.—Mother, Mrs. Ada Ruoff, Fort Pierce.

MANSFIELD, Cpl. William J., Jr.—Father, Capt. William J. Mansfield, Tampa.

POLKINGHORNE, 1st Lieut. James R.—Mother, Mrs. Maggie Polkinghorne, Pensacola.

Polkinghorne's missing in action status went unmentioned in the Pensacola newspapers but did appear with other missing Floridians in this *Miami News* June 22, 1944 article.

It was through MY loss that I truly understood HER loss. I believe when I visited Tuskegee, I not only felt my Mom's loss but also the loss of the many families of the airmen I 'knew' from her yearbook As I hold the wings James gave my Mom, I understand MY mission was to take her back to Tuskegee. Back to the last place she and James were together. The wings too have served their purpose. I believe that it was these wings' mission to guide my Mom back to James.[5]

Gustav Line Penetrated and Rome Falls

On May 11, 1944, less than a week after Polkinghorne's disappearance, Operation STRANGLE ended and Operation DIADEM, the Allied assault on Rome began. Nothing could stop the Allied juggernaut that smashed head-on into the German's fortified Gustav Line. By May 18, 1944 the Gustav Line had been fatally penetrated, followed quickly by an Allied breakout from the Anzio beachhead and the destruction of the fortified Hitler and Caesar Lines.

The coastal town of Terracina, where Polkinghorne disappeared on his final combat mission, fell on May 24, 1944. No reports filtered back to the 301st Fighter Squadron on whether he or his aircraft wreckage had been located.[6]

Now in full retreat, the Germans fought an intense rearguard action, but the Allies prevailed and entered Rome on June 4, 1944. Two days later, on June 6, 1944, Operation OVERLORD, the invasion of Europe, began with the D-Day landings at Normandy, France. Combat in Italy now dropped to an overlooked footnote in World War II history.

Glory for the 332nd Fighter Group

Meanwhile, Polkinghorne's squadronmates from the 301st Fighter Squadron slowly traded in their P-39 *Airacobra*s for the more capable Republic P-47 *Thunderbolts*. In May 1944 the 332nd Fighter Group was officially notified that it was relieved from coastal patrol assignments with the Twelfth Air Force and transferred to the Fifteenth Air Force for bomber escort duty. The frustrated fighter pilots were about to expose their fangs in actual air-to-air combat against the German Luftwaffe over the skies of Europe.

Their new base was Ramitelli, located on Italy's east coast near the Adriatic Sea, and they were assigned to the 306th Fighter Wing commanded by Brig. Gen Dean C. Strother. While Polkinghorne was still alive, Strother had visited the 301st Fighter Squadron at Montecorvino on May 3, 1944 and thrilled the pilots with a display of his North American P-51 *Mustang,* the mount in which they would soon gather their greatest fame.[7]

Polkinghorne never had the opportunity to participate in the epic air battles that so distinguished the 332nd Fighter Group as they protected long-range bombing missions into German-held territories. In the name of the President of the United States, the 332nd Fighter Group was awarded a Distinguished Unit Citation for their heroism, citing their "outstanding courage, aggressiveness, and combat technique" defending against German fighters, including ME-262s, trying to destroy the bomber formations they were protecting on a mission to Berlin on March 24, 1945.[8,9]

It was also during this period that the 332nd Fighter Group painted the tails of their assigned Republic P-47 *Thunderbolts* and North American P-51 *Mustangs* red. Per direction of Fifteen Air Force headquarters, unique identification patterns were assigned to all fighter groups to facilitate identification between groups and to prevent friendly fire by trigger-happy bomber gunners.[10]

But why was red selected for the 332nd Fighter Group's tail color? As recalled by pilot Harry Sheppard,

WAR DEPARTMENT

THE ADJUTANT GENERAL'S OFFICE

WASHINGTON 25, D. C.

IN REPLY REFER TO:

Polkinghorne, James R.
PC-N NAT 102

30 November 1944

Mrs. Maggie Polkinghorne
523 Reus Street
Pensacola, Florida

Dear Mrs. Polkinghorne:

I am again writing you concerning your son, First Lieutenant James R. Polkinghorne, 0797221, who was previously reported missing in action since 5 May 1944.

It distresses me to have to inform you that no report of any change in his status has yet been received. If at the expiration of twelve months a missing person has not been accounted for, all available information regarding the circumstances attending his disappearance is reviewed under the provisions of Public Law 490, 77th Congress, as amended, at which time a determination of his status is made. Before the twelve months' period has elapsed all data or evidence obtainable from any source which may be of any significance in the case is carefully considered. Occasionally relatives and friends of missing personnel receive communications containing pertinent and reliable information not officially reported to the War Department. If you have received any such communications and will send them or photostatic copies of them to this office, it will be greatly appreciated. After their review they will be returned to you if you so desire.

The War Department is mindful of the anguish you have so long endured and you may rest assured that, without any further request on your part, you will be advised promptly if any additional information concerning your loved one is received. Should it become necessary to establish his status in accordance with the provisions of the law cited, you will be notified of the findings shortly after the expiration of the twelve months' absence.

You have my heartfelt sympathy in your sorrow and it is my earnest hope that the fortitude which has sustained you in the past will continue through this distressing period of uncertainty.

Sincerely yours,

J. A. ULIO
Major General
The Adjutant General

In November 1944, six months after Polkinghorne had originally been declared missing, his mother received a letter from the War Department reporting that there was no change in his missing status. Although not overtly stated, the letter implied that he would be declared dead 12-months after his disappearance if no additional information was received.

TUSKEGEE
Army Air Field
BUILDINGS
for **SALE**

Tuskegee, Alabama
(For Off-Site Use Only)

The following buildings with fixtures, exclusive of personal property, are now available for disposal to priority holders under the Surplus Property Act of 1944, as amended, and War Assets Administration Regulation 5, and to certifiers under the Veteran's Emergency Housing program and to non-priority holders for removal for off site use only. Buildings will be sold with whatever permanent fixtures are located therein. These may include plumbing, heating, electrical and refrigerator systems consisting of such items as toilet fixtures, soil pipe, water pipe, boilers, radiators and connecting pipe, walk-in refrigerators, electrical fixtures, etc.

Approximately 152 T. O. Type Buildings and fixtures consisting of:

- Barracks
- Mess Halls
- Warehouses
- Theatre Buildings
- Supply Buildings
- Administration Buildings
- Recreation Buildings
- Officer's Barracks
- Latrine Buildings
- Post Exchanges
- And Others

After Tuskegee Army Air Field was closed, a series of sales were held. Apparently, even things that were tied down were sold to the public.

It was a matter of logistics. As we began to get the P-47s, we didn't have them long enough to make the transformation; we had some silver, we had some olive drab. We began to get the P-51s in, we had the checker boards, we had the candy stripes, we got the yellow tails and everything. So we scouted around, we went down to Foggia. And we found out that they had an overflow of what they called red insignia paint. So the convoy started back with red paint. Then we had a little conference. These were all maintenance people. The painters would say, 'Let's not overdo it, this thing.' So we decided to paint the tails red, the empennage and the trim tabs, and the nose spinner, which made the painters happy because they had the work to do. And this was the brightest red that I have ever seen, insignia red."[11]

Almost exactly one year after Polkinghorne's loss, the Allies entered Berlin, and by May 8, 1945, the war in Europe was officially over. In June 1945 Col. Davis returned to the United States to assume command of the 477th Composite Group and Lt. Col. George Roberts replaced him as commander of the 332nd Fighter Group, their third exchange of command together.[12]

On October 17, 1945 the 332nd Fighter Group headquarters staff, 100th Fighter Squadron and 301st Fighter Squadron arrived at Pier 15, Staten Island, New York aboard the S.S. *Levi Woodbury*, the 302nd Fighter Squadron having been inactivated in February 1945 and the 99th Fighter Squadron ordered to the 477th Composite Group at Godman Field, Kentucky.[13,14]

Thus ended nearly 30 months of continuous overseas combat duty by black military fighter pilots that began with the arrival of the 99th Fighter Squadron's in North Africa on April 24, 1943. Almost immediately the men were sent to Camp Kilmer, New Jersey for processing.[15]

Tuskegee Army Air Field Closed

With the end of World War II, preparations began for the inactivation of Tuskegee Army Air Field, but not without some controversy. There was a great fear that it would be kept open. The War Department "sought President Patterson's advice with respect to the continuance or deactivation of the Tuskegee Army Airfield."[16] After consultations with Col. Davis, Patterson recommended keeping the base open.[17] When civil rights activists found out, they vehemently protested, recognizing that the U.S. Army Air Forces would seize this opportunity to segregate all black aviators at Tuskegee,

It would indicate that the Army has either learned nothing from the recent war for democracy, or that it is determined to perpetuate the system of segregation which gnaws at the very vitals of democracy and tends to hamper that sense of unity so necessary in this country if it is to retain its position as the leading nation on earth.[18]

President Patterson subsequently withdrew his recommendation, and Tuskegee Army Air Field was not included in a list of bases to remain open under post-war U.S. Army Air Forces plans.[19,20]

In a rare display of consideration, U.S. Army Air Forces leadership decided to let those aviation cadets already enrolled in training at Tuskegee complete their course of instruction and earn their wings before permanently closing the base. On November 23, 1945 members of Class 46-C, the final training class, graduated from the Tuskegee Institute's Primary flight training school at Moton Field, ending that phase of the U.S. Army Air Forces pilot training program at Tuskegee forever.[21,22] These aviation cadets then transferred to Tuskegee Army Air Field for Basic and Advanced training.

On June 29, 1946, Class 46-C, the final class, graduated and pinned on their silver wings, four years and 11 months after

Class 42-C, the first class, had started training.[23] In total, 44 pilot classes and 992 African-American pilots graduated from Tuskegee Army Air Field.[24] Of the 2,053 aviation cadets who entered flight training, 992 received their wings, a 52% attrition rate.[25] It is estimated that nearly 14,000 ground personnel, all officially recognized as Documented Original Tuskegee Airmen (DOTA) by Tuskegee Airmen Incorporated, also served in support of the Tuskegee Airmen between 1941 and 1949.

Tuskegee Army Air Field was immediately placed in an inactive status pending transfer of all active duty support personnel. Regarding the future of the Tuskegee Institute's civilian employees associated with the aviation program, Director Washington recorded that,

> No employees were taken off the payroll before December 1st. Many were necessary through the close of the year to accomplish many things necessary to closing out such a field. Weeks before training ended I gave much attention to help personnel find other employment...just about all of the local people were placed with either the Institute or the Hospital. Practically all of the pilots who had come to us from various parts of the country, except Charles Anderson, returned to where they had been located.[26]

On December 12, 1946 Tuskegee Army Air Field, along with 31 other wartime military installations, was officially declared surplus by the War Assets Administration and offered for sale or lease.[27] The base eventually reverted to the town of Tuskegee and later into private hands.[28]

Director Washington Recognized

In formal recognition of his Herculean efforts, George L. Washington, who as Director of the Tuskegee Institute's Division of Aeronautics supervised every aspect of Tuskegee's aviation programs since 1939, was graciously granted an entire year's leave with full pay by Tuskegee's Board of Trustees.[29] The stunning success of Tuskegee's civilian and military aviation programs can be directly credited to Director Washington's extraordinary singularity of purpose and exceptional attention to detail. His efforts were perfectly complemented by President Patterson's inspired vision and Patterson's willingness to meet any perceived inequality head-on, whether it be a U.S. Army Air Forces general or the President of the United States.

1st Lt. James R. Polkinghorne Jr. Declared Dead

It was standard government policy at that time to wait at least a year before officially declaring a missing in action service member dead. In Polkinghorne's case, the notification came nearly 18

Lost Negro Flier Declared Dead

Lt. Polkinghorne Is Awarded Purple Heart

Missing in action in Italy since May 5, 1944, First Lt. James R. Polkinghorne, Jr., 22, officially has been declared dead and has been awarded posthumously the Purple Heart for wounds which resulted in his death.

The announcement of the official determination was received by his parents, 523 North Reus street, from Gen. H. H. Arnold, commanding general of the AAF. The medal was awarded by order of Maj. Gen. J. A. Ulio, adjutant general.

General Arnold, in notifying the parents, said that Lieutenant Polkinghorne was "a courageous officer whose excellent performance in the service of his country justifies your

A November 3, 1945 article in the Pensacola *Journal* reported the official death of 1st Lt. James R. Polkinghorne Jr.

months after his disappearance. In November 1945 the *Pensacola Journal* published a brief 190-word article buried deep within the paper which simply stated, "Lost Negro Flier Declared Dead,"

> Missing in action in Italy since May 5, 1944, First Lt. James R. Polkinghorne Jr., 22, has been declared dead and has been awarded posthumously the Purple Heart for wounds which resulted in his death.
>
> The announcement of the official determination was received by his parents, 523 North Reus street, from Gen. H. H. Arnold, commanding general of the AAF. The medal was awarded by order of Maj. Gen J.A. Uio, adjutant general. General Arnold, in notifying the parents, said that

This Purple Heart was presented to Polkinghorne's family and donated by them to the Museum of Florida History in Tallahassee, along with his headset, cap, and a training manual.

Lieutenant Polkinghorne was 'a courageous officer whose excellent performance in the service of his country justifies your pride in him' and that his courage and devotion to duty 'inspired those who fought with him.'

Polkinghorne attended Tuskegee Army Flying school, where he was commissioned a second lieutenant. Later, he was promoted to first lieutenant at Selfridge Field, Michigan. He was a fighter pilot and leader of his flight in the 332nd fighter group in the Mediterranean theater of operations. A large memorial scroll commemorating the death of the Negro officer was signed by President Truman and sent to the family.[30]

Polkinghorne's mother and father did not place a headstone memorializing their son in the family's plot at Holy Cross Cemetery in Pensacola. But his name does appear on the wall of the missing at the Sicily-Rome American Cemetery and Memorial.

Regretfully, Polkinghorne's official service record was destroyed in a fire at the National Personnel Records Center in 1973, but official correspondence indicates that he was awarded an Air Medal, Purple Heart and World War II victory medal in formal recognition of his heroic service to his country. [31]

Sicily-Rome American Cemetery and Memorial

The Sicily-Rome American Cemetery and Memorial are located on the northern edge of the city of Nettuno, Italy three miles south of Anzio and 38 miles south of Rome.[32] 7,861 white marble headstones commemorating American war dead are arranged in gentle arcs on green lawns under the shade of Roman pines, 488 of which contain the remains of unknown soldiers, sailors, and airmen.

Inside the cemetery's chapel, the white Carrara marble interior walls are engraved with the name, rank, organization and state of entry into military service of 3,095 missing American servicemen and women, of which one entry reflects the loss of 1st Lt. James R. Polkinghorne Jr., 301st Fighter Squadron, 332nd Fighter Group, Florida.

A temporary burial ground had been established at the site on January 24, 1944 and the permanent cemetery and memorial were completed in 1956. At the cemetery's official dedication, President Dwight D. Eisenhower, a former five-star general who served as Supreme Allied Commander in Europe during World War II, memorialized the Americans honored there,

> They died there valiantly and heroically, giving their lives that peoples of Europe might be liberated from tyranny… they rest tranquil and secure in the friendly soil of Italy. May our great debt to them, and all others who died in the cause of freedom, serve as an inspiration to all peoples to dedicate themselves to freedom and lasting peace. [33]

Post-World War II Impact of the Tuskegee Airmen

It is well-acknowledged that the Tuskegee Airmen fought two wars: the enemy overseas and racism at home. Segregated in their flight training, often led by prejudiced white officers, and subjected to irresponsible and biased reporting by those who wanted their squadrons disbanded, these brave young men persevered through all sorts of personal and professional trials. Seeking victory against the enemy abroad and victory against racism at home, they trusted that their "double-V campaign" would vanquish America's foes while allowing them to enjoy their civil rights in their own country for which they had sacrificed so dearly to protect.[34]

But while the Tuskegee Airmen's performance in combat may have opened the door of equal opportunity for black aviators, it was quickly closed in the immediate post-war era as there were few improvements in treatment for African-Americans

POLKINGHORNE JAMES R JR · 1 LT · 301 FTR SQ 332 FTR GP · FLORIDA

1st Lt. James R. Polkinghorne's name on the marble wall commemorating the missing in action at the Sicily-Rome American Cemetery in Italy.

in the U.S. military. In the fall of 1945, U.S. Army Air Force leadership recommended to the War Department the continuation of segregation in the post-war U.S. Army, which was accepted without argument.[35]

The closure of Tuskegee Army Air Field in 1946 left the U.S. Army Air Forces without a segregated flight training base to train new black pilots, although some African-American pilots did receive advanced training at other U.S. Army Air Forces training fields.[36,37] In February 1946 Gen. Carl A. Spaatz replaced Gen. Arnold as Commanding General of the U.S. Army Air Forces. Under Spaatz's leadership, black aviation cadet pilot training was "quietly integrated...without fanfare and nearly without comment at Randolph Field, Texas."[38]

In July 1947 the War Department reported that there were five black aviation cadets enrolled in initial flight training at Randolph Field and announced that "air cadets will be accepted for non-segregated training on a basis of qualification without regard to race."[39] That same month, Col. Benjamin O. Davis Jr, now commander of the 332nd Fighter Wing at Lockbourne Army Airfield in Ohio, was quoted in a newspaper article urging black youth "who desire to fly and who would like a crack at the modern jet fighter planes, to apply immediately to the Army Air Forces for air cadet training."[40]

The National Security Act of 1947, which took effect in September 1947, restructured the military and replaced the U.S. Army Air Forces with the U.S. Air Force as an independent military service equal to the U.S. Army and U.S. Navy, all under the control of the Secretary of Defense.

On July 26, 1948 President Harry S. Truman signed Executive Order 9981, terminating the doctrine of separate-but-equal rights in the U.S. Armed Forces,

WHEREAS it is essential that there be maintained in the armed services of the United States the highest standards of democracy, with equality of treatment and opportunity for all those who serve in our country's defense:

NOW THEREFORE, by virtue of the authority vested in me as President of the United States, by the Constitution and the statutes of the United States, and as Commander in Chief of the armed services, it is hereby ordered as follows:

FLORIDA AGRICULTURAL AND MECHANICAL COLLEGE

DEDICATES

THE POLKINGHORNE VILLAGE

SATURDAY MORNING, OCTOBER 30, 1948
TEN-THIRTY O'CLOCK

IN HONOR OF

THE LATE ALUMNUS JAMES R. POLKINGHORNE, JR.

DR. WILLIAM H. GRAY, JR., Presiding

The National Anthem .... The College Band

Invocation .... Dr. James Hudson, Chaplain

Our Job .... Mr. William Mitchell, Commander
State American Legion
West Palm Beach, Fla.

"Gloria"—by Lasey .... The College Band

Address .... Hon. R. A. Gray, Secretary of State

Awarding Degree Posthumously ... Colonel B. O. Davis, Commander
Lockbourne Air Base

Presentation of Memorial Plaque .... Captain Roy R. Spencer
Memphis, Tenn.

Receiving the Plaque .... Dr. & Mrs. James R. Polkinghorne, Sr.

Taps .... Bugler

"National Emblem"—by Bagley .... The College Band
(Air Salute—332nd Fighter Group)

Program from the dedication of Polkinghorne Village at Florida A&M on October 30, 1945

It is hereby declared to be the policy of the President that there shall be equality of treatment and opportunity for all persons in the armed services without regard to race, color, religion or national origin.[41]

Poem published in the May 14, 1943 edition of the *Hawks Cry*, the base newspaper of the Tuskegee Army Air Field.

Polkinghorne Tribute at Florida A&M

On October 30, 1948, a new Veterans Village was dedicated in Polkinghorne's name during Homecoming Day at his alma mater Florida A&M in Tallahassee, Florida. His mother, father and youngest sister Maggie attended, and Polkinghorne was posthumously awarded his Bachelor's degree, which was given to the family by Capt. Claude B. Govan, a squadronmate of Polkinghorne's from the 301st Fighter Squadron.[42] A Memorial Plaque was also presented to his parents from Capt. Roy R. Spencer, who graduated with Polkinghorne in Class 43-B at the Tuskegee Army Air Field and was himself a native of Tallahassee.

In tribute to one of their own, during the ceremony, a flight of eight Republic P-47 *Thunderbolts* from Ohio's Lockbourne Air Base's 332nd Fighter Wing, commanded by Col. Benjamin O. Davis Jr., Polkinghorne's fighter group commander in war-torn Italy, roared overhead.[43]

The fighters, each flown by a pilot who was closely associated with Polkinghorne during the war, most likely flew the Missing Man formation, a solemn aerial maneuver used at military funerals.[44] Just before the flight arrives over the ceremony site, one aircraft pulls up and away, leaving a vacant symbolic position for the fallen aviator, a poignant reminder for those viewing from the ground of the loss suffered by his comrades.

Polkinghorne's Epitaph

1st Lt. James R. Polkinghorne Jr. lived on this earth for 22 years, 10 months and 14 days before making the ultimate sacrifice in defense of his country, one of 81 Tuskegee Airmen killed overseas during World War II.[45,46] Yet he rarely, if ever, receives mention in various histories of the Tuskegee Airmen and he remains a nearly anonymous individual among the 355 pilot graduates from Tuskegee who saw combat overseas and earned 96 Distinguished Flying Crosses among them for extraordinary bravery.[47] 1st Lt. James R. Polkinghorne Jr. deserves to be better honored for his service to his country and to stand as a figure of hope for those who seek to overcome seemingly insurmountable obstacles in their lives.

As we seek to understand why such a fine young man had to die so young, there are no more comforting words than an open letter written by Dr. Samuel Sidat-Singh and his wife Pauline shortly after they lost their son, 2nd Lt. Wilmeth Sidat-Singh, in a flight training accident at Selfridge Army Air Field. Sidat-Singh was a squadronmate of Polkinghorne's in the 301st Fighter Squadron, and his parents wrote,

When the call from his country for duty came, he readily responded. He said that he wanted to go because he would feel guilty of shirking if another died in his stand. Today he

REPORTED LOST IN LAKE HURON

2nd Lt. Wilmeth Sidat-Singh, who was lost in a 1943 P-40 *Warhawk* accident at Selfridge Army Air Field, served in the 301st Fighter Squadron with Polkinghorne.

would want us to say to his admirers: Thank you for your loyalty in supporting me in all my efforts. I hope that I have not failed in keeping your trust. I did the best I could. I gave all that I had for my country, my life.

We are also sure that he would feel his life was not in vain, if he served to put a spark into the lives of aspiring young-sters and to impress upon them that ability, slowly but surely, receives recognition.

It is our hope that Wilmeth and thousands of others like him are not dying in vain, but that when this war is over America will be a safe place for all people, black and white, all alike; that there will emerge from these sacrifices an emancipation from racial bigotry and prejudice from inequalities of opportunities, both civic and economic; and there will be a just recognition of merit, not based upon the color of one's skin.[48] ∎

Endnotes _____

Chapter 1

1   Ancestry.com. (n.d.). U.S. WWII Draft Cards, 1940-1947. Provo, UT.

2   Gardner, L. (1925). Who's Who in American Aeronautics. Floyd Clymer Publications, Los Angeles, CA

3   Hoagland, R. (Ed.) (1932). The Blue Book of Aviation. A Biographical History of American Aviation. The Hoagland Company, Los Angeles, CA.

4   Washington, M. (1934, October). A Race Soars Upward. Opportunity: A Journal of Negro Life, XII(10), p. 301.

5   Cooper, C. & Cooper, A. (2001). Tuskegee's Heroes. Osceola, WI: MBI Publishing Company, p. 27.

6   Freydberg, E. (1994). Bessie Coleman, the Brownskin Lady Bird. New York, NY: Garland Publishing

7   Jakeman, R. (1988). America's Black Air Pioneers, 1900-1939. Maxwell, AL: Air Command and Staff College Air University

8   Snider, D. (1995). Flying to Freedom: African-American Visions of Aviation, 1910-1927 (Unpublished doctoral dissertation). Chapel Hill, SC: University of North Carolina

9   Barbour, G. (1986, April). Early Black Flyers of Western Pennsylvania, 1906-1945. The Western Pennsylvania Historical Magazine, 69(2), p. 98.

10   Lloyd, C. (2000). Eugene Bullard, Black Expatriate in Jazz-Age Paris. Athens, GA: University of Georgia Press, p. 55.

11   Lloyd, C. (2000). Eugene Bullard, Black Expatriate in Jazz-Age Paris. Athens, GA: University of Georgia Press, p. 47.

12   Lloyd, C. (2000). Eugene Bullard, Black Expatriate in Jazz-Age Paris. Athens, GA: University of Georgia Press, pp. 51-52.

13   Van Wyen, A. (1969). Naval Aviation in World War I. Washington, DC: Chief of Naval Operations.

14   Carisella, P. & Ryan, J. (1972). The Black Swallow of Death. New York, NY: Marlborough House, Inc.pp. 148-149.

15   Carisella, P. & Ryan, J. (1972). The Black Swallow of Death. New York, NY: Marlborough House, Inc., p. 162.

16   Carisella, P. & Ryan, J. (1972). The Black Swallow of Death. New York, NY: Marlborough House, Inc., p. 169.

17   Carisella, P. & Ryan, J. (1972). The Black Swallow of Death. New York, NY: Marlborough House, Inc., pp. 187-188.

18   Lloyd, C. (2000). Eugene Bullard: Black Expatriate in Jazz-Age Paris, Athens, GA: University of Georgia Press, p.59.

19   Carisella, P. & Ryan, J. (1972). The Black Swallow of Death. New York, NY: Marlborough House, Inc., pp. 187-188.

20   Lloyd, C. (2000). Eugene Bullard: Black Expatriate in Jazz-Age Paris, Athens, GA: University of Georgia Press, p.59.

21   Lloyd, C. (2000). Eugene Bullard: Black Expatriate in Jazz-Age Paris, Athens, GA: University of Georgia Press, pp. 61-62.

22   Maskel, R. (2011, March). The Unrecognized First. Air & Space Magazine. Retrieved from http://www.airspacemag.com/history-of-flight/the-unrecognized-first-79496373/

23   Holmes, K. (2013). Restoring black pilot's legacy. Retrieved from http://articles.philly.com/2013-10-14/news/42995574_1_tuskegee-airmen-photo-hart

24   The Flying Dutchman. (n.d.). Black Aviators & Emory Conrad Malick. Retrieved from http://www.buehlfield.info/aircraft-aviators/further-information-about-training-black-airmen

25   San Diego Air & Space Museum. (2011). Breaking News: First African American Pilot. Retrieved from http://www.emoryconradmalick.com/articles/SDASMlibraryArchivesNews.pdf

26   African American Registry. (n.d.). America's First Black Aviator, Emory Malick. Retrieved from http://www.aaregistry.org/historic_events/view/americas-first-black-aviator-emory-malick

27   Rich, D. (1993). Queen Bess. Washington, DC: Smithsonian Institution Press.

28   Freydberg, E. (1994). Bessie Coleman, the Brownskin Lady Bird. New York, NY: Garland Publishing, p. 76.

29   Rich, D. (1993). Queen Bess. Washington, DC: Smithsonian Institution Press, p. 32.

30   Freydberg, E. (1994). Bessie Coleman, the Brownskin Lady Bird. New York, NY: Garland Publishing, p. 82.

31   Rich, D. (1993). Queen Bess. Washington, DC: Smithsonian Institution Press, pp. 45-46.

32   Rich, D. (1993). Queen Bess. Washington, DC: Smithsonian Institution Press, pp. 55-56.

33   Freydberg, E. (1994). Bessie Coleman, the Brownskin Lady Bird. New York, NY: Garland Publishing, p. 92.

34   Rich, D. (1993). Queen Bess. Washington, DC: Smithsonian Institution Press, p. 92.

35   Freydberg, E. (1994). Bessie Coleman, the Brownskin Lady Bird. New York, NY: Garland Publishing, p. 94.

36   Rich, D. (1993). Queen Bess. Washington, DC: Smithsonian Institution Press, pp. 110-111.

37   Gubert, B., Sawyer, M. & Fannin, C. (2002). Distinguished African Americans in Aviation and Space Science. Westport, CT: Oryx Press, pp. 17-18.

38   Banning, J. (1932, December 17). The Day I Sprouted Wings. The Pittsburg Courier, p. 3.

39   Aerofiles. (2008). White's Hummingbird. Retrieved from http://www.aerofiles.com/_wh.html

40   Banning, J. (1932, December 17). The Day I Sprouted Wings. The Pittsburg Courier, p. 3.

41   Pittsburgh Courier. (1933, February 11). Local Airport Officials Pay Flyer Fine Tribute, p. 1.

42   Jakeman, R. (1992). Divided Skies. Tuscaloosa, AL: University of Alabama Press, p 63.

43   Pittsburgh Courier. (1933, February 11). Famous Coast-to-Coast Trail Blazer Killed as

Plane Crashes in West, p. 1.

44 Tucker, P. (2012). Father of the Tuskegee Airmen, John C. Robinson. Dulles, VA: Potomac Books, p.2.

45 Tucker, P. (2012). Father of the Tuskegee Airmen, John C. Robinson. Dulles, VA: Potomac Books, p.3.

46 Tucker, P. (2012). Father of the Tuskegee Airmen, John C. Robinson. Dulles, VA: Potomac Books, p.28.

47 Tucker, P. (2012). Father of the Tuskegee Airmen, John C. Robinson. Dulles, VA: Potomac Books, p.25.

48 National Register of Historic Places Registration Form. (2013). Curtiss-Wright Aeronautical University Building. Washington, DC: United States Department of the Interior, National Park Service.

49 Tucker, P. (2012). Father of the Tuskegee Airmen, John C. Robinson. Dulles, VA: Potomac Books, p.33.

50 Tucker, P. (2012). Father of the Tuskegee Airmen, John C. Robinson. Dulles, VA: Potomac Books, p.29.

51 Tucker, P. (2012). Father of the Tuskegee Airmen, John C. Robinson. Dulles, VA: Potomac Books, p.45.

52 Tucker, P. (2012). Father of the Tuskegee Airmen, John C. Robinson. Dulles, VA: Potomac Books, p.37.

53 Tucker, P. (2012). Father of the Tuskegee Airmen, John C. Robinson. Dulles, VA: Potomac Books, p.39.

54 Tucker, P. (2012). Father of the Tuskegee Airmen, John C. Robinson. Dulles, VA: Potomac Books, p. 41.

55 Tucker, P. (2012). Father of the Tuskegee Airmen, John C. Robinson. Dulles, VA: Potomac Books, p. 61.

56 Tucker, P. (2012). Father of the Tuskegee Airmen, John C. Robinson. Dulles, VA: Potomac Books, p. 33.

57 Tucker, P. (2012). Father of the Tuskegee Airmen, John C. Robinson. Dulles, VA: Potomac Books, p.71.

58 Tucker, P. (2012). Father of the Tuskegee Airmen, John C. Robinson. Dulles, VA: Potomac Books, p.99.

59 Milkias, P. & Metaferia, G. (Eds.). (2005). The Battle of Adwa, Reflections on Ethiopia's Historic Victory Against European Colonialism. New York, NY: Algoa Publishing.

60 Tucker, P. (2012). Father of the Tuskegee Airmen, John C. Robinson. Dulles, VA: Potomac Books, p. 125-127.

61 Tucker, P. (2012). Father of the Tuskegee Airmen, John C. Robinson. Dulles, VA: Potomac Books, p. 131.

62 Tucker, P. (2012). Father of the Tuskegee Airmen, John C. Robinson. Dulles, VA: Potomac Books, p. 131.

63 United Press. (1935, October 5). Negro Aviator Tells of Plane Raid on Aduwa, Shamokin News-Dispatch, p.2.

64 Tucker, P. (2012). Father of the Tuskegee Airmen, John C. Robinson. Dulles, VA: Potomac Books, p. 162.

65 Tucker, P. (2012). Father of the Tuskegee Airmen, John C. Robinson. Dulles, VA: Potomac Books, p. 161.

66 Rodgers, J. (1935, December 14). Col. Robinson States Air Duel in Clouds With Enemy Planes, Pittsburg Courier, p. 1.

67 Tucker, P. (2012). Father of the Tuskegee Airmen, John C. Robinson. Dulles, VA: Potomac Books, p. 214.

68 Tucker, P. (2012). Father of the Tuskegee Airmen, John C. Robinson. Dulles, VA: Potomac Books, pp. 40-50.

69 Tucker, P. (2012). Father of the Tuskegee Airmen, John C. Robinson. Dulles, VA: Potomac Books, p. 242-243.

70 Holway, J. (1997). Red Tails, Black Wings. Las Cruces, NM: Yuca Tree Press, p. 35.

71 Tucker, P. (2012). Father of the Tuskegee Airmen, John C. Robinson. Dulles, VA: Potomac Books, p. 31.

72 Tucker, P. (2012). Father of the Tuskegee Airmen, John C. Robinson. Dulles, VA: Potomac Books, p. 29.

73 Tucker, P. (2012). Father of the Tuskegee Airmen, John C. Robinson. Dulles, VA: Potomac Books, p. 31.

74 Tucker, P. (2012). Father of the Tuskegee Airmen, John C. Robinson. Dulles, VA: Potomac Books, p. 29.

75 National Register of Historic Places Registration Form. (2013). Curtiss-Wright Aeronautical University Building. Washington, DC: United States Department of the Interior, National Park Service, p. 31.

76 Encyclopedia of Arkansas History. (n.d.). Cornelius Robinson Coffey. Retrieved from http://www.encyclopediaofarkansas.net/encyclopedia/entry-detail.aspx?entryID=6940

77 Encyclopedia of Arkansas History. (n.d.). Cornelius Robinson Coffey. Retrieved from http://www.encyclopediaofarkansas.net/encyclopedia/entry-detail.aspx?entryID=6940

78 Golab, A. (1993, July). Black Aviator Still Flies High - Pioneer Aids Students, Chicago Sun-Times, p. 24.

79 Bragg, J. (1996). Soaring Above Setbacks. Washington, DC: Smithsonian Institution, p. 27.

80 Tucker, P. (2012). Father of the Tuskegee Airmen, John C. Robinson. Dulles, VA: Potomac Books, p. 187.

81 Tucker, P. (2012). Father of the Tuskegee Airmen, John C. Robinson. Dulles, VA: Potomac Books, p. 43.

82 Davis, E. (n.d.). Brown, Willa B. Retrieved from http://www.blackpast.org/aah/brown-willa-b-1906-1992

83 Edwards, R. (2016). Getting to Know African American Aviator: Willa Beatrice Brown. Retrieved from https://spark.adobe.com/page/7Skn28TulrP1y/

84 Edwards, R. (2016). Getting to Know African American Aviator: Willa Beatrice Brown. Retrieved from https://spark.adobe.com/page/7Skn28TulrP1y/

85 Bragg, J. (1996). Soaring Above Setbacks. Washington, DC: Smithsonian Institution, p. 28.

86 Edwards, R. (2016). Getting to Know African American Aviator: Willa Beatrice Brown. Retrieved from https://spark.adobe.com/page/7Skn28TulrP1y/

87 Hilton, B. (n.d.). Willa Brown. Retrieved from https://pioneersofflight.si.edu/content/willa-brown-0

88 Bragg, J. (1996). Soaring Above Setbacks. Washington, DC: Smithsonian Institution, p. 28.

89 Bragg, J. (1996). Soaring Above Setbacks. Washington, DC: Smithsonian Institution, p. 29.

90 Tucker, P. (2012). Father of the Tuskegee Airmen, John C. Robinson. Dulles, VA: Potomac Books, p. 46.

91 Tucker, P. (2012). Father of the Tuskegee Airmen, John C. Robinson. Dulles, VA: Potomac Books, p. 47.

92 Bragg, J. (1996). Soaring Above Setbacks. Washington, DC: Smithsonian Institution, p. 29.

93 Tucker, P. (2012). Father of the Tuskegee Airmen, John C. Robinson. Dulles, VA: Potomac Books, p. 47.

94 Bragg, J. (1996). Soaring Above Setbacks. Washington, DC: Smithsonian Institution, p. 30.

95 Bragg, J. (1996). Soaring Above Setbacks. Washington, DC: Smithsonian Institution, pp. 31-31.

96 Bragg, J. (1996). Soaring Above Setbacks. Washington, DC: Smithsonian Institution, p. 34.

97 Tucker, P. (2012). Father of the Tuskegee Airmen, John C. Robinson. Dulles, VA: Potomac Books, p. 51.

98 Bragg, J. (1996). Soaring Above Setbacks. Washington, DC: Smithsonian Institution, p. 39.

99 Kriz, M. (1996). Soaring Above Setbacks. The Autobiography of Janet Harmon Bragg. African American Aviator. Washington, DC: Smithsonian Institution Press, p. 51.

100 Bragg, J. (1996). Soaring Above Setbacks. Washington, DC: Smithsonian Institution, p. 52.

101 Bragg, J. (1996). Soaring Above Setbacks. Washington, DC: Smithsonian Institution, p. 40.

102 Freydberg, E. (1994). Bessie Coleman, the Brownskin Lady Bird. New York, NY: Garland Publishing, p. 9.

103 The Flying Dutchman Website. (n.d.). The Tuskegee Airmen. Retrieved from http://www.buehlfield.info/tuskegee-airmen

104 Holway, J. (1997). Red Tails, Black Wings. Las Cruces, NM: Yucca Tree Press, p. 33.

105 Forsyth, R. (2001). Black Flight. Breaking Barriers to Blacks in Aviation. Los Angeles, CA: AllCourt Publishing, p. 161.

106 Brock, P. (1988). Chief Anderson. Retrieved from http://people.com/archive/chief-anderson-vol-30-no-22/

107 Brock, P. (1988). Chief Anderson. Re-

trieved from http://people.com/archive/chief-anderson-vol-30-no-22/, para.9.

108 Forsyth, R. (2001). Black Flight. Breaking Barriers to Blacks in Aviation. Los Angeles, CA: AllCourt Publishing, p. 161

109 Brock, P. (1988). Chief Anderson. Retrieved from http://people.com/archive/chief-anderson-vol-30-no-22/, para.12.

110 Rasmussen, C. (2000, November 5). Early Black Pilot Found Racial Equality in the Sky. The Los Angeles Times, p. 43.

111 Hanser, K. (2016). Black Wings: The Life of American Aviation Pioneer William Powell. Retrieved from https://airandspace.si.edu/stories/editorial/black-wings-life-african-american-aviation-pioneer-william-powell

112 Collings, K. (1936, December). The American Mercury, XXXIX, 156, p. xxx.

113 Hanser, K. (2016). Black Wings: The Life of African American Aviation Pioneer William Powell. Retrieved from https://airandspace.si.edu/stories/editorial/black-wings-life-african-american-aviation-pioneer-william-powell

114 Powell, W. (1934). Black Wings. Retrieved from https://babel.hathitrust.org/cgi/pt?id=uc1.b4500439;view=1up;seq=8, p. ii.

115 Freydberg, E. (1994). Bessie Coleman. New York, NY: Garland Publishing, Inc, p. 114.

116 Jakeman, R. (1992). The Divided Skies. Tuscaloosa, AL: University of Alabama Press, p. 63

117 Jakeman, R. (1992). The Divided Skies. Tuscaloosa, AL: University of Alabama Press, p. 320.

118 Lost in Cross Country Trip. (1929, November 16). Pittsburgh Courier, p. 1.

119 Scott, P. (2009). The Blackbirds, The Story of the First All-Black Aerobatic Team. Retrieved from https://www.aopa.org/news-and-media/all-news/2009/july/pilot/the-blackbirds

120 Rasmussen, C. (2000, November 5). Early Black Pilot Found Racial Equality in the Sky. The Los Angeles Times, p. 43.

121 Scott, P. (2009). The Blackbirds, The Story of the First All-Black Aerobatic Team. Retrieved from https://www.aopa.org/news-and-media/all-news/2009/july/pilot/the-blackbirds

122 Pilot Beatrice Reeves. (1929, April 27). The

Pittsburgh Courier, p. 1.

123 Race Pilots to Tour American. (1929, April 6). The Pittsburgh Courier, p. 1.

124 Scott, P. (2009). The Blackbirds, The Story of the First All-Black Aerobatic Team. Retrieved from https://www.aopa.org/news-and-media/all-news/2009/july/pilot/the-blackbirds

125 Scott, L., & Womack, W. (1994). Double V. East Lansing, MI: Michigan State University Press, p. 37.

126 Scott, L., & Womack, W. (1994). Double V. East Lansing, MI: Michigan State University Press, p. 37.

127 Powell, W. (1937, May). The American Mercury, XLI, 161, p. 127.

128 Powell, W. (1934). Black Wings. Craftsmen of Black Wings, Los Angeles, CA: Ivan Deach, Jr, p. 147.

129 Powell, W. (1934). Black Wings. Craftsmen of Black Wings, Los Angeles, CA: Ivan Deach, Jr, p. xxxiv

130 Evans, C. (2013). Heralding the Lost History of Early Black Aviators. Retrieved from http://www.colorado.edu/asmagazine/2013/06/01/heralding-lost-history-early-black-aviators

131 Schuyler, G. (1935, September). Views and Reviews. The Pittsburgh Courier, p. 10.

132 Chamberlin, C. (1928). Record Flights. Philadelphia, PA: Dorrance and Company. pp. 232-233.

133 Chamberlin, C. (1928). Record Flights. Philadelphia, PA: Dorrance and Company. pp. 243-244.

134 Jakeman, R. (1992). The Divided Skies. Tuscaloosa, AL: University of Alabama Press, p. 59.

135 Tucker, P. (2012). Father of the Tuskegee Airmen, John C. Robinson. Dulles, VA: Potomac Books, pp. 66-67.

136 Tucker, P. (2012). Father of the Tuskegee Airmen, John C. Robinson. Dulles, VA: Potomac Books, p. 67 & 98.

137 Broadnax, S. (2007). Blue Skies, Black Wings. Westport, CT: Praeger Publishers, p. 15.

138 Jakeman, R. (1992). The Divided Skies.

Tuscaloosa, AL: University of Alabama Press, p. 59.

139 Forsyth, R. (2001). Black Flight. Los Angeles, CA: AllCourt Publishing.

140 Forsyth, R. (2001). Black Flight. Los Angeles, CA: AllCourt Publishing, p. 158.

141 Forsyth, R. (2001). Black Flight. Los Angeles, CA: AllCourt Publishing, pp. 162-163.

142 Barbour, G. (1986, April). Early Black Flyers of Western Pennsylvania, 1906-1945. The Western Pennsylvania Historical Magazine, 69(2), p. 100.

143 Barbour, G. (1986, April). Early Black Flyers of Western Pennsylvania, 1906-1945. The Western Pennsylvania Historical Magazine, 69(2), p. 100.

144 Peck, J. (1938, February). Flying in the Spanish Air Force. The Sportsman Pilot, XIX(2), p. 11.

145 Peck, J. (1938, February). Flying in the Spanish Air Force. The Sportsman Pilot, XIX(2), p. 11.

146 Mizrahi, J. (1972, April). The Phantom Brigade. Wings Magazine, 2(2), pp. 28-33.

147 Peck, J. (1938, February). Flying in the Spanish Air Force. The Sportsman Pilot, XIX(2), p. 11, 31.

148 Peck, J. (1940, May). Dogfight: A Lifetime in Forty Minutes. The New York Times Magazine, pp. 4, 20.

149 Peck, J. (1940). Armies with Wings. New York, NY: Dodd, Mead & Co. pp. 101-106.

150 Mizrahi, J. (1972, April). The Phantom Brigade. Wings Magazine, 2(2), pp. 37, 40.

151 Mizrahi, J. (1972, April). The Phantom Brigade. Wings Magazine, 2(2), p.37.

152 Herr, A. (1977). American Pilots in the Spanish Civil War. American Aviation Historical Society Journal, 22(3), pp. 162-178.

153 Peck, J. (1945, September). Radar…Magic Eye That Sees the Invisible. Popular Science, 147(3), 65-72.

154 Peck, J. (1940). Armies with Wings. New York, NY: Dodd, Mead & Co.

155 Peck, J. (1941). So You're Going to Fly. New York, NY: Dodd, Mead & Co.

Chapter 2

1   Bunch, L. (1984). In Search of a Dream: the Flight of Herman Banning and Thomas Allen. Journal of American Culture, 7(1-2), pp, 100-103.

2   Lynn, J. (1989). The Hallelujah Flight. London, UK: Robson Books Ltd.

3   Bunch, L. (1984). In Search of a Dream: The Flight of Herman Banning and Thomas Allen. Journal of American Culture, 7(1-2), p. 100.

4   Juptner, J. (Ed.). (1962). U.S. Civil Aircraft Vol. 1 Los Angeles, CA: Aero Publishers Inc., p. 149.

5   Former Ames Pilot Welcomed in New York After Noteworthy Hope. (1932, October). Ames Daily Tribune, p. 5.

6   Negro Aviators Stop Here on Trans-Continental Flight. (1932, September). St Lois Post-Dispatch, p. 22.

7   Forsythe, R. (2001). Black Flight: Breaking Barriers to Blacks in Aviation. Los Angeles, CA: AllCourt Publishing. P. 169

8   Lynn, J. (1989). The Hallelujah Flight. London, UK: Robson Books Ltd.

9   Lynn, J. (1989). The Hallelujah Flight. London, UK: Robson Books Ltd.

10 Jackman, W. & Russell, T. (1912). Flying Machines: Construction and Operations. Chicago, IL: Charles C. Thompson Co., p. 248.

11 Swopes, B. (2016). Frank Monroe Hawks. Retrieved from https://www.thisdayinaviation. com/tag/frank-monroe-hawks/

12 Bunch, L. (1984). In Search of a Dream: The Flight of Herman Banning and Thomas Allen. Journal of American Culture, 7(1-2), pp. 100-103.

13 Lynn, J. (1989). The Hallelujah Flight. London, UK: Robson Books Ltd.

14 Associated Press. (1984, February). New Museum Exhibit Marks Accomplishments of Nation's Black Fliers. The Daily Journal, p. 12.

15 Cross-Country Flight Now On. (1933, July). The Pittsburgh Courier, p. 4.

16 Washington, M. (1934, October). A Race Soars Upward. Opportunity, A Journal of Negro Life, XII(10), 300-301.

17 Forsyth, R. (2001). Black Flight. Los Angeles, CA: AllCourt Publishing, p. 188.

18 Scott, L. & Womack, W. (1994). Double V, the Civil Rights Struggle of the Tuskegee Airmen, p. 42.

19 Forsythe-Anderson Arrive on Coast After Record Flight. (1933, July). The Pittsburgh Courier, p. 1.

20 Forsyth, R. (2001). Black Flight. Los Angeles, CA: AllCourt Publishing, p. 198.

21 Atlantic City. (1933, July). The Courier News, p. 7.

22 Newark to Honor Famous Aviators. (1933, September). The Pittsburgh Courier, p. 11.

23 Forsyth, R. (2001). Black Flight. Los Angeles, CA: AllCourt Publishing, p. 202.

24 Lynn, J. (1989). The Hallelujah Flight. London, UK: Robson Books Ltd, p. 206.

25 Aviators Hop Off This Week. (1934, November). The Pittsburgh Courier, p. 4.

26 Washington, M. (1934, October). A Race Soars Upward. Opportunity, A Journal of Negro Life, XII(10), 300-301.

27 Goodwill Flyers to Get Royal Welcome. (1934, August). The Pittsburgh Courier, p.13.

28 Goodwill Flyers to Get Royal Welcome. (1934, August). The Pittsburgh Courier, p.13.

29 Pan-American Flight by Negroes Sept. 30. (1934, August). St. Louis Post-Dispatch, p. 5.

30 Tucker, P. (2012). Father of the Tuskegee Airmen, John C. Robinson. Washington, DC: Potomac Books, p. 58.

31 Brock, P. (1988). Chief Anderson. Retrieved from http://people.com/archive/chief-anderson-vol-30-no-22/, para.27.

32 Forsyth, R. (2001). Black Flight. Los Angeles, CA: AllCourt Publishing, p. 267.

33 Forsyth, R. (2001). Black Flight. Los Angeles, CA: AllCourt Publishing, p. 276.

34 Gubert, B., Sawyer, M. & Fannin, C. (2002). Distinguished African Americans in Aviation and Special Science. Westport, CT: Oryx Press, p. 126.

35 Hardesty, V. (Ed.) (1994). Black Aviator: The Story of William J. Powell. Washington, DC: Smithsonian Institution Press. P. 133.

36 Washington, M. (1934, October). A Race Soars Upward. Opportunity, A Journal of Negro Life, XII(10), p. 301.

Chapter 3

1 U.S. Army War College. (1925, October 30). The Use of Negro Man Power in War. Retrieved from http://cdm16635.contentdm.oclc.org/cdm/ref/collection/p16635coll14/id/56025

2 U.S. Army War College. (1925, October 30). The Use of Negro Man Power in War. Retrieved from http://cdm16635.contentdm.oclc.org/cdm/ref/collection/p16635coll14/id/56025

3 United States Statutes. (1938). Civil Aeronautics Act of 1938. Washington, DC: USGPO.

4 Strickland, P. (1970). The Putt-Putt Air Force: The Story of the Civilian Pilot Training Program and the War Training Service (1939-1944). Washington, DC: U.S. Federal Aviation Administration, p. 1.

5 Strickland, P. (1970). The Putt-Putt Air Force: The Story of the Civilian Pilot Training Program and the War Training Service (1939-1944). Washington, DC: U.S. Federal Aviation Administration.

6 U.S. Department of Commerce. (1941). Civil Pilot Training Manual. Washington, DC: Civil Aeronautics Administration.

7 Correll, J. (2014, January). The Feeder Force, Air Force Magazine, pp. 67-71.

8 Withington, V. (1941, March). The CPTP...? Flying and Popular Aviation, p. 72.

9 Correll, J. (2014, January). The Feeder Force, Air Force Magazine, p. 69.

10 United States Statutes. (1939). Civilian Pilot Training Act of 1939. Washington, DC: USGPO.

11 Tucker, P. (2012). Father of the Tuskegee Airmen: John C. Robinson. Washington, DC: Potomac Books. Page 221.

12 Spencer, C. (1975). Who is Chauncey Spencer? Detroit, MI: Broadside Press, p. 31.

13 Spencer, C. (1975). Who is Chauncey Spencer? Detroit, MI: Broadside Press, p. 29.

14 Spencer, C. (1975). Who is Chauncey Spencer? Detroit, MI: Broadside Press.

15 Spencer, C. (1975). Who is Chauncey Spencer? Detroit, MI: Broadside Press, p. 30.

16 Bragg, J. (1996). Soaring Above Setbacks. Washington, DC: Smithsonian Institution Press, p. 37.

17 ANP. (1939, May 6). Want to Let Gov't Know We Can Fly. The Pittsburgh Courier, p. 7.

18 Spencer, C. (1975). Who is Chauncey Spencer? Detroit, MI: Broadside Press, p. 32.

19 Spencer, C. (1975). Who is Chauncey Spencer? Detroit, MI: Broadside Press, p. 32.

20 Spencer, C. (1975). Who is Chauncey Spencer? Detroit, MI: Broadside Press, p. 32.

21 Spencer, C. (1975). Who is Chauncey Spencer? Detroit, MI: Broadside Press, p. 11.

22 Spencer, C. (1975). Who is Chauncey Spencer? Detroit, MI: Broadside Press.

23 Spencer, C. (1975). Who is Chauncey Spencer? Detroit, MI: Broadside Press, p. 32.

24 Peck, J. (1939, May 20). Good-Will Aviators Run Into Plenty of Trouble. The Pittsburgh Courier, pp. 1, 4.

25 Spencer, C. (1975). Who is Chauncey Spencer? Detroit, MI: Broadside Press, p. 33.

26 Laris, M. (2003). Freedom Flight. Retrieved from https://www.washingtonpost.com/archive/lifestyle/magazine/2003/02/16/freedom-flight

27 Washington Notables Praise 2 Aviators. (1939, May 27). The Pittsburgh Courier, p. 22.

28 Washington Notables Praise 2 Aviators. (1939, May 27). The Pittsburgh Courier, p. 22.

29 Spencer, C. (1975). Who is Chauncey Spencer? Detroit, MI: Broadside Press, p. 34.

30 Spencer, C. (1975). Who is Chauncey Spencer? Detroit, MI: Broadside Press, p. 34.

31 United States Statutes. (1939). Civiian Pilot Training Act of 1939. Washington, DC: USGPO.

32 Withington, V. (1941, March). The CPTP...? Flying and Popular Aviation, p. 58.

33 Young, D. (2003). Chicago Aviation: An Illustrated History. DeKalb, IL: Northern Illinois University Press.

34 Kraus, T. (n.d.). The CAA Helps America Prepare for World War II. Retrieved fromhttps://www.faa.gov/about/history/milestones/media/The_CAA_Helps_America_Prepare_for_World_WarII.pdf

35 Withington, V. (1941, March). The CPTP...? Flying and Popular Aviation, p. 72.

36 United States Statutes. (1936). An act to provide more effectively for the national defense by further increasing the effectiveness and efficiency of the Air Corps of the Army of the United States. Washington, DC: USGPO.

37 Schirmer, R. (1991, Spring). AAC & AAF Civil Primary Flying Schools 1939-1945 Part I. Journal American Aviation Historical Society,(36)1, pp. 2-23.

38 United States Statutes. (1936). An act to provide more effectively for the national defense by further increasing the effectiveness and efficiency of the Air Corps of the Army of the United States. Washington, DC: USGPO.

39 Broadnax, S. (2007). Blue Skies, Black Wings. Westport, CT: Praeger Publishers, p. 21.

40 Broadnax, S. (2007). Blue Skies, Black Wings. Westport, CT: Praeger Publishers, p. 21.

41 Cooper, C. & Cooper, A. (2001). Tuskegee's Heroes. Osceola, WI: MBI Publishing Company, p. 46.

42 Paszek, L. (1967, Spring). Negroes and the Air Force, 1939-1949. Military Affairs, 31 (1), pp. 1-9.

43 Paszek, L. (1967, Spring). Negroes and the Air Force, 1939-1949. Military Affairs, 31 (1), pp. 2.

44 Paszek, L. (1967, Spring). Negroes and the Air Force, 1939-1949. Military Affairs, 31 (1), pp. 1-9.

45 United States Statutes. (1940). Selective Training and Service Act of 1940.

46 Paszek, L. (1967, Spring). Negroes and the Air Force, 1939-1949. Military Affairs, 31 (1), p. 2.

47 Paszek, L. (1967, Spring). Negroes and the Air Force, 1939-1949. Military Affairs, 31 (1), pp. 2.

48 Broadnax, S. (2007). Blue Skies, Black Wings. Westport, CT: Praeger Publishers, p. 20.

Chapter 4

1   Washington, B. (1901). Up From Slavery, An Autobiography. Doubleday, Page & Co: NY, p. 1.

2   Washington, B. (1901). Up From Slavery, An Autobiography. Doubleday, Page & Co: NY, p. 110.

3   Weeks, S. (1915). History of Public School Education in Alabama. Washington, DC: Government Printing Office.

4   Moton, R. (1921). Finding a Way Out. An Autobiography. Garden City, NJ: Doubleday, Page & Company, p. 251.

5   Tucker, P. (2012). Father of the Tuskegee Airmen: John C. Robinson. Washington, DC: Potomac Books, p. 53.

6   Tucker, P. (2012). Father of the Tuskegee Airmen: John C. Robinson. Washington, DC: Potomac Books, pp. 52, 55.

7   Thomas, S. (n.d.). Pieces of our Past. Retrieved from http://courier-herald.com/ bookmark/4896763-Pieces-Of-Our-Pas-Editorial

8   Scott, L. & Womack, W. (1994). Double V. East Landing, MI: Michigan State University Press, p. 46.

9   Janet. (1936, May). John Robinson Wings His Way Down to Tuskegee. The Chicago Defender, p. 2.

10 Col. John Robinson Welcomed. (1934, May 25). Montgomery Advertiser, p. 18.

11 Tucker, P. (2012). Father of the Tuskegee Airmen: John C. Robinson. Washington, DC: Potomac Books, p. 56.

12 Tucker, P. (2012). Father of the Tuskegee Airmen: John C. Robinson. Washington, DC: Potomac Books, p. 202.

13 Tucker, P. (2012). Father of the Tuskegee Airmen: John C. Robinson. Washington, DC: Potomac Books, p. 56.

14 Tucker, P. (2012). Father of the Tuskegee Airmen: John C. Robinson. Washington, DC: Potomac Books, p. 57.

15 Sherrer, J. (1976, November). C. Alfred "Chief Anderson, The Most Famous Black Aviator in America. Retrieved from http://lestweforget.hamptonu.edu/page.cfm?uuid=9FEC34A6-CA01-7F56-073D8494ACD66F4F, para. 5.

16 Tucker, P. (2012). Father of the Tuskegee Airmen: John C. Robinson. Washington, DC: Potomac Books, p. 204.

17 Tucker, P. (2012). Father of the Tuskegee Airmen: John C. Robinson. Washington, DC: Potomac Books, p. 204.

18 Washington, G. (1972). The History of Military and Civilian Pilot Training of Negroes at Tuskegee Alabama 1939 – 1945. Washington, DC: Author, card 211.

19 Goodson, M. (Ed.) (1991). Chronicle of Faith: The Autobiography of Frederick D. Patterson. Tuscaloosa, AL: The University of Alabama Press, pp. 73-75.

20 George L. Washington. (1983, June 11). New York Times. Retrieved from http://www.nytimes.com/1983/06/11/obituaries/george-l-washington.html

21 Washington, G. (1972). The History of Military and Civilian Pilot Training of Negroes at Tuskegee Alabama 1939 – 1945. Washington, DC: Author, card 5.

22 Washington, G. (1972). The History of Military and Civilian Pilot Training of Negroes at Tuskegee Alabama 1939 – 1945. Washington, DC: Author, cards 8-11.

23 Washington, G. (1972). The History of Military and Civilian Pilot Training of Negroes at Tuskegee Alabama 1939 – 1945. Washington, DC: Author, cards 15-17.

24 Washington, G. (1972). The History of Military and Civilian Pilot Training of Negroes at Tuskegee Alabama 1939 – 1945. Washington, DC: Author, card 6.

25 Washington, G. (1972). The History of Military and Civilian Pilot Training of Negroes at Tuskegee Alabama 1939 – 1945. Washington, DC: Author, card 17.

26 Washington, G. (1972). The History of Military and Civilian Pilot Training of Negroes at Tuskegee Alabama 1939 – 1945. Washington, DC: Author, card 83.

27 Broadnax, S. (2007). Blue Skies, Black Wings. Westport, CT: Praeger Publishers, p. 25.

28 Washington, G. (1972). The History of

Military and Civilian Pilot Training of Negroes at Tuskegee Alabama 1939 – 1945. Washington, DC: Author, card 23.

29 Washington, G. (1972). The History of Military and Civilian Pilot Training of Negroes at Tuskegee Alabama 1939 – 1945. Washington, DC: Author, card 288.

30 Washington, G. (1972). The History of Military and Civilian Pilot Training of Negroes at Tuskegee Alabama 1939 – 1945. Washington, DC: Author, card 43.

31 Washington, G. (1972). The History of Military and Civilian Pilot Training of Negroes at Tuskegee Alabama 1939 – 1945. Washington, DC: Author, card 43.

32 Civil Aeronautics Administration. (1941). Civil Pilot Training Manual. Civil Aeronautics Bulletin No. 23. Second Edition. Washington, DC: United States Department of Commerce.

33 Strickland, P. (1984). The Putt-Putt Air Force: The Story of the Civilian Pilot Training Program and the War Training Service (1939-1944). Washington, DC: Department of Transportation, p. 83.

34 Washington, G. (1972). The History of Military and Civilian Pilot Training of Negroes at Tuskegee Alabama 1939 – 1945. Washington, DC: Author, card 34.

Chapter 5

1   Washington, G. (1972). The History of Military and Civilian Pilot Training of Negroes at Tuskegee Alabama 1939 – 1945. Washington, DC: Author, card 37.

2   Haulman, D. (2014, June). The Tuskegee Airfields. Air Force Magazine, pp. 60-65.

3   Washington, G. (1972). The History of Military and Civilian Pilot Training of Negroes at Tuskegee Alabama 1939 – 1945. Washington, DC: Author, cards 37-40.

4   Broadnax, S. (2007). Blue Skies, Black Wings. Westport, CT: Praeger Publishers, p. 26.

5   Bucholtz, C. (2007). 332nd Fighter Group – Tuskegee Airmen. New York: Osprey Publishing Limited.

6   Washington, G. (1972). The History of Military and Civilian Pilot Training of Negroes at Tuskegee Alabama 1939 – 1945. Washington,

DC: Author, card 41.

7   Washington, G. (1972). The History of Military and Civilian Pilot Training of Negroes at Tuskegee Alabama 1939 – 1945. Washington, DC: Author, card 121.

8   Freeman, P. (2015). Abandoned & Little-Known Airfields: Alabama, Montgomery Area. Retrieved from http://www.airfields-freeman. com/AL/Airfields_AL_Montgomery.htm#griel

9   Washington, G. (1972). The History of Military and Civilian Pilot Training of Negroes at Tuskegee Alabama 1939 – 1945. Washington, DC: Author, card 51.

10   Washington, G. (1972). The History of Military and Civilian Pilot Training of Negroes at Tuskegee Alabama 1939 – 1945. Washington, DC: Author, card 55.

11   Washington, G. (1972). The History of Military and Civilian Pilot Training of Negroes at Tuskegee Alabama 1939 – 1945. Washington, DC: Author, card 46.

12   Washington, G. (1972). The History of Military and Civilian Pilot Training of Negroes at Tuskegee Alabama 1939 – 1945. Washington, DC: Author, card 63.

13   Civil Aeronautics Administration. (1941). Civil Pilot Training Manual. Washington, DC: USGPO.

14   Washington, G. (1972). The History of Military and Civilian Pilot Training of Negroes at Tuskegee Alabama 1939 – 1945. Washington, DC: Author, card 53.

15   Washington, G. (1972). The History of Military and Civilian Pilot Training of Negroes at Tuskegee Alabama 1939 – 1945. Washington, DC: Author, card 63.

16   Strickland, P. (1984). The Putt-Putt Air Force: The Story of the Civilian Pilot Training Program and the War Training Service (1939-1944). Washington, DC: Department of Transportation, p. 81.

17   American Heritage. (1999). Waco UPF-7. Retrieved from http://www.aviation-history.com/ waco/upf-7.html

18   Washington, G. (1972). The History of Military and Civilian Pilot Training of Negroes at Tuskegee Alabama 1939 – 1945. Washington, DC: Author, card 75.

19   Washington, G. (1972). The History of

Military and Civilian Pilot Training of Negroes at Tuskegee Alabama 1939 – 1945. Washington, DC: Author, card 64.

20   Washington, G. (1972). The History of Military and Civilian Pilot Training of Negroes at Tuskegee Alabama 1939 – 1945. Washington, DC: Author, card 71.

21   Washington, G. (1972). The History of Military and Civilian Pilot Training of Negroes at Tuskegee Alabama 1939 – 1945. Washington, DC: Author, card 72.

22   Washington, G. (1972). The History of Military and Civilian Pilot Training of Negroes at Tuskegee Alabama 1939 – 1945. Washington, DC: Author, card 85.

23   Washington, G. (1972). The History of Military and Civilian Pilot Training of Negroes at Tuskegee Alabama 1939 – 1945. Washington, DC: Author, card 6.

24   Washington, G. (1972). The History of Military and Civilian Pilot Training of Negroes at Tuskegee Alabama 1939 – 1945. Washington, DC: Author, card 68.

25   Washington, G. (1972). The History of Military and Civilian Pilot Training of Negroes at Tuskegee Alabama 1939 – 1945. Washington, DC: Author, card 68.

26   Aviation Education Staff. (1984). The Putt-Putt Air Force. The story of the Civilian Pilot Training Program and the War Training Service (1939-1944). Washington, DC: Department of Transportation.

27   Tucker, P. (2012). Father of the Tuskegee Airmen John C. Robinson. Washington, DC: Potomac Books, p. 227.

28   Simmons, T. (1988). The Brown Condor: The True Adventures of John C. Robinson. Bartleby Press, Silver Spring, MD, p. 191.

29   Cooper, C. & Cooper, A. (2001). Tuskegee's Heroes. Osceola, WI: MBI Publishing Company, p. 39.

30   Cooper, C. & Cooper, A. (2001). Tuskegee's Heroes. Osceola, WI: MBI Publishing Company, p. 39.

31   Washington, G. (1972). The History of Military and Civilian Pilot Training of Negroes at Tuskegee Alabama 1939 – 1945. Washington, DC: Author, card 73.

32   Washington, G. (1972). The History of

Military and Civilian Pilot Training of Negroes at Tuskegee Alabama 1939 – 1945. Washington, DC: Author, card 81.

33   Cooper, C. & Cooper, A. (2001). Tuskegee's Heroes. Osceola, WI: MBI Publishing Company, p. 38.

34   Washington, G. (1972). The History of Military and Civilian Pilot Training of Negroes at Tuskegee Alabama 1939 – 1945. Washington, DC: Author, card 201.

35   Washington, G. (1972). The History of Military and Civilian Pilot Training of Negroes at Tuskegee Alabama 1939 – 1945. Washington, DC: Author, card 62.

36   Washington, G. (1972). The History of Military and Civilian Pilot Training of Negroes at Tuskegee Alabama 1939 – 1945. Washington, DC: Author, card 83.

37   Washington, G. (1972). The History of Military and Civilian Pilot Training of Negroes at Tuskegee Alabama 1939 – 1945. Washington, DC: Author, card 76.

38   Austin, M. (1941, March). The Negro is flying. Flying and Popular Aviation, p. 34.

39   Washington, G. (1972). The History of Military and Civilian Pilot Training of Negroes at Tuskegee Alabama 1939 – 1945. Washington, DC: Author, card 19.

40   Washington, G. (1972). The History of Military and Civilian Pilot Training of Negroes at Tuskegee Alabama 1939 – 1945. Washington, DC: Author, card 93.

41   Washington, G. (1972). The History of Military and Civilian Pilot Training of Negroes at Tuskegee Alabama 1939 – 1945. Washington, DC: Author, card 94.

42   Washington, G. (1972). The History of Military and Civilian Pilot Training of Negroes at Tuskegee Alabama 1939 – 1945. Washington, DC: Author, card 91.

43   Washington, G. (1972). The History of Military and Civilian Pilot Training of Negroes at Tuskegee Alabama 1939 – 1945. Washington, DC: Author, card 94.

44   Austin, M. (1941, March). The Negro is Flying. Flying and Popular Aviation, p.74.

45   Washington, G. (1972). The History of Military and Civilian Pilot Training of Negroes at Tuskegee Alabama 1939 – 1945. Washington,

DC: Author, card 94.

46 Washington, G. (1972). The History of Military and Civilian Pilot Training of Negroes at Tuskegee Alabama 1939 – 1945. Washington, DC: Author, card 90.

47 Washington, G. (1972). The History of Military and Civilian Pilot Training of Negroes at Tuskegee Alabama 1939 – 1945. Washington, DC: Author, card 95.

48 Goodson, M. (Ed.) (1991). Chronicle of Faith: The Autobiography of Frederick D. Patterson. Tuscaloosa, AL: The University of Alabama Press, p. 74.

49 Washington, G. (1972). The History of Military and Civilian Pilot Training of Negroes at Tuskegee Alabama 1939 – 1945. Washington, DC: Author, card 106.

50 Washington, G. (1972). The History of Military and Civilian Pilot Training of Negroes at Tuskegee Alabama 1939 – 1945. Washington, DC: Author, cards 120A, 148.

51 Washington, G. (1972). The History of Military and Civilian Pilot Training of Negroes at Tuskegee Alabama 1939 – 1945. Washington, DC: Author, card 152.

52 Washington, G. (1972). The History of Military and Civilian Pilot Training of Negroes at Tuskegee Alabama 1939 – 1945. Washington, DC: Author, Washington, card 148.

53 Craven, W. & Cate, J. (1955). The Army Air Forces in World War II, Volume Six, Men and Planes. Chicago, IL: University of Chicago Press, pp. 454-461.

54 Craven, W. & Cate, J. (1955). The Army Air Forces in World War II, Volume Six, Men and Planes. Chicago, IL: University of Chicago Press, p. 454.

55 Craven, W. & Cate, J. (1955). The Army Air Forces in World War II, Volume Six, Men and Planes. Chicago, IL: University of Chicago Press, p. 457.

56 Washington, G. (1972). The History of Military and Civilian Pilot Training of Negroes at Tuskegee Alabama 1939 – 1945. Washington, DC: Author, card 385.

57 Craven, W. & Cate, J. (1955). The Army Air Forces in World War II, Volume Six, Men and Planes. Chicago, IL: University of Chicago Press, p. 460.

58 Craven, W. & Cate, J. (1955). The Army Air Forces in World War II, Volume Six, Men and Planes. Chicago, IL: University of Chicago Press, p. 464.

Chapter 6

1 Lee, W. (2003, July). Jim Crow and Uncle Sam: The Tuskegee Flying Units and the U.S. Army Air Forces in Europe During World War II. The Journal of Military History, 69(3), pp. 787-788.

2 MacGregor, M. (1981). Integration of the Armed Forces 1940-1965. Washington, DC: Center of Military History, United States Army, p. 27.

3 Cooper, C. & Cooper, A. (2001). Tuskegee's Heroes. Osceola, WI: MBI Publishing Company, p. 52.

4 Cooper, C. & Cooper, A. (2001). Tuskegee's Heroes. Osceola, WI: MBI Publishing Company, p. 52.

5 Selective Training and Service Act of 1940, 50 U.S.C. (1941).

6 The New York Age. (1940, October 19). President Okays Jim Crowism, pp. 1, 12.

7 Moye, J. (2010). Freedom Flyers: The Tuskegee Airmen of World War II. New York, NY: Oxford University Press, p. 52.

8 Washington, G. (1972). The History of Military and Civilian Pilot Training of Negroes at Tuskegee Alabama 1939 – 1945. Washington, DC: Author, card 103.

9 Washington, G. (1972). The History of Military and Civilian Pilot Training of Negroes at Tuskegee Alabama 1939 – 1945. Washington, DC: Author, cards 119, 120.

10 Washington, G. (1972). The History of Military and Civilian Pilot Training of Negroes at Tuskegee Alabama 1939 – 1945. Washington, DC: Author, card 118.

11 Scott, L. & Womack, W. ((1994). Double V The Civil Rights Struggle of the Tuskegee Airmen. East Lansing, MI: Michigan State University Press, p. 140.

12 Tuskegee Selected to Train Flyers. (1941, January 25). The Pittsburgh Courier, p. 1.

13 McKenzie, M. (1941, January 25). Just a Bone, The Pittsburgh Courier, p. 24.

14 Hess, J. (1972), Oral History Interview with William H. Hastie. Retrieved from https://www.trumanlibrary.org/oralhist/hastie.htm, para. 15.

15 Washington, G. (1972). The History of Military and Civilian Pilot Training of Negroes at Tuskegee Alabama 1939 – 1945. Washington, DC: Author, card 133.

16 Hastie, W. (1940, December 31). Army Air Corps Plan for Negro Participation. Washington, DC: War Department, Office of the Assistant Secretary.

17 Arnold, H. (1941, January 8). Memorandum for Colonel War. Washington, DC: War Department, Office of the Chief of the Air Corps.

18 Hastie, W. (1943). On Clipped Wings, The Story of Jim Crow in the Army Air Corps. New York, NY: National Association for the Advancement of Colored People.

19 Hess, J. (1972). Oral History Interview with Judge William H. Hastie. Retrieved from https://www.trumanlibrary.org/oralhist/hastie.htm, p. 9.

20 Homan, L. & Reilly, T. (2008). Black Knights: The Story of the Tuskegee Airmen. Gretna, LA: Pelican Publishing Company, Inc., p. 28.

21 Washington, G. (1972). The History of Military and Civilian Pilot Training of Negroes at Tuskegee Alabama 1939 – 1945. Washington, DC: Author, card 101.

22 Patterson, F. (1991). Chronicles of Faith, The Autobiography of Frederick D. Patterson. Tuscaloosa, MS: University of Alabama Press, p. 78.

23 Cooper, C. & Cooper, A. (2001). Tuskegee's Heroes. Osceola, WI: MBI Publishing Company, p. 43.

24 Osur, A. (1977). Blacks in the Army Air Forces During World War II. Washington, DC: Office of Air Force History, p. 24.

25 Paszek, L. (1967, Spring). Negroes and the Air Force, 1939-1949. Military Affairs, 31 (1), pp. 1-9.

26 Paszek, L. (1967, Spring). Negroes and the Air Force, 1939-1949. Military Affairs, 31 (1), pp. 1-9.

27 Washington, G. (1972). The History of Military and Civilian Pilot Training of Negroes at Tuskegee Alabama 1939 – 1945. Washington, DC: Author, card 329.

28 Washington, G. (1972). The History of Military and Civilian Pilot Training of Negroes at Tuskegee Alabama 1939 – 1945. Washington, DC: Author, card 107.

29 Washington, G. (1972). The History of Military and Civilian Pilot Training of Negroes at Tuskegee Alabama 1939 – 1945. Washington, DC: Author, card 117.

30 Washington, G. (1972). The History of Military and Civilian Pilot Training of Negroes at Tuskegee Alabama 1939 – 1945. Washington, DC: Author, card 152.

31 Washington, G. (1972). The History of Military and Civilian Pilot Training of Negroes at Tuskegee Alabama 1939 – 1945. Washington, DC: Author, card 154.

32 Washington, G. (1972). The History of Military and Civilian Pilot Training of Negroes at Tuskegee Alabama 1939 – 1945. Washington, DC: Author, card 166.

33 Washington, G. (1972). The History of Military and Civilian Pilot Training of Negroes at Tuskegee Alabama 1939 – 1945. Washington, DC: Author, card 166.

34 Washington, G. (1972). The History of Military and Civilian Pilot Training of Negroes at Tuskegee Alabama 1939 – 1945. Washington, DC: Author, card 248.

35 Rose, R. (1975). Part I Lonely Eagles, Journal American Aviation Historical Society, Summer 1975, 20(2), pp. 118-127.

36 Washington, G. (1972). The History of Military and Civilian Pilot Training of Negroes at Tuskegee Alabama 1939 – 1945. Washington, DC: Author, card 107.

37 Craven, W. & Cate, J. (Eds.) (1955). The Army Air Forces in World War II: Volume 6 Men and Airplanes. Chicago, IL: University of Chicago Press.

38 McGahan, P. (1941, March 22). Air Corps for Form First Negro Unit. The Philadelphia Inquirer, p. 7.

39 Washington, G. (1972). The History of Military and Civilian Pilot Training of Negroes at Tuskegee Alabama 1939 – 1945. Washington, DC: Author, cards 123 to 127.

40 Paszek, L. (1967, Spring). Negroes and the Air Force, 1939-1949. Military Affairs, 31 (1), pp. 1-9.

41 War Department. (1940, December 18). Training and Establishment of Pursuit Squadron (Colored) Single Engine. Washington, DC: Office of the Chief of the Air Corps.

42 Washington, G. (1972). The History of Military and Civilian Pilot Training of Negroes at Tuskegee Alabama 1939 – 1945. Washington, DC: Author, card 222.

43 Paszek, L. (1967, Spring). Negroes and the Air Force, 1939-1949. Military Affairs, 31 (1), pp. 1-9.

44 Osur, A. (1986). Blacks in the Army Air Force During World War II: The Problems of Race Relations. Washington, DC: Office of Air Force History, p. 24.

45 Haulman, D. (2016). Tuskegee Airmen Chronology. Maxwell AFB, AL: Air Forces Historical Research Agency, p. 18.

46 Stentiford, B. (2011). Landmarks of the American Mosaic: Tuskegee Airmen. Santa Barbara, CA: ABC-CLIO, LLC.

47 Washington, G. (1972). The History of Military and Civilian Pilot Training of Negroes at Tuskegee Alabama 1939 – 1945. Washington, DC: Author, card 177.

48 Washington, G. (1972). The History of Military and Civilian Pilot Training of Negroes at Tuskegee Alabama 1939 – 1945. Washington, DC: Author, card 472.

49 Washington, G. (1972). The History of Military and Civilian Pilot Training of Negroes at Tuskegee Alabama 1939 – 1945. Washington, DC: Author, card 217.

50 Cooper, C. & Cooper, A. (2001). Tuskegee's Heroes. Osceola, WI: MBI Publishing Company.

51 Cooper, C. & Cooper, A. (2001). Tuskegee's Heroes. Osceola, WI: MBI Publishing Company, p. 23.

52 Jakeman, R. (1992). Divided Skies. Tuscaloosa, AL: University of Alabama Press.

53 Washington, G. (1972). The History of Military and Civilian Pilot Training of Negroes at Tuskegee Alabama 1939 – 1945. Washington, DC: Author, card 245.

54 Washington, G. (1972). The History of Military and Civilian Pilot Training of Negroes at Tuskegee Alabama 1939 – 1945. Washington, DC: Author, card 185.

55 Jakeman, R. (1992). Divided Skies. Tuscaloosa, AL: University of Alabama Press, p. 249.

56 Washington, G. (1972). The History of Military and Civilian Pilot Training of Negroes at Tuskegee Alabama 1939 – 1945. Washington, DC: Author, card 182.

57 Hardesty, V. (2008). Black Wings. New York, NY: Harper Collins., p. 74.

58 Brock, P. (1988). Chief Anderson. Retrieved from http://people.com/archive/chief-anderson-vol-30-no-22/, para. 18.

59 Roosevelt, E. (1941, April 1). My Day. Retrieved from https://www2.gwu.edu/~erpapers/myday/displaydoc.cfm?_y=1941&_f=md055850

60 Washington, G. (1972). The History of Military and Civilian Pilot Training of Negroes at Tuskegee Alabama 1939 – 1945. Washington, DC: Author, card 187.

61 Washington, G. (1972). The History of Military and Civilian Pilot Training of Negroes at Tuskegee Alabama 1939 – 1945. Washington, DC: Author, card 184.

62 Washington, G. (1972) The History of Military and Civilian Pilot Training of Negroes at Tuskegee Alabama 1939-1945. Washington, DC: Author, card 184.

63 Washington, G. (1972). The History of Military and Civilian Pilot Training of Negroes at Tuskegee Alabama 1939 – 1945. Washington, DC: Author, cards 187, 251.

64 Washington, G. (1972). The History of Military and Civilian Pilot Training of Negroes at Tuskegee Alabama 1939 – 1945. Washington, DC: Author, card 195.

65 Washington, G. (1972). The History of Military and Civilian Pilot Training of Negroes at Tuskegee Alabama 1939 – 1945. Washington, DC: Author, card 190.

66 Washington, G. (1972). The History of Military and Civilian Pilot Training of Negroes at Tuskegee Alabama 1939 – 1945. Washington, DC: Author, card 194.

67 Washington, G. (1972). The History of Military and Civilian Pilot Training of Negroes at Tuskegee Alabama 1939 – 1945. Washington, DC: Author, card 246.

68 Washington, G. (1972). The History of Military and Civilian Pilot Training of Negroes at Tuskegee Alabama 1939 – 1945. Washington, DC: Author, card 310.

69   Washington, G. (1972). The History of Military and Civilian Pilot Training of Negroes at Tuskegee Alabama 1939 – 1945. Washington, DC: Author, card 310.

Chapter 7

1   Craven, W. & Cate, J. (1955). The Army Air Forces in World War II, Volume Six, Men and Planes. Chicago, Il: University of Chicago Press, p. 558.

2   Holway, J. (1997). Red Tails Black Wings. Las Cruces, NW: Yucca Tree Press, p. 63.

3   Bowers, P. (1966). Boeing Aircraft Since 1916. Fallbrook, CA: Aero Publishers, pp. 219-220.

4   Caver, J., Ennels, J., Haulman, D. (2011). The Tuskegee Airmen An Illustrated History. Montgomery, AL: New South Books, p. 43.

5   Caver, J., Ennels, J., Haulman, D. (2011). The Tuskegee Airmen An Illustrated History. Montgomery, AL: New South Books, p. 53.

6   Craven, W. & Cate, J. (1955). The Army Air Forces in World War II, Volume Six, Men and Planes. Chicago, Il: University of Chicago Press, p. 577.

7   Skiles, J. (2004, May). Aviation Cadet Training. Sport Aviation, pp. 46-48.

8   Caver, J., Ennels, J., Haulman, D. (2011). The Tuskegee Airmen An Illustrated History. Montgomery, AL: New South Books, p. 76.

9   Flight Officers to Make Bow in Air Forces. (1942, August). The Montgomery Advertiser, p. 16.

10   Flight Officer New Army Rank. (1942, November). Belvidere Daily Republican, p. 4.

11   Inaugural Ceremony (1941, July 19). Programme. Tuskegee, AL: Tuskegee Institute.

12   Tucker, P. (2012). Father of the Tuskegee Airmen John C. Robinson. Washington, DC: Potomac Books, p. 231.

13   Inaugural Ceremony. (1941, July). Address by Major General Walter R. Weaver, Commanding Officer, Southeast Air Corps Training Center. Tuskegee, Al: Tuskegee Institute Bureau of Public Relations.

14   Caver, J., Ennels, J., Haulman, D. (2011). The Tuskegee Airmen An Illustrated History.

Montgomery, AL: New South Books, p. 43.

15   Davis, B. (1991). An Autobiography, Benjamin O. Davis, Jr., American. Washington, DC: Smithsonian Institution Press, p. 21.

16   Davis, B. (1991). An Autobiography, Benjamin O. Davis, Jr., American. Washington, DC: Smithsonian Institution Press, p. 70.

17   Jakeman, R. (1992). Divided Skies. Tuscaloosa, AL: University of Alabama Press, p. 273.

18   Goodson, M. (Ed.) (1991). Chronicle of Faith: The Autobiography of Frederick D. Patterson. Tuscaloosa, AL: The University of Alabama Press, p. 79.

19   Jakeman, R. (1992). Divided Skies. Tuscaloosa, AL: University of Alabama Press, p. 275.

20   Washington, G. (1972). The History of Military and Civilian Pilot Training of Negroes at Tuskegee Alabama 1939 – 1945. Washington, DC: Author, cards 239, 239.

21   Jakeman, R. (1992). Divided Skies. Tuscaloosa, AL: University of Alabama Press, p. 277.

22   Jakeman, R. (1992). Divided Skies. Tuscaloosa, AL: University of Alabama Press, p. 290.

23   Jakeman, R. (1992). Divided Skies. Tuscaloosa, AL: University of Alabama Press, p. 287.

24   Washington, G. (1972). The History of Military and Civilian Pilot Training of Negroes at Tuskegee Alabama 1939 – 1945. Washington, DC: Author, card 239.

25   Washington, G. (1972). The History of Military and Civilian Pilot Training of Negroes at Tuskegee Alabama 1939 – 1945. Washington, DC: Author, card 238.

26   Jakeman, R. (1992). Divided Skies. Tuscaloosa, AL: University of Alabama Press, p. 287.

27   Jakeman, R. (1992). Divided Skies. Tuscaloosa, AL: University of Alabama Press, p. 290.

28   Jakeman, R. (1992). Divided Skies. Tuscaloosa, AL: University of Alabama Press, pp. 285, 290.

29   Jakeman, R. (1992). Divided Skies. Tuscaloosa, AL: University of Alabama Press, p. 287.

30   Jakeman, R. (1992). Divided Skies. Tuscaloosa, AL: University of Alabama Press, p. 289.

31   Washington, G. (1972). The History of Military and Civilian Pilot Training of Negroes

at Tuskegee Alabama 1939 – 1945. Washington, DC: Author, card 384.

32   Haulman, D. (2014). The Tuskegee Airfields. Air Forces Magazine, 97(6), pp. 60-65.

33   Freeman, P. (2015). Abandoned & Little-Known Airfields: Alabama, Montgomery Area. Retrieved from http://www.airfields-freeman.com/AL/Airfields_AL_Montgomery.htm#griel

34   Kitchens, J. (1994, November/December). They Also Flew: Pioneer Black Aviation Aviators. United States Army Aviation Digest. Washington, DC: Department of the Army.

35   Washington, G. (1972). The History of Military and Civilian Pilot Training of Negroes at Tuskegee Alabama 1939 – 1945. Washington, DC: Author, card 184.

36   Washington, G. (1972). The History of Military and Civilian Pilot Training of Negroes at Tuskegee Alabama 1939 – 1945. Washington, DC: Author, card 384.

37   Haulman, D. (2014). The Tuskegee Airfields. Air Forces Magazine, 97(6), pp. 60-65.

38   Freeman, P. (2015). Abandoned & Little-Known Airfields: Alabama, Montgomery Area. Retrieved from http://www.airfields-freeman.com/AL/Airfields_AL_Montgomery.htm#griel

39   Davis, B. (1991). An Autobiography, Benjamin O. Davis, Jr., American. Washington, DC: Smithsonian Institution Press, p. 84.

40   Davis, B. (1991). An Autobiography, Benjamin O. Davis, Jr., American. Washington, DC: Smithsonian Institution Press, p. 85.

41   Washington, G. (1972). The History of Military and Civilian Pilot Training of Negroes at Tuskegee Alabama 1939 – 1945. Washington, DC: Author, card 228.

42   Jakeman, R. (1992). The Divided Skies. Tuscaloosa, AL: University of Alabama Press, p. 199.

43   Washington, G. (1972). The History of Military and Civilian Pilot Training of Negroes at Tuskegee Alabama 1939 – 1945. Washington, DC: Author, card 243.

44   Washington, G. (1972). The History of Military and Civilian Pilot Training of Negroes at Tuskegee Alabama 1939 – 1945. Washington, DC: Author, card 355.

45   Jakeman, R. (1992). The Divided Skies. Tuscaloosa, AL: The University of Alabama

Press, p. 300.

46 Washington, G. (1972). The History of Military and Civilian Pilot Training of Negroes at Tuskegee Alabama 1939 – 1945. Washington, DC: Author, card 299.

47 Davis, B. (1991). An Autobiography, Benjamin O. Davis, Jr., American. Washington, DC: Smithsonian Institution Press, p. 89.

48 The Pittsburgh Courier. (1942, September 19). Black Icarus, p. 6.

49 Jakeman, R. (1992). The Divided Skies. Tuscaloosa, AL: University of Alabama Press, p. 300.

50 Washington, G. (1972). The History of Military and Civilian Pilot Training of Negroes at Tuskegee Alabama 1939 – 1945. Washington, DC: Author, card 365.

51 Davis, B. (1991). An Autobiography, Benjamin O. Davis, Jr., American. Washington, DC: Smithsonian Institution Press, p. 86.

52 Washington, G. (1972). The History of Military and Civilian Pilot Training of Negroes at Tuskegee Alabama 1939 – 1945. Washington, DC: Author, cards 346, 356.

53 Washington, G. (1972). The History of Military and Civilian Pilot Training of Negroes at Tuskegee Alabama 1939 – 1945. Washington, DC: Author, card 330.

54 Lambert, F. (1942, June). The Negro as a Military Airman, Flying, pp. 33-34, 66-70.

55 James, R. (2013). The Double V: How Wars, Protest, and Harry Truman Desegregated America's Military. New York, NY: Bloomsbury Press, p. 165.

56 Lambert, F. (1942, June). The Negro as a Military Airman, Flying, p. 66.

57 DeBow, C. & Birnie, W. (1942, August). I Got Wings, American Magazine, pp. 28-29, 104-105.

58 Rose, R. (1975). Part II Lonely Eagles, Journal American Aviation Historical Society, Winter 1975, 20(4), 240-252.

59 Davis, B. (1991). An Autobiography, Benjamin O. Davis, Jr., American. Washington, DC: Smithsonian Institution Press, p. 89.

60 Craven, W. & Cate, J. (1955). The Army Air Forces in World War II, Volume One, Plans and Early Operations. Chicago, Il:

University of Chicago Press, p. 307.

61 Haulman, D. (2015) Tuskegee Airmen Chronology. Maxwell AFB, AL: Air Forces Historical Research Agency, p. 25.

62 Davis, B. (1991). An Autobiography, Benjamin O. Davis, Jr., American. Washington, DC: Smithsonian Institution Press, p. 88.

63 Haulman, D. (2015) Tuskegee Airmen Chronology. Maxwell AFB, AL: Air Forces Historical Research Agency, p. 26.

64 Washington, G. (1972). The History of Military and Civilian Pilot Training of Negroes at Tuskegee Alabama 1939 – 1945. Washington, DC: Author, card 372.

65 The New York Age. (1941, July 19). The Negro Pursuit Squadron, p. 6.

66 Tucker, P. (2012). Father of the Tuskegee Airmen John C. Robinson. Washington, DC: Potomac Books, p. 234.

67 Washington, G. (1972). The History of Military and Civilian Pilot Training of Negroes at Tuskegee Alabama 1939 – 1945. Washington, DC: Author, card 282.

Sidebar: Curtiss P-40 Warhawk

1 McDowell, E. (1976),. Curtiss P-40 in Action. Carrollton, TX: Squadron/Signal Publications, p. 4.

2 McDowell, E. (1976),. Curtiss P-40 in Action. Carrollton, TX: Squadron/Signal Publications, p. 5.

3 McDowell, E. (1976),. Curtiss P-40 in Action. Carrollton, TX: Squadron/Signal Publications, p. 6.

4 McDowell, E. (1976),. Curtiss P-40 in Action. Carrollton, TX: Squadron/Signal Publications, p. 6.

5 McDowell, E. (1976),. Curtiss P-40 in Action. Carrollton, TX: Squadron/Signal Publications, p. 6.

6 Robertson, B. (Ed.). (1961). United States Army and Air Force Fighters 1916-1961. Letchworth, England: Harleyford Publications Ltd, p. 48.

7 Wikipedia. (n.d.). Curtiss P-40 Warhawk. Retrieved from https://en.wikipedia.org/wiki/

Curtiss_P-40_Warhawk

8 Guttman, R. (2000, May). Hawk with Shark's Teeth, the Curtiss P-40. Aviation History, p. 44.

9 Kinzy, B. (1999). P-40 Warhawk in Detail, Part 2. Carrollton, TX: Squadron/Signal Publications, p. 5.

10 Guttman, R. (2000, May). Hawk with Shark's Teeth, the Curtiss P-40. Aviation History, p. 45.

11 Kinzy, B. (1999). P-40 Warhawk in Detail, Part 2. Carrollton, TX: Squadron/Signal Publications, p. 66.

12 Shamburger, P. & Christy, J. (1972). The Curtiss Hawks. Kalamazoo, MI: Wolverine Press, p. 144.

13 Shamburger, P. & Christy, J. (1972). The Curtiss Hawks. Kalamazoo, MI: Wolverine Press, p. 151.

14 McDowell, E. (1976),. Curtiss P-40 in Action. Carrollton, TX: Squadron/Signal Publications, p. 14.

15 Wikipedia. (n.d.). Flying Tigers. Retrieved from https://en.wikipedia.org/wiki/Flying_Tigers

16 Fox, J. (n.d.). The Flying Tigers and the Influence of Nose-Art. Retrieved from https://sites.google.com/site/aviationinamerica/home/the-flying-tigers-1

17 Ward, R. (1970). Sharkmouth 1916-1945. New York, NY: Osprey Publications Ltd.

18 Meyer, C. (2004, Summer). The Curtiss P-40 Warhawk. Flight Journal Special Issue, P-40 Warhawk, p. 17.

19 Mitchell, R. (1992). Airacobra Advantage: The Flying Cannon. Missoula, MT: Pictorial Histories Publishing Company, p. 22.

20 Meyer, C. (2004, Summer). The Curtiss P-40 Warhawk. Flight Journal Special Issue, P-40 Warhawk, p. 17.

Chapter 8

1 McGovern, J. (1976). Emergence of a City in the Modern South: Pensacola 1900-1945. p. 7.

2 Bragaw, D. (1973, January). Status of Negroes in a Southern Port City in the Progressive

Era: Pensacola, 1896-1920. Florida Historical Quarterly, LI(3), Tampa, FL: Florida Historical Society, pp. 281-282.

3   McGovern, J. (1976). Emergence of a City in the Modern South: Pensacola 1900-1945. p. 63.

4   Flint-Goodridge Hospital. (n.d.). Retrieved from https://en.wikipedia.org/wiki/Flint-Goodridge_Hospital

5   Smith, G. 1998). The Ebony Tale of Pensacola. Pensacola, Fl: Author.

6   Wilson, Maggie (Polkinghorne). Personal interview. 26 August 2017.

7   J.R. Polkinghorne Joins Council Race. (1951, April 6). The Pensacola Journal, p. 8.

8   New Drug Store and Soda Fountain. (1914, April 26). The Pensacola News-Journal, p. 3.

9   Legal Notices. (1916, September 29). The Pensacola News-Journal, p. 7.

10 Cohn, D. (2010). Race and the Census: The "Negro" Controversy. Retrieved from http://www.pewsocialtrends.org/2010/01/21/race-and-the-census-the-%E2%80%9Cnegro%E2%80%9D-controversy/

11 Wilson, Maggie (Polkinghorne). Personal interview. 26 August 2017.

12 Demo Committee Race is Swollen. (1950, May 14). The Pensacola News Journal, p. 13.

13 J.R. Polkinghorne Joins Council Race. (1951, April 6). The Pensacola Journal, p. 8.

14 Two Negroes Drop From Council Race. (1951, April 15). The Pensacola News-Journal, p. 15.

15 Nichols, G. (2007, February). Tuskegee Airmen James Polkinghorne in 'Florida Remembers WWII' Display. Gosport.

16 Florida Agricultural and Mechanical College. (1941-1942). Bulletin. Tallahassee, FL.

17 Dawson, Merle. Personal interview. December 10, 2013.

18 Nichols, G. (2007, February). Tuskegee Airmen James Polkinghorne in 'Florida Remembers WWII' Display. Gosport.

19 Begin Training. (1941, June 30). The Pensacola News Journal, p. 8.

20 TAAF To Observe Anniversary. (1945, August 4). The New York Age, p. 12.

21 Revised Schedule of Instruction. (1941, April 22). Tuskegee, AL: 66th AAF Flying Training Detachment.

22 Frazier, H. 2nd Lt. (1942, August 7). Roster of Students. Tuskegee, AL: Headquarters, 66th AAF Flying Training Detachment.

23 Wilson, Maggie (Polkinghorne). Personal interview. 26 August 2017.

24 Frazier, J. (1942, August 7). Roster of Students, Class No. 43-B. Tuskegee, AL: Headquarters, 66th AAF Flying Training Detachment.

25 Wilson, Maggie (Polkinghorne). Personal interview. 26 August 2017.

26 Haulman, D. (2014). Tuskegee Airmen Questions and Answers. Maxwell AFB, AL: Air Force Historical Research Agency, p. 7.

27 Haulman, D. (2014). Tuskegee Airmen Questions and Answers. Maxwell AFB, AL: Air Force Historical Research Agency, p. 7.

28 Homan, L. & Reilly, T. The Tuskegee Airmen. Charleston, SC: Arcadia Publishing, p. 10.

29 TAAF to Observe Anniversary. (1945, August 4). The New York Age, p. 12.

30 Tuskegee Airmen, Inc. (2016). Media Kit. Retrieved from http://tuskegeeairmen.org/wp-content/uploads/2016-TAI-Media-Kit-May-2016.pdf

31 Colasanti, A. Personal Correspondence. 9 February 2018.

32 Colasanti, A. (2008, May 30). [Letter to Christine Biggers]. Tuskegee Airmen National Historic Site, Tuskgee, AL.

33 Lomax, C. (1945, October). Specialized Course of Instruction in Aircraft Fabrics. Tuskegee, AL.

34 Colasanti, A. Personal Correspondence. 9 February 2018.

35 Bucholtz, C. (2007). 332nd Fighter Group – Tuskegee Airmen. Osprey Publishing Limited, New York, NY, p. 14.

36 McKissack, P., McKissack, F. (1995). Red-Tailed Angels. Walker Publishing Company, New York, NY, p. 71.

37 Holway, J. (1997). Red Tails Black Wings. Yucca Tree Press, Las Cruces, NM, p. 64.

38 The Ninety-Ninth Squadron. (1942, August). Time, xv(5), p.13

39 Washington, G. (1972). The History of Military and Civilian Pilot Training of Negroes at Tuskegee Alabama 1939 – 1945. Washington, DC: Author, card 382.

40 Bucholtz, C. (2007). 332nd Fighter Group – Tuskegee Airmen. Osprey Publishing Limited, New York, NY, p. 14.

41 Scott, L. & Womack, W. (1994). Double V. The Civil Rights Struggle of the Tuskegee Airmen. East Lansing, MI: Michigan State University Press, p. 191.

42 Scott, L. & Womack, W. (1994). Double V. The Civil Rights Struggle of the Tuskegee Airmen. East Lansing, MI: Michigan State University Press, p.195.

43 War Department. (1942, October to 1944, March). History of the 332nd Fighter Group. Washington, DC: U.S. Army Air Forces, p. 8.

44 War Department. (1942, October to 1944, March). History of the 332nd Fighter Group. Washington, DC: U.S. Army Air Forces, p. 7.

45 Broadnax, S. (2007). Blue Skies, Black Wings. Westport, CT: Praeger Publishers, p. 133.

46 War Department. (1942, October to 1944, March). History of the 332nd Fighter Group. Washington, DC: U.S. Army Air Forces, p. 9.

47 War Department. (13 Oct 42 to 31 Mar 44). History of the 332nd Fighter Group. U.S. Army Air Forces, p. 11.

48 Maurer, M. (Ed.) (1982). Combat Squadrons of the Air Force. Washington, DC: Officer of Air Force History, p. 365.

49 Broadnax, S. (2007). Blue Skies, Black Wings. Westport, CT: Praeger Publishers, p. 133.

50 War Department. (1942, October to 1944, March). History of the 332nd Fighter Group. Washington, DC: U.S. Army Air Forces, p. 10.

51 Scott, S. (May, 1943). History 301st Fighter Squadron. Washington, DC: U.S. Army Air Forces, p. 8.

52 McKenna, D. (2008, May). The Syracuse Walking Dream. Retrieved from http://

www.washingtoncitypaper.com/news/article/13035742/the-syracuse-walking-dream

53 War Department. (1943, May 6). Report of Aircraft Accident. Oscoda Army Air Field: U.S. Army Air Forces.

54 Scott, L. & Womack, W. (1994). Double V. East Lansing, MI: Michigan State University Press, p. 195.

55 Simmons, R. (1943, October 31). Morale Chief Spurs Colored Selfridge Unit, Chicago Tribune, p. 137.

56 War Department. (13 Oct 42 to 31 Mar 44). History of the 332nd Fighter Group. U.S. Army Air Forces, p. 3.

57 War Department. (1943, May 25). Report of Aircraft Accident. Oscoda Army Air Field: U.S. Army Air Forces.

58 War Department. (1943, May 25). Report of Aircraft Accident. Oscoda Army Air Field: U.S. Army Air Forces

59 War Department. (1943, June 29). Report of Aircraft Accident. Oscoda Army Air Field: U.S. Army Air Forces

60 War Department. (1943, June 29). Report of Aircraft Accident. Oscoda Army Air Field: U.S. Army Air Forces

61 Davis, B. (1991), An Autobiography, Benjamin O. Davis, Jr., American. Washington, DC: Smithsonian Institute Press, p. 89.

62 Holway, J. (1997). Red Tails Black Wings. Yucca Tree Press, Las Cruces, NM, p. 77.

63 Washington, G. (1972). The History of Military and Civilian Pilot Training of Negroes at Tuskegee Alabama 1939 – 1945. Washington, DC: Author, card 416.

64 Washington, G. (1972). The History of Military and Civilian Pilot Training of Negroes at Tuskegee Alabama 1939 – 1945. Washington, DC: Author, card 416.

65 Wikipedia. (n.d.) Northwest African Tactical Air Force. Retrieved from https://en.wikipedia.org/wiki/Northwest_African_Tactical_Air_Force#cite_note-2

Chapter 9

1 Davis, B. (1991). An Autobiography, Benjamin O. Davis, Jr., American. Washington, DC: Smithsonian Institution Press, p. 95.

2 Davis, B. (1991). An Autobiography, Benjamin O. Davis, Jr., American. Washington, DC: Smithsonian Institution Press, p. 94

3 Davis, B. (1991). An Autobiography, Benjamin O. Davis, Jr., American. Washington, DC: Smithsonian Institution Press, p. 98.

4 Davis, B. (1991). An Autobiography, Benjamin O. Davis, Jr., American. Washington, DC: Smithsonian Institution Press, p. 97.

5 Kaiser, D. (n.d.). NATAF Organization for Operation Husky, the Invasion of Sicily. Retrieved from http://www.warwingsart.com/12thAirForce/nataf.html

6 Davis, B. (1991). An Autobiography, Benjamin O. Davis, Jr., American. Washington, DC: Smithsonian Institution Press, p. 36.

7 Homan, L. & Reilly, T. (2008). Black Knights: The Story of the Tuskegee Airmen. Gretna, LA: Pelican Publishing Company, Inc., p. 99.

8 Negro Pilots Pass First Combat Test. (1943, June 24). The Daily Telegram, p. 1.

9 Francis, C. (1955). The Tuskegee Airmen. Boston, MA: Bruce Humphries, Inc., p. 36.

10 Holway, J. (1997). Red Tails Black Wings. Las Cruces, NM: Yucca Tree Press, p. 92.

11 Davis, B. (1991). An Autobiography, Benjamin O. Davis, Jr., American. Washington, DC: Smithsonian Institution Press, p. 99.

12 Davis, B. (1991). An Autobiography, Benjamin O. Davis, Jr., American. Washington, DC: Smithsonian Institution Press, p. 99.

13 Davis, B. (1991). An Autobiography, Benjamin O. Davis, Jr., American. Washington, DC: Smithsonian Institution Press, p. 102.

14 Stimson, Davis Meet in Tunisia. (1943, August 14). Pittsburgh Courier, p. 1.

15 House, E. (1943, September 16). Combat Efficiency of the 99th Pursuit Squadron. Headquarters XII Air Support Command. In Stentiford, B. (2012), Tuskegee Airmen. Santa Barbara, CA: ABC-CLIO, LLC, pp. 160-161.

16 Lee, U. (1963). The Employment of Negro Troops. Washinton, DC: U.S. Army Center of Military History, p. 453.

17 Davis, B. (1991). An Autobiography, Benjamin O. Davis, Jr., American. Washington, DC: Smithsonian Institution Press, p. 103.

18 Davis, B. (1991). An Autobiography, Benjamin O. Davis, Jr., American. Washington, DC: Smithsonian Institution Press, p. 103.

19 David Home, Lauds '99th.' (1943, September 18). Pittsburgh Courier, pp. 1, 4.

20 Wener, L. (1943, September 25). Experiment Successful, The New York Age, p. 6.

21 David Home, Lauds '99th.' (1943, September 18). Pittsburgh Courier, pp. 1, 4.

22 Rouzeau, E. (1943, September 18). Rouzeau Tells How Our Boys Fight Germans. Pittsburgh Courier, p. i.

23 Experiment Proved? (1943, September). Time, XLII(12), pp. 66,68.

24 Davis, B. (1991). An Autobiography, Benjamin O. Davis, Jr., American. Washington, DC: Smithsonian Institution Press, p. 104.

25 Time Casts Doubts. (1943, September 25). The Pittsburgh Courier, p. 6.

26 Davis, A. (1943, October). Letters. Time, XLII(16), pp. 8, 11.

27 Mjagkj, N. (Ed.). Organizing Black America: An Encyclopedia of African American Associations. New York, NY: Garland Publishing, Inc., p. 161.

28 Davis, B. (1991). An Autobiography, Benjamin O. Davis, Jr., American. Washington, DC: Smithsonian Institution Press, p. 105.

29 Davis, B. (1991). An Autobiography, Benjamin O. Davis, Jr., American. Washington, DC: Smithsonian Institution Press, p. 105.

30 Haulman, D. (2013, July). Tuskgee Airmen Chronology. Maxwell AFB: Air Force Historical Research Agency.

31 Scott, S. & Womack, W. (1994). Double V. East Lansing, MI: Michigan State University Press, p. 188.

32 U.S. Army Air Forces. (1944, March). Operations of the 99th Fighter Squadron Compared with Other P40 Squadrons in MTO. Air Force Historical Research Agency, Maxwell AFB, Alabama.

33 Bucholtz, C. (2007). 332nd Fighter Group – Tuskegee Airmen. New York, NY: Osprey Publishing, p. 27.

Sidebar:
Bell P-39 Airacobra

1   U.S.A.A.F. Resource Center. P-39 Aira-cobra Design & Development. Retrieved from http://www.warbirdsresourcegroup.org/URG/p39_design.html

2   Mitchell, R. (1992). Airacobra Advantage: The Flying Cannon. Missoula, MT: Pictorial Histories Publishing Company.

3   Trimble, R. (1982, December). Bell's Iron Dog. Air Classics, 18(12), pp. 29-,31 64-77.

4   Wainwright, M. (2008, June). Airacobra! Air Classics, (44)6, p. 22.

5   Trimble, R. (1982, December). Bell's Iron Dog. Air Classics, 18(12), p. 64.

6   Trimble, R. (1982, December). Bell's Iron Dog. Air Classics, 18(12), p. 70.

7   Mitchell, R. (1992). Airacobra Advantage: The Flying Cannon. Missoula, MT: Pictorial Histories Publishing Company, p. 12.

8   O'Leary, M. (2004, September). Airacobra. Air Classics (40)9, p. 32.

9   Mitchell, R. (1992). Airacobra Advantage: The Flying Cannon. Missoula, MT: Pictorial Histories Publishing Company, p. 35.

10 Mitchell, R. (1992). Airacobra Advantage: The Flying Cannon. Missoula, MT: Pictorial Histories Publishing Company, p. 2.

11 Mitchell, R. (1992). Airacobra Advantage: The Flying Cannon. Missoula, MT: Pictorial Histories Publishing Company, p. 37.

12 Trimble, R. (1982, December). Bell's Iron Dog. Air Classics, 18(12), pp. 29.

13 Mitchell, R. (1992). Airacobra Advantage: The Flying Cannon. Missoula, MT: Pictorial Histories Publishing Company, p. 12.

14 O'Leary, M. (2004, September). Airacobra. Air Classics (40)9, p. 57.

15 Mitchell, R. (1992). Airacobra Advantage: The Flying Cannon. Missoula, MT: Pictorial Histories Publishing Company, p. 13.

16 Mitchell, R. (1992). Airacobra Advantage: The Flying Cannon. Missoula, MT: Pictorial Histories Publishing Company, p. 22.

Chapter 10

1   War Department. (June 1943 to March 1944). History of the 332nd Fighter Group. U.S. Army Air Forces, p. 15.

2   War Department. (October 19 42 to August 1943). History of the 332nd Fighter Group. U.S. Army Air Forces, p. 16.

3   War Department. (October 1942 to August 1943). History of the 332nd Fighter Group. U.S. Army Air Forces, p. 15.

4   War Department. (October 1942 to August 1943). History of the 332nd Fighter Group. U.S. Army Air Forces, p. 16.

5   War Department. (June 1943 to March 1944). History of the 332nd Fighter Group. U.S. Army Air Forces, p. 21.

6   Holway, J. (1997). Red Tails Black Wings. Las Cruces, NM: Yucca Tree Press, p. 123.

7   Saccone, G. (1987). Training of the Tuskegee Airman. Champaign-Urbana: University of Illinois, p. 74.

8   Holway, J. (1997). Red Tails Black Wings. Las Cruces, NM: Yucca Tree Press, p. 123.

9   Holway, J. (1997). Red Tails Black Wings. Las Cruces, NM: Yucca Tree Press, p. 124.

10 Schooling Selfridge Pilots, Ground Crews in New P-39 Pursuit Planes. (1943, October 23). The Pittsburgh Courier, p. 2.

11 War Department. (June 1943 to March 1944). History of the 332nd Fighter Group. U.S. Army Air Forces, p. 27.

12 Davis, B. (1991). An Autobiography, Benjamin O. Davis, Jr., American. Washington, DC: Smithsonian Institution Press, p. 110.

13 Davis, B. (1991). An Autobiography, Benjamin O. Davis, Jr., American. Washington, DC: Smithsonian Institution Press, p. 113.

14 Davis, B. (1991). An Autobiography, Benjamin O. Davis, Jr., American. Washington, DC: Smithsonian Institution Press, p. 111.

15 War Department. (June 1943 to March 1944). History of the 332nd Fighter Group. U.S. Army Air Forces, p. 29.

16 War Department. (June 1943 to March 1944). History of the 332nd Fighter Group. U.S. Army Air Forces, p. 29.

17 War Department. (June 1943 to March 1944). History of the 332nd Fighter Group. U.S. Army Air Forces, p. 32.

18 War Department. (13 Oct 42 to 31 Mar 44). History of the 332nd Fighter Group. U.S. Army Air Forces, section 2

19 War Department. (June 1943 to March 1944). History of the 332nd Fighter Group. U.S. Army Air Forces, p. 33.

20 War Department. (June 1943 to March 1944). History of the 332nd Fighter Group. U.S. Army Air Forces, p. 29.

21 Scott, S. (1943, July). History of the 301st Fighter Squadron. U.S. Army Air Forces, p. 17.

22 Nichols, G. (2007, February). Tuskegee Airmen James Polkinghorne in 'Florida Remembers WWII' Display. Gosport.

23 War Department. (June 1943 to March 1944). History of the 332nd Fighter Group. U.S. Army Air Forces, p. 34.

24 War Department. (June 1943 to March 1944). History of the 332nd Fighter Group. U.S. Army Air Forces, p. 34.

25 War Department. (June 1943 to March 1944). History of the 332nd Fighter Group. U.S. Army Air Forces, p. 35.

26 Scott, S. (1943, July). History of the 301st Fighter Squadron. U.S. Army Air Forces, p. 18.

27 War Department. (June 1943 to March 1944). History of the 332nd Fighter Group. U.S. Army Air Forces, pp. 30,33.

28 War Department. (June 1943 to March 1944). History of the 332nd Fighter Group. U.S. Army Air Forces, pp. 35,36.

29 War Department. (June 1943 to March 1944). History of the 332nd Fighter Group. U.S. Army Air Forces, p. 36.

30 War Department. (June 1943 to March 1944). History of the 332nd Fighter Group. U.S. Army Air Forces, p. 36.

31 Wrecksite. (n.d.). SS Clark Mills. Retrieved from http://www.wrecksite.eu/wreck.aspx?37150

32 Scott, S. (1943, July). History of the 301st

Fighter Squadron. U.S. Army Air Forces, p. 19.

33 Gandy, S. (2011). Down on the Ground, The Diary of an Enlisted Tuskegee Airmen, Denver, CO: Outskirts Press, pp. 5-8.

34 Fifth Army History. (1944). Part V The Drive to Rome. Italy, Headquarters Fifth Army, p. 211.

35 Fifth Army History. (1944). Part V The Drive to Rome. Italy, Headquarters Fifth Army, p. 157.

36 Rose, R. (1975). Part II Lonely Eagles, Journal American Aviation Historical Society, Winter 1975, 20(4), pp. 240-252.

37 Tucker, G. (1944, February 25). Negro Air Squadron Clicks on Downbeat, Pittsburgh Post-Gazette, p. 5.

38 Negro Fighter Squadron Praised by Arnold. (1944, February 6). Deadwood Pioneer-Times, p. 1.

39 Army & Navy. (1944, February). Sweet Victories, Time Magazine, XLIII(7), pp. 68-70.

40 War Department. (June 1943 to March 1944). History of the 332nd Fighter Group. U.S. Army Air Forces, p. 37.

41 Bucholtz, C. (2007). 332nd Fighter Group – Tuskegee Airmen. Osprey Publishing Limited, New York, NY, p. 37.

42 Gandy, S. (2011). Down on the Ground, The Diary of an Enlisted Tuskegee Airmen, Denver, CO: Outskirts Press, pp. 5-8.

43 Busby, J. (1944, February). War Diary, HQ 332nd Ftr Gp. U.S. Army Air Forces, p. 1.

44 British 8th Army Patrols Join Yanks. (1943, September 17). St. Louis Post-Dispatch, p. 9

45 Allies Using Big Airfield Near Salerno. (1943, September 19). The Greenville News, p. 1.

46 Busby, J. (1944, February). War Diary, HQ 332nd Ftr Gp. U.S. Army Air Forces, p. 1.

47 Davis, B. (1991). An Autobiography, Benjamin O. Davis, Jr., American. Washington, DC: Smithsonian Institution Press, p. 116.

48 Mitchell, R. (1992). Airacobra Advantage: The Flying Cannon. Missoula, MT: Pictorial Histories Publishing Company, p. 37.

49 Hatchett, M. (1944, March). War Diary

of the 301st Fighter Squadron. U.S. Army Air Forces, p. 1

50 Busby, J. (1944, February). War Diary, HQ 332nd Ftr Gp. U.S. Army Air Forces, p. 3.

51 Mitchell, R. (1992). Airacobra Advantage: The Flying Cannon. Missoula, MT: Pictorial Histories Publishing Company, p. 37.

52 U.S. Army Air Forces. (1944, March). Operations of the 99th Fighter Squadron Compared with Other P40 Squadrons in MTO. Air Force Historical Research Agency, Maxwell AFB, Alabama.

53 Davis, B. (1991). An Autobiography, Benjamin O. Davis, Jr., American. Washington, DC: Smithsonian Institution Press, p. 119.

54 Guttman, J. (1999, March). Charles Mc-Gee, Tuskegee and Beyond. Aviation History (9)4, pp. 39-44,67.

55 Holway, J. (1997). Red Tails Black Wings. Las Cruces, NM: Yucca Tree Press, p. 144.

56 Holway, J. (1997). Red Tails Black Wings. Las Cruces, NM: Yucca Tree Press, p. 145.

57 Holway, J. (1997). Red Tails Black Wings. Las Cruces, NM: Yucca Tree Press, p. 145.

58 O'Leary, M. (2004, September). Airacobra. Air Classics (40)9, p. 41.

59 Dial, J. (1967). The Bell P-39 Airacobra. Leatherhead, England: Profile Publications Ltd, p. 8.

60 Homan, L., Reilly, T. (1998). The Tuskegee Airmen.Charleston, SC: Arcadia Publishing, p. 116.

61 Scott, S. (1944, February). History of the 301st Fighter Squadron. U.S. Army Air Forces, p. 21.

62 Scott, S. (1944, February). History of the 301st Fighter Squadron. U.S. Army Air Forces, p. 23.

63 Craven, W. & Cate, J. (1951). The Army Air Forces in World War II. Volume Three Europe. Chicago, IL: University of Chicago Press, p. 269.

64 War Department. (1944, March 7). Report of Aircraft Accident. U.S. Army Air Forces.

65 War Department. (1944, March 7). Report of Aircraft Accident. U.S. Army Air Forces.

66 Jackson, W. (1969). The Battle for Rome. New York, NY: Bonanza Books, p. 24.

67 Craven, W. & Cate, J. (1951). The Army Air Forces in World War II. Volume Three Europe. Chicago, IL: University of Chicago Press, p. 373.

68 Craven, W. & Cate, J. (1951). The Army Air Forces in World War II. Volume Three Europe. Chicago, IL: University of Chicago Press, p. 378.

69 Craven, W. & Cate, J. (1951). The Army Air Forces in World War II. Volume Three Europe. Chicago, IL: University of Chicago Press, p.393.

70 Craven, W. & Cate, J. (1951). The Army Air Forces in World War II. Volume Three Europe. Chicago, IL: University of Chicago Press, p. 342.

71 Craven, W. & Cate, J. (1951). The Army Air Forces in World War II. Volume Three Europe. Chicago, IL: University of Chicago Press, p. 343.

72 Craven, W. & Cate, J. (1951). The Army Air Forces in World War II. Volume Three Europe. Chicago, IL: University of Chicago Press, p.351.

73 Scott, S. (1943, July). History of the 301st Fighter Squadron. U.S. Army Air Forces, p. 23.

74 War Department. (June 1943 to March 1944). History of the 332nd Fighter Group. U.S. Army Air Forces, p. 47.

75 Davis, B. (1991). An Autobiography, Benjamin O. Davis, Jr., American. Washington, DC: Smithsonian Institution Press, p. 116.

76 War Department. (June 1943 to March 1944). History of the 332nd Fighter Group. U.S. Army Air Forces, p. 47.

77 Davis, B. (1991). An Autobiography, Benjamin O. Davis, Jr., American. Washington, DC: Smithsonian Institution Press, pp. 116-117.

78 Rose, R. (1975). Part II Lonely Eagles, Journal American Aviation Historical Society, Winter 1975, 20(4), pp. 240-252.

79 Holway, J. (1997). Red Tails Black Wings. Las Cruces, NM: Yucca Tree Press, p. 148.

80   Hatchett, M. (1944, March). War Diary, 301st Fighter Squadron. U.S. Army Air Forces, p. 2.

81   Davis, B. (1991). An Autobiography, Benjamin O. Davis, Jr., American. Washington, DC: Smithsonian Institution Press, p. 117.

82   Kaiser, D. (n.d.). The Mount Vesuvius Eruption of March 1944. Retrieved from http://www.warwingsart.com/12thAirForce/Vesuvius.html

83   Holway, J. (1997). Red Tails Black Wings. Las Cruces, NM: Yucca Tree Press, p. 145.

84   Pratt, S. (2016). March 17, 1944: The most recent eruption of Mount Vesuvius. Retrieved from http://www.earthmagazine.org/article/benchmarks-march-17-1944-most-recent-eruption-mount-vesuvius

85   Busby, J. (1944, March). War Diary, HQ 332nd Ftr Gp. U.S. Army Air Forces, p. 1.

86   War Diary. (1944, March). 332nd Fighter Group. U.S. Army Air Forces.

87   Statistical Control Division. (1944, March 20). Operations of the 99th Fighter Squadron Compared with other P-40 Squadrons in MTO, 3 July 1943-31 January 1944. AFSHRC.

88   O'Leary, M. (2004, September). Airacobra. Air Classics (40)9, p. 59.

89   Homan, L., Reilly, T. (1998). The Tuskegee Airmen. Charleston, SC: Arcadia Publishing, , p. 116.

Chapter 11

1   War Department. (March 1944 to April 1944). History of the 332nd Fighter Group. U.S. Army Air Forces, p.4.

2   Haulman, D. (2015). Tuskegee Airmen Chronology. Maxwell AFB, AL: Air Force Historical Research Agency, p. 69.

3   Rose, R. (1975). Part II Lonely Eagles, Journal American Aviation Historical Society, Winter 1975, 20(4), pp. 240-252.

4   War Department. (March 1944 to April 1944). History of the 332nd Fighter Group. U.S. Army Air Forces, p.6.

5   War Department. (March 1944 to April 1944). History of the 332nd Fighter Group. U.S. Army Air Forces, p.12.

6   War Diary. (1944, April). 332nd Fighter Group. U.S. Army Air Forces, sheet no. 1.

7   Jackson, W. (1969). The Battle for Rome. New York, NY: Bonanza Books.

8   Fifth Army. (1944). Fifth Army History Part V, the Drive to Rome. p. 84.

9   Jackson, W. (1969). The Battle for Rome. New York, NY: Bonanza Books, p. 46.

10   Fifth Army. (1944). Fifth Army History Part V, the Drive to Rome. p. 11.

11   Technical Manual. (1943, June 29). German 88-mm Anti-aircraft Gun Material. Washington, DC: War Department.

12   Werrell, K. (1988). Archie, Flak, AAA, and SAM. Maxwell AFB, Alabama: Air University Press.

13   Dean, F. (n.d.). Flak Guns in the Brenner Pass. Retrieved from http://www.budslc.com/ww2/brenner.htm

14   Baer, D. (n.d.). German Anti-Aircraft Flak. Retrieved from http://www.scharch.org/Dick_Baer/German%20Enemy/German%20Anti-aircraft%20Flak.htm

15   Anderson, T. (2004, Summer). Flying Tanks of the Desert. Flight Journal Special Issue, P-40 Warhawk, p. 66.

16   Harrington, O. (1944, May 6). Enemy Flak Flips Fliers, The Pittsburgh Courier, p. 5.

17   Harrington, O. (1944, May 6). Destroys Enemy Supply Line in Blistering Air Offensive, The Pittsburgh Courier, p. 1.

18   West Point Grad Headed Fighter Squadron in Italy. (1944, July 15). The Pittsburgh Courier, p. 1.

19   Harrington, O. (1944, May 6). Destroys Enemy Supply Line in Blistering Air Offensive, The Pittsburgh Courier, p. 1.

20   War Diary. (1944, April). 332nd Fighter Group. U.S. Army Air Forces.

21   Nichols, G. (2007, February). Tuskegee Airmen James Polkinghorne in 'Florida Remembers WWII' Display. Gosport.

22   Nichols, G. (2007, February). Tuskegee Airmen James Polkinghorne in 'Florida Remembers WWII' Display. Gosport.

23   War Diary. (1944, May). 332nd Fighter Group. U.S. Army Air Forces.

24   F-16 Net Forum, Spazsinbad. (2013, February). First F-35A four-ship flies over Eglin. Retrieved from http://www.f-16.net/forum/viewtopic.php?t=22125

25   Commanding Officer, 301st Fighter Squadron. (1944, May 7). Transmittal of Missing Air Crew Report. U.S. Army Air Forces.

26   Commanding Officer, 301st Fighter Squadron. (1944, May 7). Transmittal of Missing Air Crew Report. U.S. Army Air Forces.

27   Commanding Officer, 301st Fighter Squadron. (1944, May 7). Transmittal of Missing Air Crew Report. U.S. Army Air Forces.

28   Scurlock, R. 1944, May). War Diary, 301st Fighter Squadron. U.S. Army Air Forces, p. 1.

29   War Diary. (1944, May). 332nd Fighter Group. U.S. Army Air Forces.

Chapter 12

1   Wilson, M. Personal Interview. 26 August 2017.

2   Lozare, N. (2002, November). Wentworth reflects life during war, Pensacola News Journal, p. 1.

3   Colasanti, A. Personal Interview. 1 February 2018.

4   Colasanti, A. (2008, May 30). [Letter to Christine Biggers]. Tuskegee Airmen National Historic Site, Tuskgee, AL.

5   Colasanti, A. (2008, May 30). [Letter to Christine Biggers]. Tuskegee Airmen National Historic Site, Tuskgee, AL.

6   Jackson, W. (1969). The Battle for Rome. New York, NY: Bonanza Books.

7   Hatchett, M. (1944, May). War Diary, 301st Fighter Squadron. U.S. Army Air Forces, p. 1.

8   332nd Fighter Groups Awarded Distinguished Unit Citation. (1945, November 3). The New York Age, p. 3.

9   Haulman, D. (2016, February 26). Tuskegee Airman Chronology. Maxwell AFB, AL: Air Force Historical Research Agency, p. 106-107.

10   Springs, R. (2012). The Origin of the

Tuskegee Airmen Red Tails Designation. Nicholasville, Ky: Gen. Noel Parrish Chapter of T.A.I.

11 Homan, L. & Reilly, T. (2001). Black Knights, the Story of the Tuskegee Airmen. Gretna, LA: Pelican Publishing Company, p. 129.

12 332nd Group Returns to States. (1945, October 27). The New York Age, p. 12.

13 332nd Fighter Group Returns to States. (1945, October 27). The New York Age, p. 12.

14 Haulman, D. (2015, October 29). Tuskegee Airman Chronology. Maxwell AFB, AL: Air Force Historical Research Agency, p. 121.

15 332nd Fighter Group Returns to States. (1945, October 27). The New York Age, p. 12.

16 Washington, G. (1972). The History of Military and Civilian Pilot Training of Negroes at Tuskegee Alabama 1939 – 1945. Washington, DC: Author, card 465.

17 Washington, G. (1972). The History of Military and Civilian Pilot Training of Negroes at Tuskegee Alabama 1939 – 1945. Washington, DC: Author, card 465.

18 Negro Aviators. (1945, September 29). The Pittsburgh Courier, p. 6.

19 Washington, G. (1972). The History of Military and Civilian Pilot Training of Negroes at Tuskegee Alabama 1939 – 1945. Washington, DC: Author, card 466.

20 Army Won't Retain TAAF. (1945, October 27). The Pittsburgh Courier, p. 3.

21 Washington, G. (1972). The History of Military and Civilian Pilot Training of Negroes at Tuskegee Alabama 1939 – 1945. Washington, DC: Author, card 471.

22 Haulman, D. (2015, October 29). Tuskegee Airman Chronology. Maxwell AFB, AL: Air Force Historical Research Agency, p. 126.

23 Haulman, D. (2015, October 29). Tuskegee Airman Chronology. Maxwell AFB, AL: Air Force Historical Research Agency, p. 128.

24 Haulman, D. (2014, September). Tuskegee Airmen Questions and Answers. Maxwell AFB, AL: Air Force Historical Research Agency, p. 5.

25 Haulman, D. (2014, September). Tuskegee Airmen Questions and Answers. Maxwell AFB, AL: Air Force Historical Research Agency, p. 6.

26 Washington, G. (1972). The History of Military and Civilian Pilot Training of Negroes at Tuskegee Alabama 1939 – 1945. Washington, DC: Author, card 473.

27 Tuskegee Army Airfield Declared Surplus. (1946, December 13). The Anniston Star, p. 6.

28 Washington, G. (1972). The History of Military and Civilian Pilot Training of Negroes at Tuskegee Alabama 1939 – 1945. Washington, DC: Author, card 485.

29 Washington, G. (1972). The History of Military and Civilian Pilot Training of Negroes at Tuskegee Alabama 1939 – 1945. Washington, DC: Author, card 478.

30 Lost Negro Flier Declared Dead. (1945, November). Pensacola News Journal.

31 Young, A. (September, 2018). Polkinghorne, James Reed [Letter to Leo Murphy]. St. Louis, MO: National Personnel Records Center.

32 American Battle Monuments Commission. (n.d.). Sicily-Rome American Cemetery and Memorial. Arlington, VA.

33 American Battle Monuments Commission. (n.d.). Sicily-Rome American Cemetery and Memorial. Arlington, VA.

34 Scott, L. & Womack, W. (1994). Double V, The Civil Rights Struggle of the Tuskegee Airmen. East Lansing, MI: Michigan State University Press.

35 Paszek, L. (1967, Spring). Negroes and the Air Force, 1939-1949. Military Affairs, 31 (1), pp. 1-9.

36 Gropman, A. (1985). The Air Force Integrates 1945-1964. Washington, DC: Office of Air Force History, United States Air Force, p. 284.

37 Haulman, D. (2016, February 26). Tuskegee Airman Chronology. Maxwell AFB, AL: Air Force Historical Research Agency, p. 133, 142.

38 Gropman, A. (1985). The Air Force Integrates 1945-1964. Washington, DC: Office of Air Force History, United States Air Force, p. 77, 284.

39 War Department. (1947, July 12). 5 Negro Aviation Cadets at Randolph. The Pittsburgh Courier, p. 1

40 Graves, L. (1947, July 12). Need More Pilots for Jet Plane Fighter Group, Col. Davis Says. The Pittsburgh Courier, p. 21.

41 Truman, H. (1948, July). Executive Order 998. Retrieved from https://www.trumanlibrary.org/9981a.htm

42 Variety of Activities Mark Homecoming. (1948, November 5). Tampa Bay Times, p. 27.

43 A&M Observes Homecoming Day. (1948, October). The Daily Democrat. Tallahassee, FL.

44 Variety of Activities Mark Homecoming. (1948, November 5). Tampa Bay Times, p. 27.

45 Homan, L, & Reilly, T. (2001). Black Knights, the Story of the Tuskegee Airmen. Gretna, LA: Pelican Publishing Company, p. 176

46 Haulman, D. (2014, September). Tuskegee Airmen Questions and Answers. Maxwell AFB, AL: Air Force Historical Research Agency, p. 17.

47 Haulman, D. (2014, September). Tuskegee Airmen Questions and Answers. Maxwell AFB, AL: Air Force Historical Research Agency, p. 17.

48 Sidat-Singh, S. (1943, July 10). Letters to the Editor, Dr. Sidat-Singh Speaks. The New York Age, pp. 6,8.

Image Credits _____

Index

CPSIA information can be obtained
at www.ICGtesting.com
Printed in the USA
LVHW102200011219
639097LV00009B/666/P